Resource Published by the Society of Wine Educators

SOCIETY of WINE EDUCATORS

CERTIFIED SPECIALIST OF SPIRITS

STUDY GUIDE 2019

ABOUT THE SOCIETY OF WINE EDUCATORS

The Society of Wine Educators (SWE) is a membership-based nonprofit organization focused on providing wine and spirits education along with the conferral of several certifications. The Society is internationally recognized, and its programs are highly regarded for both their quality and relevance to the industry.

The mission of the SWE is to set the standard for quality and responsible wine and spirits education and professional certification.

With its diverse programs, SWE is unique among educational programs in the wine and spirits field. Each year, the Society presents an annual conference with over 50 educational sessions and significant opportunities for professional interaction. Education and networking are further enhanced through symposiums, the Society's newsletter, and robust social media efforts.

SWE offers four professional credentials for those seeking to certify their wine and spirits knowledge, including the Certified Specialist of Wine (CSW), the Certified Specialist of Spirits (CSS), the Certified Wine Educator (CWE), and the Certified Spirits Educator (CSE). In addition, the Hospitality/Beverage Specialist Certificate is available, offered both as a self-study guide and an online class.

SWE members include the following types of individuals:
- Educators offering classes and tastings
- Instructors in public and private colleges, universities, and hospitality schools
- Importers, distributors, and producers
- Retailers, restaurateurs, and hoteliers
- Industry consultants
- Sommeliers, wine stewards, bartenders, and mixologists
- Culinary and hospitality school students
- Wine and spirits industry media professionals
- Wine and spirits enthusiasts

For more information about the Society's educational and membership programs, please contact us.

Society of Wine Educators
1612 K Street NW, Suite 700
Washington, DC 20006, USA
Telephone: (202) 408-8777
Website: www.societyofwineeducators.org

ACKNOWLEDGMENTS

The Society is grateful to the following people and organizations for their generosity in providing SWE with permission to use their figures and images throughout this publication:

- Alès, Philippe: Photo of the alembic still at the Bénédictine Museum
- Avarim Photography: Photo of washbacks at Glenfiddich Distillery
- Delonge, Jeff: Photo of peat stacks on Harris Island
- Dohrendorf, Thomas: Photo of bottles of Brazilian rum
- Glencairn Crystal: Photo of "The Official Glass for Whisky"
- Flood, Kyle: Photo of classic Gin and Tonic
- Harris, Scott E.: Photo of hybrid still at Catoctin Creek Distillery
- Ireton, Rob: Photo of Carpano Antica Formula Vermouth
- Ivanovich, Stefan: Photo of fermentation tanks at Domaine de Séverin, Cadet, Guadeloupe
- Kellor, Gernot: Photo of Black Friars Distillery
- Lembeck, William: Diagrams and drawings in chapter 1; maps
- Mahmood, Khalid: Photo of raw sugarcane juice
- Rosier Photography: Photo of the grounds of the House of Martell; photo of cognac aging at Martell
- Ryan, Jack: Photo of limoncello for sale in Capri
- Thomas, Ken: Photo of Woodford Reserve Rackhouse
- Worth, John: Photo of London dry gins

INTRODUCTION

The Certified Specialist of Spirits (CSS) certification represents the Society of Wine Educators' recognition that the holder has attained an in-depth knowledge about distillation and the major spirits categories, as well as the art of service as it applies to distilled spirits. The CSS Certification Exam was first given in 2008, with the first CSS Study Guide published in that same year. The Society would like to acknowledge and thank the Brown-Forman Corporation for its support and funding of the initial program.

This Study Guide is designed to help candidates who are seeking the CSS certification prepare for the corresponding examination. The guide is written to demonstrate the degree of familiarity with the various topics that is appropriate for beverage professionals to possess.

The information needed to pass the hundred-question exam is contained in this Study Guide, although many questions on the examination will require the candidate to interpret this information or to use multiple pieces of data together to draw a conclusion. Candidates are expected to read the CSS Study Guide in its entirety to prepare for the exam. All of the information contained in the body of the book (chapters 1–12) is considered fair game for the examination.

ORGANIZATION OF THE CSS STUDY GUIDE

The Study Guide begins with an overview of spirits in general, spirit production, and the sensory evaluation of spirits. The guide then proceeds with chapters dedicated to the major categories of spirits. These include vodka and other neutral spirits, gin and other flavored spirits, whiskey (whisky), brandy and other fruit-based spirits, rum, tequila and other agave-based spirits, and liqueurs. A chapter on vermouth, amari, and bitters is included—even though some of these products are technically defined as aromatized wines rather than spirits, they make up an important part of the sales and service of distilled spirits. The final chapters include information on setting up a bar and mixology. Plus, there's an important discussion on the impact of alcohol on health.

Additional resources are provided in four appendices. These include a glossary of spirit terms, a list of books and websites recommended for additional study, and the Society of Wine Educators' Spirits Tasting Rationale. Appendix C includes a selection of cocktail and mixed drink recipes. Please note that the CSS Exam does not test the candidate's knowledge of specific recipes that are included in this appendix. Rather, these are provided to serve as a useful reference.

A NOTE ABOUT THE MAPS

The maps included in this Study Guide are available electronically on the SWE blog, *Wine, Wit, and Wisdom*. The address is http://winewitandwisdomswe.com/swe-wine-maps/cssspirits-maps/.

Candidates are encouraged to access these maps electronically and to download full-page copies of the maps for use in study. The maps and diagrams are considered an integral part of the material in this Study Guide. Candidates should expect that information from the maps will be included in the CSS Exam.

RESOURCES FOR CSS CANDIDATES

The Society of Wine Educators offers many resources for CSS students and exam candidates, including the following:

Webinars: Monthly SWEbinars are available at no charge and to the public, covering CSS- and CSW-related topics. For more information, including the schedule, see the SWEbinar webpage at SWE's blog, http://winewitandwisdomswe.com/.

Online Prep Classes: Several times a year, SWE offers guided, ten-week online prep classes covering the CSS Study Guide. These classes are offered free of charge for professional members of SWE who hold a current CSS Exam attendance credit. For more information, contact Jane Nickles at jnickles@societyofwineeducators.org.

Workbook: A workbook designed to accompany this Study Guide is available for purchase through Amazon.com. For other purchase options, please contact SWE's Home Office.

Study Guide Updates: To assist all members of the adult beverage industry so that they may keep up with the ever-changing world of wine and spirits, SWE maintains "Study Guide Updates" pages for both the CSS and CSW Study Guides. Any changes that occur in the regulatory landscape, or elsewhere, that affect the information in the Study Guides will be updated on these pages. To access our Study Guide Updates page, see http://winewitandwisdomswe.com/study-guide-updates/.

CSS Exams: The CSS Exam consists of 100 multiple-choice questions, with all question content drawn exclusively from the CSS Study Guide. Candidates are provided with one (1) hour in which to complete the exam. CSS Exams are offered throughout the world, by appointment, at Pearson VUE Testing Centers. To find a Pearson VUE Center near you, use the search function on SWE's landing page at the Pearson VUE website: http://www.pearsonvue.com/societyofwineeducators/.

Exams based on the 2019 version of the CSS Study Guide will be available at Pearson Vue Testing Centers through December 30, 2021.

The Certified Spirits Educator Certification: SWE has recently launched a higher-level spirits certification, the Certified Spirits Educator (CSE). The CSE Exam is a unique certification that tests a candidate's knowledge of spirits, as well as his or her tasting acumen and teaching ability. This intense undertaking consists of a theory exam, two tasting exams, and a presentation skills demonstration, along with requiring candidates to provide evidence of Responsible Beverage Alcohol Service certification. All candidates pursuing the CSE certification must already possess the Certified Specialist of Spirits (CSS) certification. Candidates who successfully pass all components of the CSE Exam are entitled to use the CSE post-nominal as part of their professional signature. They will also receive a certificate (suitable for framing) and a CSE lapel pin. More information on the CSE is available on the SWE website.

© 2019 The Society of Wine Educators
All rights reserved. No part of this publication may be reproduced or utilized in any form or by any means, electronic or mechanical, including photocopying and recording, or by any information storage and retrieval system, without permission in writing from the publisher.

This publication is intended to provide accurate information with regard to the subject matter covered; however, the world of alcoholic beverages is a volatile one, and facts, figures, laws, consumption levels, and other information regarding these products are all liable to change over time. Please contact the Society of Wine Educators if you have any questions or comments about the contents of this guide.

Printed in the United States of America

TABLE OF CONTENTS

Chapter 1:	Spirit Production	7
Chapter 2:	The Sensory Evaluation of Spirits	21
Chapter 3:	Vodka and Other Neutral Spirits	29
Chapter 4:	Gin and Other Flavored Spirits	41
Chapter 5:	Whiskey	55
Chapter 6:	Brandy and Other Fruit-Based Spirits	85
Chapter 7:	Rum and Other Sugarcane-Based Spirits	109
Chapter 8:	Tequila and Other Agave-Based Beverages	127
Chapter 9:	Liqueurs	141
Chapter 10:	Vermouth, Amari, and Bitters	155
Chapter 11:	Mixology	179
Chapter 12:	Impact of Alcohol on Health	195

Additional Resources 199

Appendix A:	Glossary of Spirits-Related Terms	201
Appendix B:	Bibliography and Supplementary Reading	209
Appendix C:	Cocktail and Mixed Drink Recipes	213
Appendix D:	The Society of Wine Educators' Spirits Tasting Rationale	219

SOCIETY of WINE EDUCATORS

CHAPTER ONE SPIRIT PRODUCTION

SPIRIT PRODUCTION

CHAPTER ONE

LEARNING OBJECTIVES

After studying this chapter, the candidate should be able to do the following:
- Describe the processes of fermentation and distillation as they apply to the production of alcoholic beverages.
- Discuss the various types of stills and the impact that their use can have on the various styles of distilled beverages.
- Identify and describe the processes of spirit maturation, including aging in oak and other post-distillation procedures.
- Identify and describe the categorization of distilled spirits and other alcoholic beverages.

Spirits are defined as beverages in which the alcohol content has been concentrated by the process of distillation. Whereas beer and wine are produced solely by fermentation, generally resulting in alcohol levels of up to about 16%, spirits are produced using a fermented liquid that is further processed via distillation.

In the production of spirits, the distillation process separates the alcohol in a fermented liquid from the rest of the liquid, generally through the use of heat. This process may produce an alcohol content of nearly 100% after multiple distillations.

Nearly any fermentable product can be used to create a spirit. Given this fact, spirits are produced from a myriad of ingredients, including grapes, grains, fruit, plants, and honey. In addition to the wide variety of base ingredients used, spirits are made according to a number of specific distillation processes, aging regimens, and finishing procedures.

This chapter explains the general process of distillation as well as post-distillation procedures that are common to the production of many types and styles of spirits. Information specific to each type of spirit is covered in subsequent chapters.

HISTORY OF DISTILLED SPIRITS

Spirits, historically known as ardent spirits, are distilled beverages that contain alcohol. The word *ardent* comes from the Latin *ardere,* which means "to burn" and connotes the application of heat in the distillation process.

Distillation is essentially the process by which two or more liquids are separated into smaller parts of desired purity and concentration through the use of heat applied to the liquid. The term *distill* comes from the Latin *destillare,* which translates as "trickle down" and refers to the drops of condensed liquid that form during the distillation process.

Our word *alcohol* stems from the Arabic *al-ko'hl.* It is generally accepted that the earlier eighth-century meaning of al-ko'hl is "spirit," as in a ghost or ethereal body. However, it otherwise means "essence"—a further reference to the separation and purification obtained by distillation.

Figure 1.1: *The Alchemist's Laboratory* (engraving pictured in the book *Amphitheatrum Sapientiae Aeternae* by Heinrich Khunrath de Vries [1595])

Distillation is believed to have a long history. The ancient Chinese, Egyptians, and Mesopotamians distilled alcohol for medicines and perfumes long before the Common Era (CE). As early as 3500 BCE, Indian Sanskrit documents showed evidence of several different types of alcohols. Later, Aristotle (384–322 BCE), the great Greek philosopher, stated in his tome *Meteorology* that "sea water can be made potable by distillation; wine and other liquids can be submitted to the same process." There are many such references to distilled spirits in ancient writings.

The more modern history of distillation is considered to have originated with the Arabs or Saracens. They gave us the words *alcohol* and *alembic,* the latter meaning a "still." The first mention of distillation in this context can be traced back to the tenth century. It is attributed to an Arabian alchemist named Albukassen.

The Arabic method of distillation was transmitted to western Europe through the Moorish invasions. Later, in the thirteenth century, a Majorcan chemist and philosopher by the name of Raymon Llull (or Raymond Lully) described the process of distillation. Similarly, the Celts of Eire and Scotia were producing a potable spirit which they called *uisge beatha* or *uisge baugh* ("water of life"), from which the word *whiskey* is derived.

The stimulant and digestive qualities of alcoholic beverages ensured their development over the centuries. In addition, for much of human history, most sources of water, particularly those in densely populated areas, were unfit for human consumption. Due to these unsanitary conditions, alcohol was often safer to drink than water. As human population centers increased, moderate consumption of alcoholic beverages acted as a valuable "social lubricant" and helped to ameliorate harsh living conditions.

THE PRODUCTION OF DISTILLED SPIRITS

Simply put, a spirit is the product of an initial fermentation followed by the distillation of that fermented liquid, resulting in a high-alcohol beverage. As with other alcoholic beverages, spirits contain ethanol, which is commonly known as ethyl alcohol. This alcohol is a product of the initial fermentation process whereby sugar is converted to alcohol through the metabolic action of yeast.

Alcohol is a general term for any organic chemical in which a hydroxyl (OH) radical (called a hydroxyl grouping) is affixed to a carbon atom, which, in turn, may be bound to other carbon atoms and single hydrogen atoms. There are innumerable combinations of this sort; however, in the alcoholic beverage industry, *alcohol* designates ethyl alcohol. This alcohol is potable, meaning that a person may consume it in moderation without suffering any undesirable effects. Other alcohols, such as methanol, are also present in fermented products and can be extremely toxic in more than trace amounts.

BASE INGREDIENTS

Alcoholic spirits may be produced using a variety of different base ingredients. Depending on the choice of base ingredient, the production process of a spirit consists of either two or three main stages. Like wine, spirits are frequently produced from grapes or other fruits. Spirits may also be produced from other natural sugar-based materials such as honey, sugarcane, or molasses. When starting with ingredients that contain readily available sugars such as these, only two stages are required, as the available sugars are converted into alcohol relatively easily.

Spirits produced from starchy materials such as rice, potatoes, or grains require a conversion process in order to convert the starch into a fermentable form of sugar. This conversion, known as *saccharification,* is typically accomplished by heating the starch to trigger the production of specific enzymes which, in turn, cause the chemical conversion of the starch into fermentable sugars.

FERMENTATION

Fermentation, in the context of beverage alcohol, is the action of yeast on the sugars in a solution. The yeast consumes and metabolizes the sugar and, in the process, converts the sugar into ethyl alcohol, carbon dioxide, and energy in the form of heat.

When using a base material of grapes or fruit, the fermentation process results in a "wine" ranging, in general, from 8% to 14% alcohol. Starchy grains that have undergone an enzymatic conversion ferment into a "beer" with roughly 5% to 10% alcohol. The balance of each liquid (86–95%) is made up of water. However, the liquid will also contain acids, aldehydes, esters, and other compounds that were created during the fermentation process. These compounds, known as *congeners,* are important in spirit production as they add distinct aromas and flavors to the finished product.

After fermentation is complete, both types of fermented liquids will contain spent (used up) yeast cells in the mixture. These dead yeast cells are known as *lees*. While they are often discarded, there are times when the lees are used to impart additional flavor to a spirit, the details of which will be addressed in the relevant chapters.

Figure 1.2: *The Medical Alchemist* by Franz Christoph Graz Janneck (1703–1761) (showing a rudimentary distillation apparatus)

Fermentation may also create small amounts of other alcohols, such as *methanol (methyl alcohol)* and a range of compounds collectively referred to as *fusel oils* which contain small amounts of amyl alcohol, n-propyl, and isobutyl alcohols.

DISTILLATION

Once the initial ferment—now referred to as wine, distiller's beer, or wash—has been obtained, the distillation process can begin. This second or third stage of the production process concentrates the alcohol to a desired degree and, in some cases, separates it almost completely from the water and the other dissolved components. The equipment used in the process is known as a *spirit still*.

Distillation is a complex process. However, the process is based on one simple fact. Water has a higher *boiling point* than ethyl alcohol; therefore, the alcohol in a solution will "boil off" before the water even begins to boil. The boiling point of pure water is 212°F/100°C, while that of pure ethyl alcohol is 173°F/78°C.

As heat is applied to a solution of water and ethyl alcohol, the temperature of the heated liquid slowly rises. When the temperature reaches a point where the alcohol is above 173°F (78°C), the alcohol (along with some water) will transform from the liquid state into a gas. This is known as *vaporization*.

The vaporized alcohol and water are then captured in a closed vessel and cooled. As they cool, the vapors will return to liquid form; the resulting liquid will thus have a higher concentration of alcohol than the original alcohol-water mixture.

Boiling Points: In order to understand distillation, it is important to also understand boiling points. A liquid does not have to boil in order to be vaporized. As long as the concentration of a component in the liquid is greater than its concentration in the air above it, that component will evaporate into the air.

Essentially, the boiling point of a liquid is the highest temperature it may reach before it vaporizes completely. Water vaporizes very slowly at room temperature, and more quickly as heat is applied. When heat is applied, the water's temperature continues to rise until it reaches 212°F (100°C). At this point, it stays at that temperature until all the water is vaporized (turned to steam). The same thing happens when ethyl alcohol is heated. When its temperature rises to 173°F (78°C), which is its boiling point, the ethyl alcohol stays at that temperature until all of it is vaporized.

Miscible Liquids: It is also important to note that a solution of liquids has very different characteristics than the individual liquids of which it is composed. In this regard, a solution of water and ethyl alcohol, each of which are *miscible* (meaning that they dissolve in one another), acts like a new, single liquid. Accordingly, the miscible liquid has its own boiling point somewhere between those of the individual components. For example, a solution of 10% ethyl alcohol in water boils at 197°F (92°C), while a solution of 30% ethyl alcohol in water boils at 183°F (84°C).

Figure 1.3: Pot Stills at the Glendronach Distillery in Edinburgh, Scotland

Potential Alcohol by Volume: If, in distillation, the separation could be carried out to the point where only the alcohol remained, then the resultant spirit would be pure, or absolute, alcohol with an alcohol level of 100%. However, in commercial distillation, the final mixture never reaches more than 96.5% alcohol by volume (abv). To achieve 100% alcohol by volume, a dehydration procedure would have to be carried out in laboratory conditions.

Congeners: The preceding explanation of distillation has been simplified by using the example of a solution made of only ethyl alcohol and water. However, in reality, there are many other compounds present in a fermented solution. These compounds, known as congeners, are responsible for much of the aroma and flavor—besides that of pure ethyl alcohol and water—of individual spirits. These compounds include acids, esters, aldehydes, fusel oils, and alcohols (other than ethanol) that are developed during fermentation. During distillation, congeners may vaporize and blend in with the ethanol–water vapors; however, each specific congener will react differently based on three factors: boiling point, solubility (in ethanol and water), and specific gravity.

Congeners contribute to the overall flavor of a product even though they may be present in miniscule quantities and are often measurable in terms as small as *parts per million*. While many of these congeners contribute to favorable aromas and flavors, some of them can be undesirable. As such, one of the many jobs of the master distiller is the control of congeners during the production process. During distillation, the type and level of congeners that will remain in the finished product can be controlled via the shape, size, and type of still used as well as by the cut points and the manner in which the distillate is allowed to exit the still.

Heads, Tails, and Hearts: The first part of the distillate to come off the still is known as the *heads*, or *foreshots*. Foreshots contain compounds known as *low boilers* because of their lower boiling point. The heads are generally redistilled or discarded, as many of these compounds are nonpotable. Similarly, the last part of the distillate, known as the *tails*, or *feints*, includes compounds called *high boilers*, which may be poisonous. The tails are redistilled or discarded as well.

The center part of the distillate is known as the *heart*, or the potable spirit. This is the distiller's main focus, as it is this portion that contains a variety of preferred congeners.

The points of separation between the heads and heart and between the heart and tails are referred to as *cut points*. The cuts may also be described as those points where the flow of the vapors in a distillation run are re-directed. Specific cut points vary based on the type of spirit being produced and the level of congeners desired by the distiller. The distiller has learned from experience at what temperatures and alcohol levels these congeners can be concentrated or reduced. As such, he or she can control the amount that is left in the final product.

This is one of the many times when the distiller's role combines both art and science. Distillates that are low or lacking in congeners are purer and cleaner, but they may have little to no character. Distillates with a greater concentration of congeners have more character and may contain traces of the base material.

Reflux: During distillation, heat is used to turn a liquid into vapors and, depending on the shape, size, and format of the still, portions of the vapor will be drawn off the still to be condensed into the distillate. However, some of the vapor will cool, turn back into liquid form, and drop back down into the boiling liquid. This process is known as reflux. The shape, size, temperature, and format of the still will influence which elements of the liquid are passed on the condenser and which are returned to the still.

Rectification: Rectification is the process of concentrating the alcohol content in a liquid by repeated distillation. This process is a type of *fractional distillation* (referring to component parts, or fractions). While modern pot stills are sometimes fitted with a few rectification plates, rectification is typically discussed in terms of column still distillation. A column still may contain a rectification column with a number of rectification plates—sometimes even more than 40.

Rectification plates (each of which can hold a small amount of liquid) maximize the interaction between alcoholic vapors and the liquid in the still by forcing the vapors up through a series of liquid layers, allowing just the more volatile components to reach the top of the still. The level of rectification refers to the proof and concentration of congeners in a distilled spirit; those that are highly rectified are almost pure ethyl alcohol with a minimum level of congeners.

Proof: Before the production of distilled spirits became a science, early distillers had a very simple method for determining the potable strength of the distillate. Equal quantities of spirit and gunpowder were mixed, and a flame was applied to the mixture. If the gunpowder failed to burn or only sparked, then the spirit was too weak; if it burned too brightly, then the spirit was too strong. If the mixture burned evenly with a blue flame, it was said to have been proven to be 100% pure. Today, it is known that 100% pure is the equivalent of approximately 50% alcohol by volume.

The term *proof* has been adopted to accurately describe the strength of alcoholic beverages. In the United States, a 100 proof spirit is one containing 50% alcohol by volume at a temperature of 60°F (15.5°C).

It is generally a requirement to list the amount of alcohol in a spirit on the product's label in terms of the percentage of alcohol by volume. For distilled spirits, the proof measurement is now commonly placed after the alcohol by volume measurement, such as 40% abv (or, simply, 40% alcohol) and 80 proof (or 80°).

TYPES OF STILLS

Different types of stills have been developed over the years, with each type having special attributes and thus producing different products. The four most common types of stills are the pot still, the column still, the multiple column still, and the hybrid still.

THE POT STILL

Although modern science has made distillation increasingly efficient, a particular type of spirit still known as the *pot still* is very much the same as the one used by the original distillers many centuries ago. Reduced to its two essential parts, it consists of the still itself and a *worm condenser*. The still itself is a metal pot, usually copper or stainless steel. It consists of a broad rounded bottom, a long tapered swan's neck, and a *lyne arm* that transfers the vapors from the still to the condenser. The worm condenser is a spiral metal tube that is connected to the still by a metal pipe. The worm passes through a jacket that contains cold water, which assists in rapid condensation of the vapors.

A pot still works in what is known as a *batch process*. To start the process, a batch of fermented wine or beer is loaded into the pot, and a fire is lit below. As the vapors come off the still, they are condensed and collected at the relatively low alcohol strength of approximately 25% alcohol by volume. This first batch off the still is known as *brouillis* (from the French meaning to "brew" or "boil") in the context of brandy production and as *low wines* in whiskey production.

To prepare for the next stage in the process, the pot is cleaned out. The residue may be put aside for use in a future batch of spirits. The first distillate is then reinserted into the clean pot and redistilled to produce a distillate with a higher concentration of alcohol. This process may be repeated three or even four times, with the final results typically having an alcoholic concentration between 55% and 70% alcohol by volume.

While all pot stills work in a similar fashion, there are several variables that come into play with regard to the finished spirit. Some of these are discussed below.

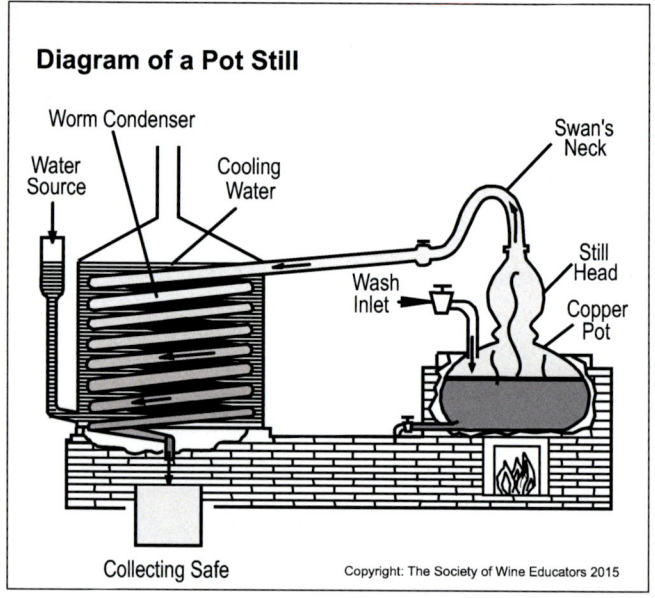

Figure 1.4: Diagram of a Pot Still

Materials: Pot stills are usually made from copper, which acts as a catalyst during the distillation process. As the vapors travel up the still, the copper pulls heavy elements away from them.

Shape and Size: The shape and size of the still, particularly the height of the still and swan's neck, as well as the angle of the lyne arm can have a large impact on the style of the resulting distillate. A higher (taller) still and a lyne arm that angles up as it leads away from the body of the still will result in more reflux as vapors re-condense and are returned to the bottom of the still. This will lead to a lighter, more refined distillate.

On the other hand, a shorter still and a lyne arm that slopes downward as it leads away from the still will allow for more of the heavier vapors to escape, leading to less reflux. This will result in a heavier, more congener-laden distillate.

Speed: The speed of the distillation run will further influence the character of the finished spirit. A faster run will result in a heavier spirit, as the interaction between the copper and the vapor will be limited. A slower run will permit more of this interaction and also promote reflux, resulting in a lighter spirit.

Given its batch process, the simple pot still rarely produces alcohol concentrations greater than 70% alcohol by volume (140 proof). Consequently, the spirits produced via pot still are generally less pure and have a higher concentration of congeners. Such spirits are therefore quite flavorful with distinct characteristics. Compared to other, more modern forms of the still, a pot still may be considered inefficient, as its use requires significant time and labor to carry out multiple distillations. This can obviously lead to increased costs of production. The pot still, however, continues to be used in commercial distillation. It is appreciated for the historic accuracy and artisanal qualities of its products.

THE COLUMN STILL

Not surprisingly, after centuries of pot still use, people began to search for a more efficient method of distillation. In 1826, Robert Stein, a member of a famous Scotch whisky-distilling family, invented the column still. It was later perfected by Aeneas Coffey, whose patent replaced Stein's. This type of still, also known as a continuous still, is made up of a distillation column or columns.

Coffey's name is now connected with this type of still, which is sometimes referred to as a *Coffey still* or *patent still*. In 1830, Coffey began using this new type of still at his recently-opened Dock Distillery (located in Dublin). Within four years, he closed the distillery and dedicated all of his time to creating and installing stills in other distilleries (mostly in London, as the Irish preferred the style of spirit created via pot still). The main advantage of this new type of still was its continuous nature, which vastly improved efficiency in terms of labor and also imparted the ability to distill to higher alcohol strengths.

Parts of a Column Still: A simplified diagram of a continuous distillation column is shown in figure 1.5. The column consists of a long tube known as the *analyzer*. The analyzer includes the *stripping section* below the feed tube and a *rectifying section* above the feed tube. At the top is a condenser, and at the bottom is an optional *reboiler*, as well as a steam inlet and a *liquid return*. The liquid return contains a mixture of condensate water and some wash from which not all of the alcohol was removed.

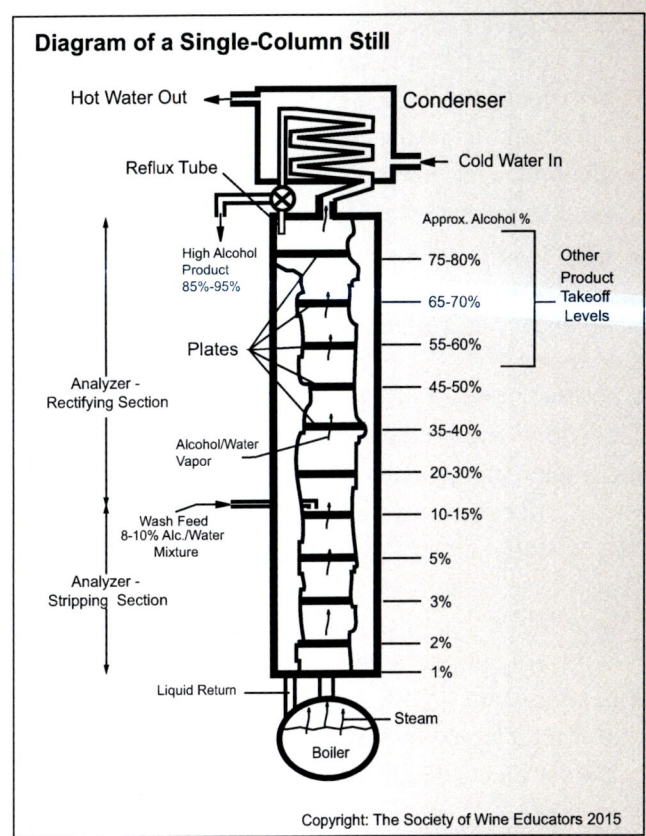

Figure 1.5: Diagram of a Single-Column Still

The Column Still Distillation Process: Column still distillation involves the following processes:

- A continuous inflow of wash.
- A continuous outflow of spent wash.
- An output of concentrated alcoholic liquid that can be tapped at various levels in the rectifying section.
- An output of highly concentrated alcohol vapor. This vapor is condensed and then partially withdrawn as a final product, while much of it is recirculated to the top plate as reflux. The reflux flow is required to produce a downward-flowing liquid, which is essential in supplying liquid to the rectifying section.
- The downward-flowing liquid settles on each plate in a shallow pool, the height of which is controlled by the dam level of a pipe connecting each plate to the one below, known as a *downcomer pipe*. As the liquid level rises, the overflow goes into the downcomer pipe and sinks to the next plate below. Meanwhile, the vapor bubbles up through holes in the plate, which are small enough so that the bubbles prevent the liquid from flowing through.

- At each plate level, the bubbling vapor from below (initially at lower alcoholic concentration) is in contact with the plate liquid (at a higher concentration). Thus, vapor with increased alcoholic concentration leaves the surface of each successive plate while progressing upward through the column, and the liquid at each plate—giving up alcohol to the bubbling vapors—flows downward in an ever-decreasing alcoholic concentration.

With the increased efficiency of this type of still, the distiller can produce a spirit at a much purer and higher strength (90–96.5% alcohol by volume). Such spirits generally have fewer congeners and, consequently, fewer flavor characteristics.

THE MULTIPLE COLUMN STILL

When a very pure-strength spirit is desired, along with significant efficiency, the basic column still can be further adapted by adding more columns. This type of still is called a multiple column still.

The initial set of columns acts in much the same way as a single column still does, with the spirit (at 94% alcohol by volume) passed on to a *hydroselector column*. Within the hydroselector column, also referred to as a *purifier column*, hot water is added to the spirit, which changes the vapor/liquid equilibrium and permits the volatile components of the liquid to vaporize more easily. In this manner, the aldehydes, esters, and other congeners can be removed from the spirit, creating a purer product.

The resulting solution is then passed on to another set of columns, known as *rectifiers*, for further distillation. This final distillation process removes the added water and brings the alcohol up to the desired strength, eventually coming off the still at 96.5% alcohol by volume.

THE HYBRID STILL

Given that each type of still has its advantages and disadvantages, there are some producers of premium spirits who prefer to use the traditional pot still. However, as previously mentioned, these stills are limited to outputting an alcoholic concentration of about 70% alcohol by volume, even when two batch distillations are used. Although a third or fourth batch distillation could produce the alcoholic purity desired in a higher-proof spirit, this procedure is time-consuming, very energy-inefficient, and expensive.

Accordingly, a hybrid still (sometimes called a pot and column still) is used to achieve the desired results. This type of still is basically designed as a rectifying column still sitting on top of a heated pot still so that the initial distillate is transferred from the pot still to the column for distillation to a higher concentration. There are many shapes, sizes, and configurations of hybrid stills in use.

One difference between a hybrid still and the continuous still is that in a hybrid still, as the alcoholic vapor is boiled off from the wash, the concentration of alcohol in the wash diminishes. Concurrently, as the wash loses its alcohol, the drawn-off product also loses its concentration. To prevent this from occurring, more reflux must be allowed to drain back into the column to refresh the loss of liquid and to increase the alcohol concentration in the upper plates.

The basic advantage of this still is its simplicity of design, construction, and operation. The disadvantage is its lower distillation efficiency. Typically, a hybrid distillation unit requires about three times as much energy as an equivalent continuous distillation still. However, it is more efficient than a pot still alone.

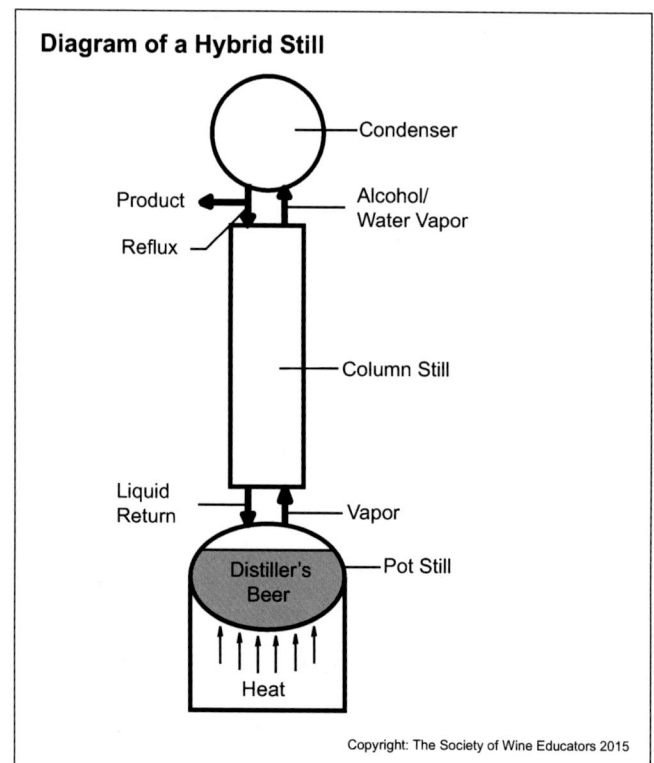

Figure 1.6: Diagram of a Hybrid Still

Figure 1.7: Hybrid Still at Catoctin Creek Distillery

THE MATURATION OF DISTILLED SPIRITS

Regardless of the type of still used for distillation and the raw materials used for the initial fermentation, all newly distilled spirits, known as *new-make spirits*, are colorless, or water-white. They possess a sharp, biting aroma and taste, which will mellow if the spirit is given time to mature.

At this point, some spirits are ready to be finished by being reduced in strength and bottled, at which point they are ready for consumption. However, it is common for many types of spirits to be treated with a variety of post-distillation processes before being bottled. Such post-distillation treatments include coloring or filtration, and may occur in stainless steel containers or large wooden vats. These treatments are usually fairly short in duration, typically lasting less than two months. Many spirit categories, including some types of vodka, gin, soft fruit brandies, and plata (blanco) tequila, include such unaged expressions.

Aging in Oak: Many styles of whiskey, rum, tequila, grape brandy, and apple brandy are typically oak aged. Oak aging of spirits can last anywhere from several months to several decades, allowing the spirit to evolve over time. Oak maturation involves six processes: extraction, evaporation, oxidation, concentration, filtration, and coloration.

Oak is the common name for several hundred different species of trees in the genus *Quercus*, native to the Northern Hemisphere. American white oak, *Quercus alba*, is often used to mature spirits. The use of this type of oak stems partly from the abundance of oak forests found throughout the United States, especially in the Ozarks.

Beyond its availability, this type of oak is prized for its strength, resilience, and ability to be bent into the shape of a barrel. Its high tannin content makes it resistant to insects and fungus, which adds to its durability. While not as tightly grained as French oak, the pores of American oak are small enough to make the barrel leak-proof yet still able to allow the contents to slowly evaporate through the walls of the barrel, also allowing small amounts of oxygen to enter.

Oak heartwood contains the following three structural components:
- *Cellulose:* Cellulose is an organic compound whose strength and chemical resistance provides structural integrity to the oak, permitting it to keep its shape and durability for years. It makes up 40% of the mass of the wood.

Figure 1.8: Barrels of Bourbon Whiskey Aging in the Jim Beam Rackhouse

- *Hemicellulose:* Another organic compound, hemicellulose is found in almost all plant cell walls, along with cellulose. It is composed of many different sugars with lower molecular weights than those found in cellulose, which accounts for its easy solubility in alcohol. It makes up approximately 25% of the mass of wood. Hemicellulose is responsible for the *red layer* that forms in charred oak barrels.
- *Lignin:* Found in all woods, lignin helps cement the cellulose fiber cells in the wood together, providing rigidity to the wood structure. Its greatest contribution to the maturation of a spirit is that it is the source of a group of organic compounds called *methoxyphenols*. The methoxyphenols group includes vanillin and syringol, which smell and taste like vanilla. Lignin makes up approximately 25–30% of the mass of the wood.

The remaining 5–10% of the oak's mass is predominantly composed of tannins, which are astringent, bitter *polyphenolic compounds*, and small amounts of coconut-flavored lactones and volatile phenolic acids. Although small in quantity, these volatile acids can provide over four hundred aromatic and flavor combinations to the matured spirit. Consequently, with time in wood, the spirit will transform in color, aroma, taste, and character.

The Processes of Oak Aging: The specific chemistry involved in the maturation of spirits in oak is quite complicated. The processes of extraction, evaporation, oxidation, concentration, filtration, and coloration all take place simultaneously, but they are discussed here one at a time.

- *Extraction:* When an oak barrel is untreated, very little extraction of congeners can take place. However, if the wood is exposed to heat, thereby altering its composition, extraction can more readily occur. Thus, the interior wood surface of an oak barrel is often either toasted, or burned and charred. These actions change the chemical composition of the hemicellulose, lignin, and tannins in the wood. The hemicellulose will form into the red layer—a caramelized layer of sugars just below the charred surface. This red layer can provide a range of seemingly sweet aromas and flavors—such as chocolate, butterscotch, and caramel—to spirits.

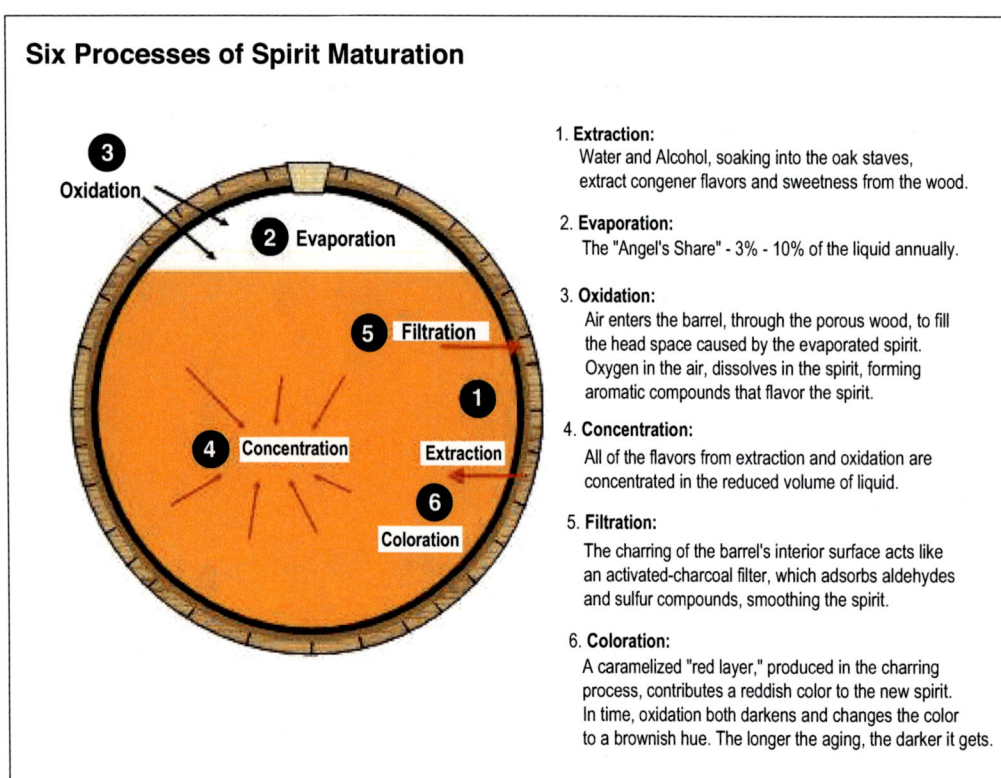

Figure 1.9: Diagram of the Six Processes of Spirit Maturation

- *Evaporation:* Because of the permeable nature of the oak, some of the liquid in the barrel will evaporate through the pores in the wood. Depending on the temperature and humidity at the location where the barrels are stored, there is an approximate 3% loss of liquid annually. This can be much higher in warmer climates. This loss is sometimes called the *angel's share*, since the components in the spirit leave the barrel and travel skyward. In areas of high humidity, such as Scotland, the alcohol in the spirit will evaporate more readily than the water. As a result, the spirit's proof decreases as it ages. In less humid regions, the water loss is greater than the alcohol loss, and so the spirit's proof increases with time. In both cases, however, there is a net loss of total volume. Temperature will also impact the rate of evaporation, which may occur much more quickly in hotter regions than in cooler ones.
- *Oxidation:* The semiporous nature of the oak allows oxygen to seep through the wood and enter the barrel. The oxygen dissolves in the spirit and causes a desirable oxidation of the spirit's components. Over time, additional esters are formed, and aldehydes and acids increase.
- *Concentration:* As mentioned above, evaporation of the alcohol and water reduces the total volume of spirit remaining in the barrel. Thus, the unchanged, original components of the spirit are concentrated over time in the barrel, along with the newly extracted and oxidized constituents.
- *Filtration:* When the inside of the barrel is charred, a layer of charcoal is produced. This charcoal acts as a means by which to filter the spirit.
- *Coloration:* The charring process somewhat degrades the tannins in the wood, which may give the spirit a reddish color that deepens as it ages in the barrel. In addition, the spirit's color may turn brown with exposure to oxygen via the process of oxidation. The longer a spirit ages, the more color it takes on. Spirits that are aged for only a brief period will be much lighter in natural color than those aged for several years.

At the end of the maturation process, the colorless, harsh new-make spirit has been converted into a tawny-hued, mellower, sweeter-tasting, and more multifaceted flavorful spirit.

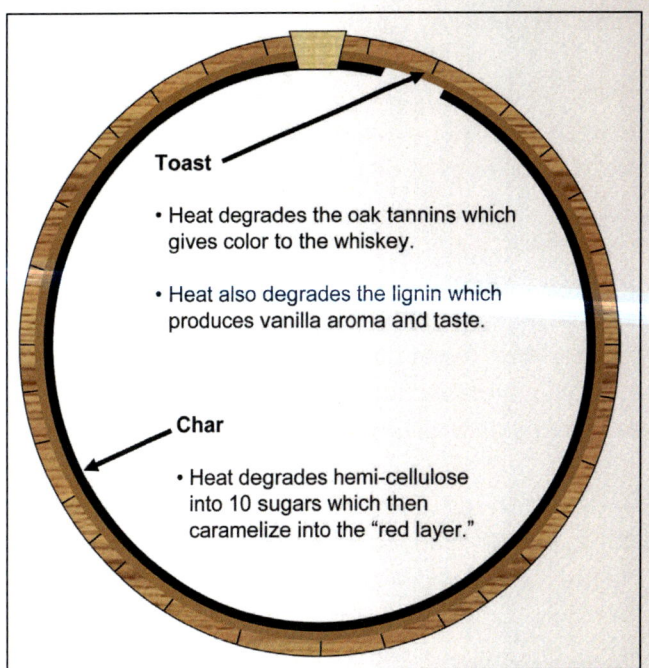

Figure 1.10: Diagram – Charring the Barrel

POST-DISTILLATION PROCESSES

Colorings and Other Additives: While many spirits get their color from the maturation process, other spirits are allowed to contain coloring agents. Such color is usually derived from caramel, which is added in order to create a consistently colored product. Other spirits, namely liqueurs and some flavored spirits, may be flavored post-distillation (although many are flavored during distillation, as well). The specifics of these spirits are covered in the later chapters.

Filtration: A spirit may be filtered to remove impurities, color, or both. *Filtration* most commonly involves the use of activated charcoal, which absorbs the harsher characteristics of the spirit. In addition, many spirits undergo a process known as *chill filtration*. Chill filtration removes components common to many spirits that can cause a spirit to appear hazy or dull. Matured spirits, in particular, are likely candidates for chill filtration. To carry out this process, the spirit is chilled, which causes a haze to form that can then be removed. With all types of filtration, care must be taken to avoid filtering out desirable components that contribute to body and flavor along with those components that are unwanted.

Blending: In some cases, the finished spirit will be taken from a single batch or cask. However, in many cases, the finished spirit will be a blend of many different spirits or batches, blended from among casks, ages, or even distilleries.

Some blended spirits contain many dozens of different component spirits. The job of the master blender is extremely important, as the blending process helps to maintain the house style of a particular spirit and allows the producer to create complexity and balance in the final product.

Bottling Strength: Most spirits when taken off the still have an alcohol concentration of 58–96.5% by volume, which is generally reduced prior to bottling. To reduce the alcohol concentration after filtration or aging, high-quality water that is often demineralized, or a mixture of water and spirit, is added to the spirit. For certain types of spirits, this process must be done very carefully and slowly to avoid a negative impact on the final product. Some spirits that have been matured for a long period of time will lose alcohol strength naturally via evaporation, and will thus need little to no dilution before bottling. Most spirits are bottled at 37 to 43% alcohol by volume.

SPIRIT CATEGORIES

While they make up a large, diverse group of products, spirits can be categorized according to the base ingredient used in the production process. A brief overview of the main spirit categories is provided below. A more detailed discussion of each spirit category follows in its respective chapter.

Vodka and Other Neutral Spirits: Vodka is typically a clear, water-white spirit with a relatively neutral flavor profile. It may be produced from any fermentable base material. In fact, the US definition requires that vodka be distilled so as to be without distinctive character, aroma, taste, or color. Despite this definition, some vodka can be distinguished depending on the base material and water source used. Vodkas are permitted to be flavored, broadening the variety of vodkas found in the market. Still, the neutral character of many styles of vodka makes it ideal in cocktails and mixed drinks.

Other spirits are obtained by distilling various fermented starchy or sugar-containing products in a process similar to that of making vodka. Distilled from a mash of rice, potato, sweet potato, wheat, barley, tapioca, or sugar, Soju (from Korea), shōchū (from Japan), and baijiu (also called shaojiu; from China) are the most widely produced spirit types in the world. Like vodka, most versions are colorless, somewhat neutral spirits.

Gin and Other Flavored Spirits: Gin is a flavored spirit typically produced by either redistilling or compounding a high-proof neutral spirit in the presence of juniper berries and other botanicals. Styles of gins include London dry gin, Plymouth gin, and Old Tom gin. A wide range of juniper-flavored spirits, including Genever, Steinhäger, and fruit-flavored gins, are also produced. This category also includes other flavored spirits, such as akvavit flavored with caraway seeds, and anise-flavored spirits such as pastis and absinthe.

Brandy and Other Fruit-Based Spirits: Brandy is produced by distilling wine or a fermented mash of fruit. Brandies distilled from fruits are usually clear and may be aged or unaged; these include kirsch or kirschwasser (from cherries), pear brandy and slivovitz, mirabelle and quetsch (from plums), and others. Brandies distilled from grapes, such as cognac and armagnac, and most versions of calvados or apple brandy are usually aged in wood. Spirits may also be produced from the grape skins that remain after winemaking. These spirits are referred to as pomace brandies.

Whiskey: Whiskey is a spirit obtained from the distillation of a fermented mash of grain. Well-known examples include Scotch whisky, Irish whiskey, Canadian whisky, bourbon, and Tennessee whiskey. Whiskey is also increasingly produced in other regions of the world such as Japan, India, and New Zealand. (Note: Different spellings are intentional and based on tradition.)

Rum and Other Sugarcane-Based Spirits: These spirits are obtained from the distillation of a fermented mash of sugar, sugarcane juice, or molasses. They may be aged or unaged. A variety of production methods are used to make rum; and many styles exist—most of which depend on the

Figure 1.11: Hybrid Still in Use at Distillerie Mavela in Corsica

traditions of the country or region of production. Industrial rum, rhum agricole, and cachaça are all examples of types of rum. Other spirits, such as those based on sugar beets or made from a combination of sugarcane and other ingredients, are part of the broader definition of this category as well.

Tequila and Other Agave-Based Spirits: Tequila is produced exclusively in Mexico by fermenting and distilling the cooked sap of the blue agave plant. Mezcal was the original name for all beverages distilled from agave, but today it refers to a specific spirit distilled from a number of agave varieties. Mezcal generally has a smokier flavor than tequila. A variety of beverages based on many members of the agave family are also included in this category.

Liqueurs: These are sweetened, flavored spirits made from any type of base spirit. Their flavors are obtained by compounding, infusing, or redistilling with fruits, fruit juices, spices, flowers, or other natural flavorings. Liqueurs must contain at least 2.5% sugar by weight in the United States, with EU requirements calling for higher levels of sugar. Liqueurs may even contain up to about 35% sugar, making some of them quite sweet. Liqueurs are categorized by their main flavoring component, such as fruit, botanicals, or cream. Amaretto, crème de cacao, crème de menthe, Sambuca, and triple sec are all examples of this type of spirit.

Amari and Cocktail Bitters: Amari, or bittered spirits, form a broad category of distilled spirits, originally derived as "elixirs" or medicines and flavored with bittering agents. Many of these are also sweetened and "overlap" with products in the liqueur family. Well-known examples of bittered spirits include Chartreuse, Fernet, and Campari. Cocktail bitters, while based on distilled spirits, are not considered beverages per se, but they are used in very small amounts as food and cocktail flavorings. Well-known examples of cocktail bitters include Peychaud's, Fee Brothers, and Angostura bitters.

Note: Vermouth and other aromatized wines, although not distilled and therefore not technically classified as spirits, are also included in this Study Guide. Because of their popularity as aperitifs and digestifs and their use in cocktail recipes, these products play a large role in the bar business in general, and in the sales and service of alcoholic beverages in particular. Vermouth, vini amari, quinquina, and americano are some examples of aromatized wines that are covered in chapter 10, along with bittered spirits and cocktail bitters.

THE DEFINITION AND LABELING OF DISTILLED SPIRITS

The alcoholic beverage industry is highly regulated, particularly in regards to the production, distribution, marketing, and consumption of alcoholic beverages. In addition, many specific spirits or spirit categories are precisely defined as to permitted or required base materials, methods of production, aging, packaging, labeling, and even sensory characteristics.

Such definitions are set out by a range of legislative bodies throughout the world, including the Alcohol and Tobacco Tax and Trade Bureau (TTB) of the US Government, the *Norma Oficial Mexicana* (Official Mexican Standard) of Mexico, and the Food and Drug Regulations of Canada. In addition, the European Union (EU) maintains regulations as to the "scope, definition, and categories of spirit drinks" and provides additional standards for certain beverages that have earned protected geographical indication (PGI) or protected designation of origin (PDO) status. Specific spirits defined as such will be discussed in the chapters that follow.

CHAPTER TWO THE SENSORY EVALUATION OF SPIRITS

THE SENSORY EVALUATION OF SPIRITS

CHAPTER TWO

LEARNING OBJECTIVES

After studying this chapter, the candidate should be able to do the following:
- Describe the process of the sensory evaluation of spirits as used by beverage professionals.
- Discuss the ideal setup of a distilled beverage tasting, including proper logistics, glassware, and the choice of beverage(s).
- Identify visual clues regarding the type and quality of distilled spirits.
- Recognize and describe the aromas, flavors, and tactile sensations exhibited by distilled spirits.
- Describe how complexity, finish, and quality are revealed during the spirits evaluation process.

Beverage professionals are generally well-versed in the sensory evaluation of wine. A well-trained wine taster is taught to conduct a detailed visual observation, swirl a glass to coax out the aromas, smell the wine using deliberate inhales, and finally roll the wine around the palate while drawing in gulps of air.

While the knowledge and skill developed as a wine taster is certainly transferable to the sensory evaluation of spirits, the high alcohol content of most spirits requires a different sort of tasting methodology. The tasting procedure that follows is the preferred method used by the Society of Wine Educators. It is similar to those used by other groups of wine and spirits professionals.

It is quite useful to take notes during the spirit tasting process. For this purpose, the Society of Wine Educators' Spirits Tasting Rationale, a detailed outline for recording tasting notes, is located in appendix D.

Glassware: An ideal glass for a general spirit tasting is stemmed, tulip-shaped, and made of standard thin, clear glass. As for any type of professional tasting, the glasses should be clean, dry, and odor-free. A capacity of 6–8 ounces (177–237 ml) is enough to hold a 1- to 1¼-ounce (30–37 ml) serving of spirits throughout the tasting process without spilling. A typical liqueur, port, or white wine tasting glass will serve the purpose, although dedicated tasters may want to invest in a collection of specialty spirit tasting glasses such as those made by Riedel, Schott Zwiesel, and a variety of other producers.

There is a variety of specialty glasses on the market designed for whiskey tasting. The glasses vary a bit by shape and size, but they can be grouped into those shaped like a sherry-tasting copita; those shaped like a typical white wine tasting glass; "tulip-shaped" glasses with a short stem; and wide-bowled tumblers. Two examples of whiskey tasting glasses are the "official glass for whisky" created by the Scotch Whisky Heritage Centre and produced by Glencairn Crystal, and the Scotch Malt Society's whisky glass. Many other brands are available as well.

Figure 2.1: The "Official Glass for Whisky," Created by the Scotch Whisky Heritage Centre

There are also a variety of specialty brandy tasting glasses available, most of which are a variation on the standard brandy snifter or the typical spirit tasting glass. Many brandy experts recommend using a standard tulip-shaped tasting glass or a smaller variation on the brandy snifter for serious tastings, so as not to expose too much of the surface of the spirit to air.

The Spirits: Ideally, spirits should be evaluated in flights of similar products—and no more than six to eight samples at a time. In most cases, spirits should be poured in order of alcohol by volume, from lowest to highest, and in order of age, from youngest to oldest.

Spirit tasting can quickly lead to palate fatigue. For obvious reasons, samples should be limited. A pour of 1 to 1¼ ounces (30–37 ml) should suffice. Bottled water (preferably distilled or demineralized) and dry, unsalted crackers are helpful to cleanse and refresh the palate between samples. Needless to say, while a small amount of each spirit may be swallowed to experience the full range of sensations, spitting is highly recommended.

Spirits can be evaluated effectively either chilled or at room temperature. For those spirits such as whiskey and brandy that are traditionally served at room temperature, this is the obvious choice. For spirits such as vodka and gin (which are best enjoyed chilled), the spirits may be served either at room temperature or chilled. Obviously, the products will show differently at different serving temperatures. There are many different points of view on the subject; some say that room temperature reveals the true nature of the spirit, while others prefer to taste the spirit in the manner in which it will be served. The choice is up to the organizers of a tasting event. However, once a method is chosen, it should be used consistently throughout the event, keeping in mind that tasting the same spirit, both chilled and at room temperature, could make for an interesting compare-and-contrast.

Figure 2.2: Irish Whiskey in Barrels at Old Midleton Distillery, Showing the Color at Different Stages of Barrel Aging

Appearance: The first step of evaluating spirits is to give the spirits a visual examination in a well-lit room, while holding the spirit against a standard white background. Tipping the glass to look through the spirit at both the *meniscu*s (edge) and *eye* (middle) is a good way to reveal color and clarity.

Through the process of distillation, all spirits start off as colorless. The actual color of the finished spirit can be the result of three processes: time aged in wood, the addition of caramel colorings or sweetening agents, and/or the addition of natural or artificial colorings.

For high-quality spirits, color is generally a factor of aging; however, in many cases, there is no way to know if a particular spirit's color is due to aging or caramel coloring. In addition, some spirits that have been aged in barrels for a short period of time, perhaps even up to a year or more, are filtered to remove the color acquired by aging.

Table 2.1: The SWE Spirits Tasting Rationale – Appearance

APPEARANCE						
Clarity:	Brilliant	Clear	Dull	Hazy	Cloudy	
Hue:	Water-White	Pale	Light Yellow	Yellow-Gold	Deep Gold	Copper
	Tawny	Amber	Mahogany	Molasses	Brown	
Colored Spirits:	Light Green	Dark Green	Clear Blue	Dark Blue	Purple	
	Pink	Red	Orange	Yellow	Black	
	Other:					
Depth:	Water-White	Pale	Medium	Deep	Opaque	
Legs:	Fast	Slight	Medium	Pronounced	Slow	
Other Observations:						

White spirits are usually clear or watery in color, perhaps with a slight platinum hue. Some white spirits may appear to have a bit of a gray tint when put under a light; this color may be an indication of the type of distillation or character of the spirit, as those spirits produced via pot still may appear to be duller than those produced via continuous distillation.

Aged tequilas, brandies, and whiskeys may range in color from light yellow to dark amber. The longer the time spent in the barrel, the darker the natural coloring will be. However, it is sometimes possible that a coloring is added to aged spirits, particularly blends. With practice, one can develop an instinct about whether the color of a spirit has been naturally derived through aging or has been artificially added.

Unlike with some types of wine, it is not expected that a spirit would have sediment; so, any foreign-appearing objects should be investigated. Most spirits are also not expected to have a cloudy or hazy appearance, known as *turbidity*, although there certainly are some exceptions. As we shall see in the later chapters, some spirits, such as absinthe, ouzo, and raki, experience *louching,* or cloudiness, when mixed with water. This is one good reason to sample spirits both with and without water, as is discussed in further detail below.

Figure 2.3: Pastis Charbay Displaying the Louche Effect

The way that the "tears" or "legs" run down the sides of the glass after giving the glass a swirl—in terms of thick, thin, fast, or slow—may also reveal something about a beverage. A spirit with slowly running tears is likely to be more viscous than the spirit with faster-running tears. Viscosity may also be a function of age, with an aged spirit being more viscous than a younger spirit. Spirits that are higher in alcohol will tend to have slowly running tears as well. However, slow-running tears may also be a function of sweetness; thus, a freshly produced, brightly colored, highly sweetened bottom-shelf liqueur may have the slowest tears of all.

Aromas: Unlike wine, which sometimes needs to have its aromas brought forth, aromatics from spirits fairly jump out of the glass, propelled forward by the alcohol. Thus, it is ideal to approach the aromatics of each spirit in two steps. First, without swirling the glass, take a series of quick, gentle sniffs, positioning the surface of the spirit in the glass three to four inches below your nose. Be mindful of the shape and size of the glass; this may mean keeping the glass directly below your nose or else allowing for a few inches in between the rim of the glass and your nose. Keeping the mouth slightly open will help eliminate a rush of alcohol into your nose and eyes.

At this point, you can measure the intensity of the aromas. If you can detect and describe the aromas of the spirit at a distance of six inches (15 cm) from your nose, then they can be classified as "intense." If they are detected at three inches (7.5 cm) of distance or so, then this represents "medium" intensity. If it requires that your mouth be at the rim of the glass while breathing in to detect any aromatics, then the aromatic intensity may be described as "light." Analyze every spirit in the flight in this manner, pausing between products to rest your senses and to take notes.

After a break of three to five minutes, during which both the taster and the spirits should be allowed to rest undisturbed, begin the second round. This round should be an in-depth examination of the aromas of each spirit, beginning with deeper, longer inhalations—always remembering to keep the mouth open.

Begin by smelling each glass in its undisturbed state, and then give the spirit a good roll around the glass. Most spirits professionals suggest a gentle "roll" as opposed to a more agitated "swirl" in order to prevent the spirit from releasing too much alcohol that will "hover" over the surface of the liquid in the glass—which does, in fact, mask some of the aromas. Note the differences in both the aromas and their intensity brought about by the motion. Let the spirit rest for a minute or so while you write your notes, and then smell it again just to make sure you haven't missed any subtleties.

Spirit aromas are diverse and somewhat unique to each spirit category. However, aromas can be loosely categorized for ease of recognition and identification. These categories include grain, fruity, floral, botanical, sweet aromatics, spice, oak/wood, nutty, and rancio (oxidized), as well as the catchall "other" category. The words used to describe these aromas have numerous variations in terminology and usage.

A tasting discussion specific to each spirit category is included in the chapters that follow. Of course, while it is an interesting and almost academic endeavor to test your skill in the recognition and identification of spirit aromas, the main item of interest in the sensory evaluation of spirits is to note whether or not you find the aroma appealing and pleasurable. In other words, does it make you want to take a sip?

Flavors: As is the case for analyzing aromatics, it is good practice to assess the in-mouth impressions of a spirit in two steps. The high alcohol content of a distilled spirit is likely to be somewhat shocking to the palate upon its first impression; therefore, it helps if you condition the palate before assessing the first spirit in a flight. This can be done with a quick sip. Take a small amount of the first spirit in your mouth; let it sit on your tongue for a few seconds; quickly "swish" it around your mouth to coat the entire palate, including the gums; and then quickly spit it out. Allow the heat to dissipate for a few seconds as you breathe in through your mouth. This will both prepare your palate to assess the spirit and "cleanse" the palate of any lingering impact from tasting a previous spirit.

After a rest of a minute or so, take a second sip, gently roll the liquid over the palate to coat the entire mouth, take a quick inhale, and let the spirit rest on the middle of your tongue for a few seconds. Next, tilt your head down and allow the spirit to pool by your front teeth for about five to ten seconds. Holding the spirit in your mouth for a full ten seconds enables it to warm, which further enables you to discern aromas and flavors. If you find the spirit overly intense, shorten the length of time—there is no need to experience displeasure. Next, "chew" the spirit for a few seconds and, after a pause, swallow or spit (spitting is recommended). Quickly inhale through the mouth and, with lips closed, exhale through the nose.

Table 2.2: The SWE Spirits Tasting Rationale – Conditions and Aromas

CONDITIONS AND AROMAS

Condition:	Clean	Fresh	Stale	Unclean/Faulty		
Aroma Intensity:	Neutral	Light	Medium	Intense		
Aromas						
Grain:	Malt	Bran	Cereal	Corn	Wheat	Biscuit
	Other:					
Fruity:	Citrus	Tropical Fruit	Tree Fruit	Dried Fruit	Candied Fruit	Orange Peel
	Other:					
Floral:	Rose	Violet	Perfume	Orange Blossom	Dried Flowers	
	Other:					
Botanical:	Herbal	Vegetal	Juniper	Tobacco	Peat	Seaweed
	Other:					
Sweet Aromatics:	Caramel	Honey	Maple	Molasses	Burnt Sugar	Toffee Vanilla
	Other:					
Spice:	Clove	Nutmeg	Anise	Cinnamon	White Pepper	Black Pepper
	Other:					
Oak/Wood:	Oak	Cedar	Sawdust	Coffee	Pine	Char
	Other:					
Nutty:	Walnut	Hazelnut	Praline	Almond	Marzipan	Coconut
	Other:					
Rancio:	Leather	Smoke	Earthy	Acetaldehyde	Ash	Tar
	Other:					

Other:

You can now proceed to evaluate the spirit based on its basic taste components of sweetness, acidity, and bitterness. Does it have no discernible sweetness, as is true with many spirits, or is there a level of sweetness? Some spirits, primarily liqueurs, may be sweet to very sweet. One must take care in assessing unsweetened spirits, as a perception of sweetness can be deceiving. This is because high levels of alcohol can mimic the taste of sweetness in a large percentage of tasters. Some studies show that up to 50% of the population perceives alcohol as having a "sweet" taste. Furthermore, the perception of sweetness can be derived from the charring of the barrel, as the lignins may have caramelized and formed vanilla- and coconut-flavored compounds.

Acidity is generally sensed on the sides of the tongue. It may be soft or smooth, crisp like green apples, or even sharp like lemons. The level of acidity can be determined by noting the salivary reaction of your palate; the more highly acidic, the more you will salivate.

Most spirits will have some bitterness apparent because of their alcohol content, unless this bitterness is well-masked by sweetness. Bitterness is generally experienced on the back of the palate. It is a long-lasting sensation. The slight taste of bitterness may underlie the finish of the spirit. Bitterness is, of course, an inherent taste component for the wide array of spirits and aromatized wines that have bittering agents added to them. These products will be discussed in detail in chapter 10.

This is a good time to consider the actual flavors of the spirit, which may or may not mirror the aromas you experienced. In other words, you can absolutely expect a gin with the aroma of juniper to have the flavor of juniper. However, it is also likely that a gin with rich juniper aromas will have a spicy, coriander-like flavor on the palate. Also note the intensity of the flavors, which might range from delicate and subtle to rich and intense. Mainly, however, notice if the spirit appeals to you. It may not be "easy drinking," but it should be pleasurable.

Dilution: Some tasters find it beneficial to go through the steps of aroma and flavor evaluation one more time after diluting the spirit with a bit of distilled water. This dilution allows the aromas to blossom. Also, by reducing the alcoholic strength of the spirit, dilution may allow some of the background flavors to come forward. Some experts recommend diluting the spirit by just a few drops; others dilute to a standard alcohol by volume, such as 20%.

Body: The in-mouth impression registered by the sense of touch is known by various terms, such as body or "mouthfeel." Mouthfeel may be described in terms of texture, such as silky, soft, smooth, or rough; by weight, such as light, medium, or heavy; or by viscosity, such as thick or thin.

Table 2.3: The SWE Spirits Tasting Rationale – Palate

PALATE						
Sweetness:	None	Light	Moderate	Sweet	Very Sweet	
Acidity:	None	Light	Moderate	Sharp	Sour	
Bitterness:	None	Light	Moderate	Sharp	Astringent	
Alcohol:	Soft	Smooth	Warm	Pronounced	Hot	Harsh
Body:	Light	Medium	Full			
Flavors:						
Flavor Intensity:	Light	Medium	Full			

Finish: Just as in wine tasting, the sensations—in terms of scent, flavors, and tactile impressions—that a spirit leaves after one spits or swallows is a large part of the overall impression. The sensations of some spirits may quickly disappear, but most will linger on the palate. In general, a longer finish correlates with a higher-quality spirit, although you may not tend to agree if you find the flavor of the finish unappealing!

When evaluating the finish, you may notice an array of aromas and flavors that may or may not mirror those sensed before. In terms of taste impressions, sweetness tends to fade quickly, acidity will remain for a while, and bitterness lasts the longest of all. A slight hint of bitterness in the back of the mouth, or a warm sensation in the mouth and throat, is often the final sensation left at the end of the finish.

Overall Impressions: After an analytical tasting, one should take a moment to savor the spirit and reflect on its overall impression. The most important question one should ask, of course, is whether the spirit is pleasurable—or, to put it in more casual terms, did you like it? If so, what is it about this spirit that is enjoyable? If not, what is it about the spirit that is unpleasant? Also consider how this drink could be best enjoyed—served neat, chilled, on the rocks, or in a specific mixed drink or cocktail.

Complexity: Spirits that are one-dimensional or linear may reveal only a few simple aromas and flavors and may be described as "uninteresting." Well-made spirits, however, will show a variety of aromas, flavors, and textures gleaned from the base materials and the production processes of fermentation, distillation, and aging, among others. Complex spirits will continue to change and reveal an array of sensations over the course of a tasting. They will also hold the taster's interest—sometimes for a very long time.

Quality: It is also a good idea to keep in mind that a high-quality, well-made spirit will not necessarily appeal to everyone, as most people have their (sometimes inexplicable) individual likes and dislikes. Thus, it is meaningful to consider whether the spirit is a good example of its type (or not), and if it offers a good value for its price point. Premium-priced spirits should be able to offer something in terms of "expressiveness" that is not available in a less expensive brand.

Table 2.4: The SWE Spirits Tasting Rationale – Finish

FINISH					
Length:	Short	Medium	Long	Lingering	
Aftertaste:	Warm	Smooth	Pleasant	Harsh	Unpleasant

Table 2.5: The SWE Spirits Tasting Rationale – Overall Impressions

OVERALL IMPRESSIONS					
Complexity:	Simple/None	Some complexity	Moderate Complexity	Very Complex	
Quality:	Faulty	Acceptable	Good	Very Good	Excellent	Exceptional
Maturity:	Unaged	1-2 Years	3-5 Years	6-10 Years	Mature	Very Old

CHAPTER THREE: VODKA AND OTHER NEUTRAL SPIRITS

VODKA AND OTHER NEUTRAL SPIRITS

CHAPTER THREE

LEARNING OBJECTIVES

After studying this chapter, the candidate should be able to do the following:
- Define vodka in terms of base materials, distillation processes, maturation, and other post-distillation procedures.
- Describe the main differences between American vodka and European vodka.
- Discuss the "flavored vodka" phenomenon.
- Recall and describe other neutral spirits, including high-proof neutral spirits, baijiu, shōchū, and soju.
- Discuss the sensory evaluation of vodka and the typical procedures for the serving of vodka and vodka-based drinks.

Given the popularity of vodka today and the seemingly infinite varieties of brands and flavors available, it is difficult to believe that it did not begin to show up in American cocktails until shortly after World War II. Despite its recent entry into the United States, Vodka is the largest-selling spirit (by volume) in the US spirits market and, despite the strong growth seen in the whiskey category, is likely to continue this dominance in the foreseeable future.

Vodka is a clear, unaged spirit that is often considered to be completely neutral, meaning that it is without distinct characteristics, flavor, color, or aroma. This is, however, somewhat mistaken in that vodka produced in the United States often has traces of flavor from both the ethyl alcohol present and the type of water used in its production. Moreover, vodka produced outside of the United States is often made in ways that allow its raw materials to express themselves, and many imported vodkas will exhibit subtle flavors, textures, and aromas.

This chapter begins with an overview of vodka, including a short history of the spirit and a standard definition—both from a United States and European viewpoint. It then proceeds to a discussion of basic production techniques, followed by a discussion of vodka's taste and style. The chapter concludes with a discussion of other neutral spirits produced around the world, information on flavored vodkas, and a short note on tasting and serving vodka.

DEFINITION OF VODKA

In order to adequately discuss the United States Standards of Identity for vodka, one must first define "neutral spirits." Accordingly, in the United States, neutral spirits are defined as:
- Distilled spirits produced from any material
- Spirits distilled at or above 190 proof (95% alcohol by volume) and bottled at not less than 80 proof (40% alcohol by volume)

In the United States, vodka is thus defined as:
- Neutral spirits so distilled, or so treated after distillation with charcoal or other materials, so as to be without distinctive character, aroma, taste, or color

It is noteworthy that in the United States, the category of vodka and neutral spirits is the only spirit category that is required to be distilled at or above 190 proof.

The European Union has slightly different standards for vodka, which include the following:
- It must be produced from potatoes, cereals, and/or other agricultural raw materials.
- It must be distilled and/or rectified so that the organoleptic characteristics of the raw materials used and the by-products formed in fermentation are "selectively reduced."
- It may be redistilled or treated with activated charcoal or other appropriate materials.

- It must be bottled at a minimum of 37.5% alcohol by volume (75 proof).
- Flavorings that are to be found naturally in distilled products may be added (these include glycerol and sugar).
- Other flavorings that may give the product "special organoleptic characteristics" may also be added.
- If produced from base materials other than potatoes or grains, the name of the base materials must be stated on the label.

Note: Flavored vodka, now produced in a wide range of flavors ranging from the "standards," such as lemon, orange, and vanilla, to more modern interpretations, such as peanut butter and birthday cake, is based on neutral vodka (sometimes referred to as *original vodka*), as defined above. Flavored vodkas require additional production steps and have slightly different legally defined standards than those for original vodka; these products are discussed later in this chapter.

HISTORY OF VODKA

The origins of vodka are difficult to pinpoint. Depending on which sources you believe, the first documented production was either in eighth-century Poland or ninth-century Russia. If one places the origin in Russia, then it makes sense that the typical archaic description of ardent spirits, "water of life," was eventually reduced to simply *voda*, the Russian word for water. It is believed that in the fourteenth century, the diminutive form of the word—*vodka*, interpreted as *little water*—began to be used in reference to the spirit.

An alternate theory refers to the Polish word *wódka*, the earliest known mention of which can be found dating to 1405 in the Akta Grotskie court documents of the Palatine of Sandomierz, Poland. It is used there in reference to a medicinal drink.

Whichever version one believes, it is well documented that by the 1500s, vodka began to be used as a beverage as well as a chemist's distillate for medicines and perfumes throughout the regions known today as eastern Europe and Russia.

The earliest vodkas were distilled from the most plentiful and, hence, least expensive locally sourced grain. They were often harsh and unpleasantly flavored because of poor fermentation and rudimentary distillation methods. Thus, it became common practice to mask these flavors with herbs and spices.

In the late eighteenth and early nineteenth centuries, distillers in and around Poland began to utilize a newly introduced food source from the New World—the potato—as the base material for their vodka. Despite the higher costs of potatoes, people appreciated the smoother, more palatable product; potatoes thus began to be widely used in the production of higher-quality vodka.

Additionally, in the 1870s it was discovered that the element carbon, in the form of charcoal, could remove most or all of the unwanted aromas and flavors by way of a filtration process. This set the standard for the relatively colorless and subtly flavored vodka that is available today.

Unlike many other spirits, vodka wasn't brought to the United States until the early twentieth century. Its earliest introduction was an indirect result of the rise of communism in Russia. The chain of events began in the late 1890s when the tsar nationalized the Russian vodka industry, and Vladimir Smirnov was forced to sell off his successful factory as well as the Smirnov vodka brand.

Later, during the October Revolution of 1917, the Smirnov family was forced to flee the country. They eventually landed in Constantinople (now Istanbul) and established a vodka production facility there. The family later moved to Lwów (now called Lviv, Ukraine) and started to sell the vodka under the name Smirnoff (a French-style spelling of the family name). The family eventually built another distillery in Paris, but neither enterprise matched the success the company had known in Russia.

In the 1930s, Vladimir Smirnov sold the rights to produce and market vodka under the Smirnoff name and with the Smirnoff formula to Rudolph Kunett. Mr. Kunett was a former Russian who, after fleeing the country in the 1920s, had become a successful businessman in New York. The Kunetts and the Smirnovs had done business together before. (Prior to the Russian Revolution, the Kunetts supplied grain to the Smirnovs.)

Smirnoff vodka began to be produced in the United States in 1933. Smirnoff was thus established as the first and only American-made vodka for many years. Now, over eighty years later, the brand has retained both its name and the distinction of being one of the largest-selling spirit brands in both the United States and the world.

Figure 3.1: The Once-Popular "Midday Pick-Me-Up"

Vodka did not become widely consumed in America until the late 1940s, after World War II. Up until this time, vodka was considered an exotic specialty consumed almost exclusively by Eastern European immigrants who preferred to drink their vodka straight, ice-cold, and in one gulp from a small glass.

With the rise of American cocktail culture in the 1950s, it was discovered that vodka's relatively indistinct flavor blended exceedingly well with fruit juices and other mixers. Therefore, vodka's popularity began its rise as the Screwdriver (vodka and orange juice), the Bloody Mary (vodka and spiced tomato juice), and the Moscow Mule (vodka and ginger beer served in a chilled copper mug) all became part of the American cocktail scene.

Vodka developed further popularity as it became well-known that—when taken as a midday "pick-me-up" or with a "three-Martini lunch"—it left little telltale evidence on one's breath. The Smirnoff Company even touted this benefit in their advertisements, stating, "Smirnoff leaves you breathless."

With its many uses—with a variety of mixers, as a ready substitute for gin in the Martini, and, eventually, as a product to be consumed straight or on the rocks—vodka became the most widely consumed type of spirit in the United States. Vodka also benefited from the 1960s' and 1970s' "counterculture" movement, and from the timing of the easing of the Cold War tensions between the United States and the Soviet Union. These events allowed for the importation of Stolichnaya vodka from Russia, in return for the establishment of a Pepsi production facility in the USSR. As a result, vodka came to be perceived as "cool" and "cutting edge."

Vodka's commercial success in the United States now includes brands from the Baltics, Canada, England, Finland, France, Germany, Israel, the Netherlands, Norway, Poland, Russia, Sweden, and Ukraine, along with brands from many enterprising distilleries in the United States. Today's vodka consumer has an estimated number of more than fifteen hundred products from which to choose.

Table 3.1: Top-Selling Vodka Brands

Top-Selling Vodka Brands (Global Sales)	
Rank	Brand
1.	Smirnoff
2.	Absolut
3.	Khortytsa
4.	Khlibnyi Dar
5.	Svedka
6.	Five Lakes
7.	Skyy
8.	Morosha
9.	Medoff
10.	Magic Moments
11.	Stolichnaya
12.	Soplica
13.	Grey Goose
14.	Russian Standard
15.	Belenkaya

Source: Drinks International (2018)

THE EU VODKA WARS

As we have seen, vodka has been produced and consumed by the countries of the Vodka Belt—Poland, Belarus, Ukraine, and Russia; the Baltic States of Latvia, Estonia, and Lithuania; and the Nordic states of Finland, Sweden, Norway, and Iceland—for centuries. These vodkas are traditionally made from grains or potatoes, with the majority made from a mix of grains. Some of the finest examples are made from potatoes—particularly Poland's unique, high-starch *Stobrawa* variety.

However, in 2003, a brand of French-produced vodka known as *Cîroc* was introduced. While Cîroc is produced using grapes as the base material, it still qualified to be labeled as vodka under the legal standards of the European Union. This did not sit well with those EU member-countries that had long-standing traditions of grain- or potato-based vodka production.

As a result, on February 20, 2006, Poland—with the backing of the EU vodka belt countries and Germany—requested that the European Commission revise the definition of vodka to include just those spirits produced from grains, potatoes, or sugar beets. Vodka, it was argued, was entitled to the same protections as to base ingredients and manufacturing processes as those granted to whiskies and brandies—and as such, should be granted the same assurances as to the quality and originality of the product. The opposition, which included other EU producers of vodka (such as France and the United Kingdom), countered with an argument that such restrictions would dissuade innovation and competition, and could be seen as an attempt to monopolize the vodka market by the Vodka Belt countries.

After significant deliberation, Horst Schenllhardt, Member of the European Parliament (MEP) from Germany suggested a compromise: the EU definition of vodka could be written so as to include those products distilled from (1) cereals and/or potatoes, and/or those produced from (2) "other agricultural raw materials." Those vodkas produced from "other agricultural raw materials" (such as grapes, carrots, or onions) must state the base material on the label. This proposal—known as The Schnellhardt Compromise—passed in 2007, and forms the basis for the EU vodka definition today.

This decision led many of the traditional vodka-producing countries of the EU to form organizations at the national level in order to pursue regulation and protections for the quality and character of their vodka. Of these, the most visible is Poland, which has been awarded a protected geographical indication (PGI) for its vodka. According to the standards of the PGI, Polish vodka must be made exclusively in Poland from Polish-grown grains or potatoes. Bottles meeting these criteria are able to display the PGI statement as well as a trademarked "Polska Wódka/Polish Vodka" symbol on their labels.

Estonian vodka received protected geographical indication status for its vodka in October of 2017. According to the standards, vodka so defined must be produced from 100% Estonian raw materials and water. Other EU countries pursuing national standards and/or PGI status for vodka include Sweden (*Svensk Vodka*/Swedish Vodka), Finland (*Suomalainen Vodka/Finsk Vodka*/Vodka of Finland), Norway (Norsk Vodka/Norwegian Vodka) and Lithuania (*Originali lietuviška degtinė*/Original Lithuanian vodka).

THE PRODUCTION OF VODKA

Vodka is unique in that, unlike most of the other spirit types, it has no required source of ingredients or required geographic area of production. Moreover, it is neutral in style as a result of having been distilled to a very high proof and, quite often, consequently filtered, as well as being generally unaged. Therefore, its production generally ends without the benefit of time in casks or other vessels that may impart flavors.

Base Materials: As previously mentioned, vodka has always been distilled from the most plentiful and least expensive materials, including potatoes and various grains, primarily corn. There are no restrictions on what may be used to produce vodka, with the exception of the EU standard that it be an agricultural product. There are even versions produced using grapes, sugarcane, or sugar beets. The majority of vodkas, however, are made from a mixture of grains. Similar to those used for other grain-based spirits, grains used to produce vodkas must first undergo the conversion process.

The choice of base material, and its impact on the final product, is discussed later in this chapter under the heading "Discussing Vodka's Taste and Style."

Fermentation: Fermentation is conducted quickly. Many producers use ionized, softened, or demineralized water to further reduce unwanted flavors. Depending on the water source used during this process, the water's acidic or basic content impacts the mouthfeel of the finished spirit.

Distillation: Since vodka is essentially ethyl alcohol that is reduced in proof to bottling strength, it is often distilled in an energy-efficient column still at proofs over 190. This still boils off almost all congeners to an indistinguishable level, giving vodka its "neutral spirit" designation. It should be noted, however, that neither US nor EU standards require a specific distillation method. Most vodka is produced using column still distillation, but the possibilities include a range of methods such as hybrid stills, a combination of pot still and column still distillation, or even multiple alembic distillations.

Filtration: Vodka is often processed after distillation to further neutralize its character. However, contrary to popular belief, vodka is not required to be filtered or further processed after distillation. Even in the case of American vodka, which is expected to be "without distinctive character, aroma, taste, or color," the standard allows for this to be accomplished via the manner in which the spirit is "distilled, or so treated after distillation." The American standards also mention the use of "charcoal or other materials."

Examples of charcoal filtration procedures include the following:
- Neutral spirits flow continuously through tanks containing no less than 1½ pounds (0.68 kg) of vegetal charcoal for each gallon (3.8 liters) of spirits, for a minimum period of eight hours.
- A mixture of spirits and new charcoal in a tank filled with no less than six pounds (2.7 kg) of new charcoal for every one hundred gallons (378 liters) of neutral spirit is agitated for a minimum of eight hours.

Other filtration agents may be used, such as crushed limestone; precious metals such as silver, gold, and platinum, which are praised for their catalytic actions; and crushed industrial diamonds.

Figure 3.2: Vodka on the Bottling Line in Ulyanovsk, Russia

Bottling: Vodka is bottled in a variety of alcoholic strengths, from as low as 37.5% alcohol by volume (the European minimum standard) or 40% alcohol by volume (the United States' minimum standard). It may be bottled at levels of alcohol ranging up to 50% by volume or higher, if desired, for a particular marketing purpose. While vodka is typically not aged before bottling, aging is permitted. Some specialty vodka products—both traditional and modern—are aged.

DISCUSSING VODKA'S TASTE AND STYLE

With vodka's distillation to a very high proof and potential further processing, almost all of the congeners are removed from the resulting spirit. This is in direct contrast to other spirits, such as whiskey and brandy, which are distilled at lower proofs in order to retain congener flavors. However, this should not be interpreted to mean that vodka is without taste or character. Even in the most processed of vodkas, some congeners remain, and all vodkas have the potential of displaying the flavor and character of the water used to cut the spirit before bottling.

The Taste and Style of American Vodka: Although American vodka is defined as a neutral spirit, it should not be perceived to be as neutral as water. Instead, it should be considered as neutral as pure ethyl alcohol, which does have a slight aroma as well as a somewhat sweet taste and harsh, burning aftertaste on the tongue and in the throat. It is, however, colorless like water.

Hypothetically, American vodka should be nearly congener-free. However, laboratory analysis shows that most brands contain one or more congeners in such concentration that they can surpass the sensory threshold of the average adult.

The Taste and Style of European Vodka: As noted earlier in this chapter, the EU laws governing vodka allow for the spirit to be bottled at a lower alcohol level than regulated by the United States. EU laws also allow for the addition of "small quantities of flavorings," which may include glycerin and sugar. Both of these factors may provide European vodka with specific flavor properties as well as a richer mouthfeel compared to American versions.

The Role of Congeners: Many vodka brands today have a discernible presence of residual congeners, especially those that are produced according to the EU rules. Modern vodka producers believe that these residual congeners identify their brand. Only a very few brands have no discernible characteristic other than that of ethanol. Desirable congeners commonly found in modern vodka include ethyl laurate, which gives fruity and floral aromas, and ethyl myristate and ethyl palmitate—both of which provide a waxy flavor and character.

Figure 3.3: Vodka on Store Shelves

The Choice of Base Ingredients: While the choice of the raw materials used in the production of vodka has generally been based on availability and cost, there are some historical or commercial associations, such as the following:
- Russia: Wheat
- Poland: Rye or potato
- Sweden: Winter wheat
- Finland: Barley

Vodka has the potential to exhibit certain flavors and styles according to its base materials. While the degree of distillation and filtration will, of course, limit this influence, the potential remains for the following characterizations:
- Wheat and barley base: Highly acidic, and lighter in body
- Rye or rye blends: Spicier character, more robust in flavor
- Potato base: Full-bodied, creamier on the palate
- Corn: Delicate

In the past, it would have been unusual for the source material to be mentioned on the label. However, today, in the ever-more-crowded vodka category, some premium brands see this as a way of differentiating themselves from their competitors. Table 3.2 lists some of the most common brands of vodka and the typical base ingredient(s) from which they are distilled.

FLAVORED VODKA

The wildly popular category of flavored vodka, while considered to be a modern trend, can actually trace its origins back to some of the earliest vodkas produced in eastern Europe, particularly in the vodka strongholds of Russia and Poland.

Infusions and mixtures of herbs, grasses, spices, leaves, honey, and flowers were initially used to disguise the unpleasant flavor of primitive vodka. However, these flavored spirits eventually became popular for their own sake, leading to the long-standing tradition of flavored vodkas produced in Russia, Poland, and throughout Eastern Europe. Some of these include the following:
- **Pertsovka** is a Russian term for vodka flavored with red chili pepper, with a resulting distinctive hot spiciness. Traditionally, the flavor would have also included honey.

- **Zubrówka** is a Polish vodka flavored with bison grass. Often, the vodka would be tinged yellow in the process. The result isn't grassy but often floral and somewhat herbal and sweet. This style of vodka is also popular in Belarus, where it is known as *Zubrovka*.
- **Okhotnichya,** also known as hunter's vodka, is a Russian vodka flavored with a blend of spices, often with ginger as a top note and backed by citrus peel, black pepper, red pepper, cloves, anise, and a bitter herb called tormentil. It is traditionally blended with some kind of fortified white wine.
- **Kubanskaya** is Russian vodka flavored with dried lemon and orange peels and, sometimes, honey.
- **Starka,** traditionally from Poland and Lithuania, is a vodka that is aged in oak casks and often flavored with spices and herbs. This tradition of aged vodka dates from as early as the fifteenth century, when, upon the birth of a child, the father would fill an oak vat that previously held wine with vodka, seal it, and bury it—with the intention of unearthing it at the child's wedding. The result was vodka that took on some of the characteristics of whiskey. The term *starka* refers to the aging process but also means "old woman"—a somewhat whimsical reference when applied to an aged spirit. Modern versions of oak-aged vodka, usually made from pure vodka spirit without the addition of flavorings, offer the drinker a mellower experience than whiskey, but with some of whiskey's characteristic vanilla, allspice, nutmeg, and smoky aromas. The color is amber as a result of the contact with oak.
- **Krupnik** is a Polish term for vodka that is flavored with clover honey and herbs. This style of flavored vodka is also traditional to and popular in Lithuania, where it is known as *Krupnikas*. It is often quite sweet and is sometimes heated before serving.

Table 3.2: Vodka by Typical Base Ingredient

VODKA BY TYPICAL BASE INGREDIENT	
Base Ingredient	Representative Brands
Rye	Belvedere (Poland)
	Potocki (Poland)
	Wyborowa (Poland)
	Zytnia (Poland)
Wheat	Absolut (Sweden)
	Grey Goose (France)
	Ketel One (The Netherlands)
	Sputnik (Russia)
Barley	Finlandia (Finland)
	Koskenforva (Finland)
Corn	Smirnoff (USA)
	Tito's (USA)
Grain (Combination)	Charbay (USA)
	Iceberg (Canada)
	Ikon (Russia)
	Jewel of Russia (Russia)
	Polstar (Iceland)
	Skyy (USA)
	Stolichnaya (Russia)
Potato	Chopin (Poland)
	Luksusowa (Poland)
	Monopolowa (Austria)
	Teton Glacier (USA)
Blend	Ultimat (Poland)
Grapes	Cîroc (France)

As Russian and European distillers began to extend their flavorings to include citrus, berry, and other fruits and spices, the category became so well liked that American producers began to adopt the idea. They have since added flavored versions to their brands. Colors, as well as flavors, are sometimes added to attract the eye of the consumer and reinforce the perception of the named flavor.

Originally, these flavors were based on typical foodstuffs such as lemon, orange, vanilla, pear, berry, horseradish, and pepper. However, today it seems that vodka producers, both established firms and entrepreneurs, are constantly searching for the next "hot" flavor and have developed many creative flavors, such as salted caramel, peanut butter, whipped cream, bacon, and smoked salmon.

Such new flavors are usually introduced with much advertising and marketing fanfare, along with spectacularly designed bottles and labels. This explosion of new products has carried the vodka category to new heights, further ensuring vodka's continued popularity in the spirits market. Some of these flavors are categorized in table 3.3.

It is important to note that in both the United States and Europe, the category of flavored spirits, which includes flavored vodka, has slightly different regulations as opposed to the original or unflavored spirit.

In the United States, the following standards apply to a flavored vodka product:
- It must be made with vodka to which natural flavorings have been added, with or without the addition of sugar.
- It must be bottled at no less than 30% alcohol by volume (60 proof).
- It must be labeled with the name of the predominant flavor as part of the designation, for example, "blueberry-flavored vodka."
- It may contain wine, but if the total amount of wine exceeds 2.5% of the total volume, the types and percentages of the wine must be stated on the label.

Figure 3.4: Export Bottle of Zubrówka

Table 3.3: Representative Types of Flavored Vodka

Fruits		Spices and Herbs	Other	
Apple	Lemon	Basil	Amaretto	Pecan
Banana	Lime	Black Pepper	Bacon	Piña Colada
Berry	Lychee	Chili Pepper	Bison Grass	Pumpkin Pie
Blackberry	Mandarin Orange	Chipotle Pepper	Bubble Gum	Punch
Black Cherry	Mango	Cilantro	Butterscotch	Red Licorice
Black Currant	Melon	Cinnamon	Cake	Root Beer
Blood Orange	Orange	Dill	Caramel	Rose
Blueberry	Passion Fruit	Fennel	Coffee	Salted Caramel
Buddha's Hand	Peach	Ginger	Cola	Smoked Salmon
Cherry	Pear	Horseradish	Cotton Candy	Sriracha
Citrus	Pineapple	Lemongrass	Cucumber	Tea
Coconut	Pomegranate	Mint	Espresso	Tobacco
Cranberry	Raspberry	Rosemary	Fresh-Cut Grass	Whipped Cream
Dragon Fruit	Rhubarb	Vanilla	Hibiscus	
Fig	Strawberry		Honey	
Grape	Tangerine		Lemonade	
Grapefruit	Tomato		Marshmallow	
Huckleberry	Watermelon		Maple Syrup	
Kiwi			Peanut Butter	

It may be noted that the United States Standards of Identity include a similar set of standards for products labeled as flavored brandy, gin, rum, or whiskey.

As flavored vodka produced in the United States can be bottled at 30% alcohol by volume and can therefore have more water in the blend, some brands have touted certain flavors as a "light" or "low-calorie" option. The required "natural" flavorings are also highlighted on some brands, but one should not assume that this means the flavor is derived from an actual fruit, herb, or spice. As many commercial flavoring essences are classified as "natural," these essences are predominantly used to flavor vodka.

There are, however, certain brands that use a maceration method to extract flavors from real food sources. As this process can be expensive and requires specific expertise, the maceration method is only financially practical for premium brands.

The European standards for flavored vodka are quite similar to the EU standards for unflavored ("original") vodka. They are specified as follows:
- In the European Union, flavored vodka is defined as vodka that has been given a predominant flavor *other than that of the raw materials.* It may be sweetened, blended, matured, or colored.
- It must be bottled at a minimum of 37.5% alcohol by volume (75 proof)—the same standard that applies to unflavored vodka produced in the European Union.

OTHER NEUTRAL SPIRITS

Many types of neutral spirits are produced; however, they are usually made for use in the production of some other final product. These spirits are known variously as a "new-make spirit," a "rectified spirit," or an "eau-de-vie." These spirits may also be produced to be added to a blend, as is done in the production of whiskey, brandy, and some liqueurs.

Neutral spirits are simply highly concentrated ethanol, typically around 95% alcohol by volume, and are made from a variety of source materials including grain, corn, or sugar beets. If produced exclusively from grains, then it may be referred to as a "neutral grain spirit." While most of these are made as part of a separate spirit-production process, there are a few types of high-proof neutral spirits bottled for sale and consumption. These products include the following:
- **Everclear:** Perhaps best known as a favorite of the college party set, this is an American neutral grain spirit produced by the company Luxco. Everclear, generally located "behind the counter" in liquor stores, is bottled in two versions—one at 75.5% alcohol by volume (151 proof) and one at 95% alcohol by volume (190 proof).
- **Primaspirit:** This is a type of neutral grain spirit produced in Germany, bottled at 95.6% alcohol by volume (191.2 proof). Primaspirit is sold primarily for use in homemade liqueurs. It also goes by the name of neutralalkohol.
- **Spirytus Rektyfikowany:** This rectified spirit from Poland is made from grain and/or potatoes. It is commonly used for homemade liqueurs but is sometimes consumed in an undiluted form. It is bottled at 96% alcohol by volume (192 proof).

BAIJIU, SHŌCHŪ, AND SOJU

Vodka-like spirits have been popular in many Asian countries for a very long time. The production and consumption of such products dates back to the earliest instances of distillation, as the practice spread eastward from its beginnings in the Middle East and Europe.

Baijiu

Baijiu, a Chinese spirit (sometimes called shaojiu), is most commonly made from sorghum, but local variations may use such base materials as barley, millet, or glutinous rice. With a history dating back several millennia, baijiu is the world's most consumed spirit, accounting for almost one-third of all spirits sold worldwide. However, it is not widely available outside of China.

Baijiu is generally bottled at a relatively high proof for an Asian spirit, often between 40% and 60% alcohol by volume; some variations have an even higher proof. Traditionally, it is bottled in ceramic crocks or bottles. It is often served warm or at room temperature, and poured into small ceramic cups. A dizzying variety of baijiu is sold in China, both in flavored and unflavored forms. Some infused versions are even considered to have certain medicinal properties.

Figure 3.5: Baijiu Produced Locally in Haikou, Hainan, China (The numbers represent the alcohol levels, followed by the price.)

The conversion of starch to sugar, in this and many other types of Asian liquors, is accomplished by compressing a mash of the base material into bales or bricks, followed by storing it in a damp environment so that it becomes filled with mold spores and yeasts. This is called the *qu*. After about a month, it is mixed with fresh grains and water to start the process of saccharification. During saccharification, the enzymes within the qu break down the starches into their component sugars, and the yeasts start the fermentation process. The resulting mash can then be distilled using traditional Chinese wooden stills or a more modern pot or column still.

The resulting spirit is sometimes mixed with more grain and qu, refermented, and distilled a second time in order to concentrate the alcohol. It can then be aged, usually in earthenware urns, to mellow the flavors. After a period as short as a few months or as long as several years, the baijiu is bottled.

Every local province has its own tradition and variant of baijiu, so, for a Westerner, the task of deciphering the bottlings can be daunting. While each variant can have a distinctive flavor profile, they are often commonly grouped into "fragrance" categories. For instance, the "sauce" fragrance has a pungent character with a solvent-like aroma, while the "light" fragrance is more delicate and mellow. There is also a "thick" fragrance, which is unctuous and sweet-tasting, as well as a "rice" fragrance, and a "honey" fragrance.

The more popular, unflavored versions of baijiu include the following:

- **Moutai:** From the town of Maotai in Guizhou, this baijiu was a favorite of Mao Zedong, who served it at state dinners during Richard Nixon's 1972 visit to China. Moutai, which is based on sorghum and a wheat qu, undergoes seven cycles of fermentation and distillation.
- **Erguotou:** Erguotou is the version most commonly associated with Beijing. Erguotou is bottled under the popular brand Red Star. Inexpensive but with a high alcohol content, it is a favorite among the working class.
- **Luzhou Laojiao:** Produced in the Sichuan province, this version is known for its complexity and unique aromas, attributed to the yellow clay cellars where the mash is stored until use.
- **Wuliangye:** Produced in the city of Yibin in the Sichuan province, Wuliangye is often called "five grain drink," as it is produced using sorghum, corn, wheat, rice, and glutinous rice.

Flavored varieties of baijiu, which may be sweetened, are made using flowers, tea, honey, and Chinese medicinal herbs.

Shōchū

Shōchū is a Japanese spirit that derives its name from a word that means "burned liquor." Common varieties use barley, buckwheat, rice, or sweet potatoes as the base material, but some of the more industrial-style preparations are produced using molasses or sugar.

Single-distilled versions have a relatively low alcohol content of around 25% alcohol by volume, while column still versions that undergo multiple distillations may be bottled at closer to 35% alcohol by volume. Depending on the variety of shōchū, it can be aged for as little as one month before bottling, or it may be aged up to three years or longer.

Figure 3.6: Shōchū Produced by Nikaidō Brewery, Located in Ōita Prefecture

Fermentation is achieved using a mold called a kōji in order to induce saccharization of the base materials. There are three types of kōji mold used, each of which imparts its own distinctive characteristics in the final product:

- **White Kōji:** White kōji is the most common and has the least impact on the resulting shōchū, giving it a subtle, sweet taste.
- **Yellow Kōji:** Yellow kōji, the type used to produce sake, provides a lush, fruity taste. This type of kōji is extremely sensitive to warm temperatures.
- **Black Kōji:** Black kōji is prized for its ability to help extract the most character from the base materials and, as such, is considered to be the highest quality, despite its prolific tendency to cover every surface of the production facility with a layer of black mold.

Moromitori shōchū is the most common single-distilled version of shōchū. It is named for the two-stage fermentation method that produces the moromi—the low-alcohol mash that is then distilled. There are many types, named for their base material. The most common varieties are as follows:

- **Rice Shōchū:** Rice shōchū, or komejōchū, is produced in areas that are also well-known for sake production.
- **Sweet Potato Shōchū:** Sweet potato shōchū, or imojōchū, has a strong, almost smoky character.
- **Barley Shōchū**: Barley shōchū, or mugijōchū, has a mellow flavor that makes it easy to drink.
- **Soba Shōchū:** Soba (buckwheat) shōchū, or sobajōchū, is a fairly recent variant that is often used in blended shōchū because of its mild taste.
- **Blended Shōchū**: Blended shōchū is generally made with a blend of the more strongly flavored single-distillation shōchū and a less expensive multiple-distilled shōchū. Blends sell at a less expensive price point and retain some of the flavors and aromas of the single-distilled product.
- **Kasutori Shōchū:** Kasutori shōchū is produced using the lees left over from the fermentation of sake.

Soju

Soju is a Korean distilled spirit made from rice, barley, or wheat, although modern variants may incorporate sweet potatoes, as well. The alcohol content of soju varies widely, from as low as 16% alcohol by volume to as much as 45% alcohol by volume. Some versions are produced via single distillation, but soju is most commonly produced using a continuous still distillation.

Jinro is the most widely distributed brand of soju and, as such, is among the best-selling brands of spirits in the world. Variations include diluted and undiluted versions as well as a variety of flavored and unflavored styles. Soju may be consumed straight or used in cocktails as a replacement for vodka.

TASTING AND SERVING VODKA

Vodka is considered by many to be the ultimate base for mixed drinks and cocktails. It is happily consumed across the globe in the Cosmopolitan, the Bloody Mary, the Black Russian, some versions of the Martini (although gin aficionados will argue the point), and countless other drinks. High-quality vodkas are also enjoyed straight up or on the rocks.

Vodka is most often enjoyed chilled, so while tasting a sample at room temperature is certainly an option, vodka is likely to show at its best when well chilled. Ideally, chilled vodka should be stored in the freezer overnight in order to allow its viscosity and flavors to shine.

An interesting approach to vodka tasting is to group vodkas by base ingredient—potato, wheat, rye, barley, or grain—or to do a comparative tasting across the range. Another tasting could group vodkas by region of origin, such as Poland, Russia, America, and western Europe.

Unflavored vodkas are generally crystal clear and should have excellent clarity. The color of flavored vodka may, of course, reflect its flavoring.

Good vodkas are often subtle in aroma and flavor; however, some styles of vodka (particularly European) show aromas and flavors reminiscent of the base ingredient. Many styles of vodka will have light aromas of mineral, charcoal, or grain. Wheat vodkas may show aromas of anise or licorice, and rye vodka may have a nutty scent. A medicinal or solvent-like aroma may indicate low-quality vodka.

Upon tasting, even the best vodka will impart a noticeable "burn" of alcohol, although it should not be unpleasant or overly intense. Note if the vodka seems sweet or dry, light-bodied or chewy, and delicate and subtle or intense. Vodka can be any of these. Vodka may retain the flavors of its base ingredient, however subtle, and is often described as spicy, creamy, or sharp.

If vodkas produced from a variety of raw materials are tasted, it may be noted that those from a wheat and barley base are highly acidic and comparatively lighter in body. Those produced from rye or rye blends will seem spicier, with a robust flavor. Potato-based vodkas are likely to be full-bodied and creamy on the palate, while corn vodkas have the most delicate of flavors.

Good vodka should finish dry, with a hint of flavor (likely mineral, but this varies by brand and style). A bit of sharpness, perhaps just a "bite," is acceptable and even expected in the finish of vodka.

Table 3.4: Tasting Vodka – Typical Flavors and Aromas

TASTING VODKA – TYPICAL FLAVORS AND AROMAS	
Fruity	Grapefruit, Orange, Lemon, Lime
Floral	Rose Petals, Violet, Dried Flowers, Perfume
Sweet Aromatics	Honey, Vanilla Bean, Marshmallow
Fermented	Wine, Rum, Whiskey
Solvent	Soapy, Linalool, Ethanol
Grain/Cereal	Grain, Biscuit, Cooked White Rice, Potato, Corn, Rye
Spice	Anise, Licorice
Mineral	Charcoal, Slate, Mineral
Other	Nutty, Coffee, Herbal, Tobacco

Table 3.5: Tasting Vodka – Typical Descriptors for Palate and Style

TASTING VODKA – TYPICAL DESCRIPTORS FOR PALATE AND STYLE	
Style	Clean, Smooth, Neutral, Shows Flavor of Base Ingredient (Europe)
Palate	Creamy, Spicy, Oily, Chewy
Other	Warm, Sharp, Dry, Bitter, Delicate, Complex

GIN AND OTHER FLAVORED SPIRITS

LEARNING OBJECTIVES

After studying this chapter, the candidate should be able to do the following:
- Define gin in terms of base materials, distillation processes, maturation, and other post-distillation procedures.
- Identify the various botanicals used in the production of gin.
- Define the London dry, Plymouth, and Old Tom styles of gin.
- Describe the various juniper-flavored spirit drinks, including Steinhäger, genever, and wacholder.
- Identify and discuss the various anise-flavored spirits, such as raki, absinthe, Pernod, pastis, and ouzo.
- Identify and discuss other flavored spirits including pacharán and akvavit.
- Discuss the sensory evaluation of gin and the typical procedures for the serving of gin and gin-based drinks.

Gin is essentially a neutral spirit flavored with juniper berries as well as a wide range of other herbs, spices, roots, flowers, seeds, and leaves. Gin has its origins in Holland, Germany, and England, but today it can be produced anywhere in the world. Several styles of gin are produced. All have the juniper flavor in common, but they are unique in terms of distillation techniques, botanical recipes, and, in some cases, maturation processes.

This chapter begins with an overview of gin, including a standard definition, history, basic production techniques, and a discussion of botanical flavorings. It then proceeds to describe the leading styles of gin, including London dry gin—the most popular and widely distributed. It continues with a discussion of juniper-flavored spirit drinks, which are a range of beverages related to gin but, according to strict US and EU standards, are classified in a different category, generally because of their lower levels of alcohol. The chapter concludes with a discussion of anise-flavored spirits and other uniquely flavored beverages produced throughout the world.

DEFINITION OF GIN

According to the United States Standards of Identity, gin is defined as follows:
- It is a spirit that derives its main characteristic flavor from juniper berries.
- It is bottled at no less than 40% alcohol by volume (80 proof).
- "Distilled gin" is defined as a subcategory of gin that must be produced exclusively using original distillation or redistillation.
- The following products are defined as types of gin and therefore must adhere to the standards set for gin: dry gin, London dry gin, geneva gin, Holland gin, Tom gin, and Old Tom gin.

According to the US standards, gin may be produced using any of the following procedures:
- Original distillation from mash
- Redistillation of distilled spirits
- Mixing neutral spirits with or over juniper berries and other aromatics (neutral spirits being defined as "distilled spirits produced from any material at or above 190 proof")
- Mixing neutral spirits over extracts derived from infusions, percolations, or maceration of such materials
- Mixing gin and neutral spirits

The EU definition of gin has slightly different specifications:
- It must be a juniper-flavored spirit drink of agricultural origin.
- It must be bottled at a minimum of 37.5% alcohol by volume.

- Only natural flavorings may be used.
- The predominant flavor must be juniper.
- "Distilled gin" is defined as a subcategory of gin that must be produced via original distillation or redistillation using a spirit distilled at a minimum of 192 proof.
- "London gin" is defined as a subcategory of distilled gin whose flavor is introduced exclusively through redistillation in traditional stills and which contains less than 0.1 gram of sugar per liter and no added ingredients aside from water. This type of spirit may also be called London dry gin.

The European Union also recognizes juniper-flavored spirit drinks as a separate product category. Juniper-flavored spirit drinks are based on the earliest styles of gin and may be bottled at a minimum of 30% alcohol by volume. Being, in general, too low in alcohol to be classified as true gins, genever, Steinhäger, and wacholder are all recognized by the European Union as types of juniper-flavored spirits.

HISTORY OF GIN

The Dutch physician Franciscus Sylvius is often credited with the invention of gin in the mid-seventeenth century; however, it seems that juniper-infused spirits were produced long before Dr. Sylvius was even born. It has been claimed that British soldiers fighting in the Eighty Years War against the Spanish were drinking genever—widely referred to as "Dutch courage" for its calming effect—as early as 1585, and that a recipe for genever appears in a thirteenth-century encyclopedia, *Der Naturen Bloeme,* written in Bruges. The term g*enever* was based on the Dutch word for juniper and over the years became shortened to *gin*.

Nevertheless, the good Doctor Sylvius, a professor of medicine at Holland's University of Leyden, can at the very least be acknowledged for popularizing a medicinal tonic made with neutral spirits and the oil of the juniper berry. The juniper berry was believed to cure all sorts of ailments afflicting the bladder, kidneys, and circulatory system. Soon, "gin tonic" became a popular cure.

A few years later, during the 1689–1702 reign of King William III of England (known as William III of Orange), duties and taxes on French imported wines and brandies were raised, while the excise tax on English distilled spirits was lowered. This incentive led English distillers to make their own versions of gin based on the successful production methods invented by the Dutch. The English mass-produced their gin using inexpensive corn spirits blended with juniper berries and other flavorings. The flavorings masked the crude spirit's harsh taste and, at the same time, produced a very inexpensive beverage.

Not long after the English monarchy began to allow unlicensed production of gin for the masses, the "gin craze" commenced. The gin craze was a period between 1720 and 1751 when the per capita consumption of distilled spirits almost tripled. Centered in London, this urban phenomenon created a web of thousands of "dram shops," where gin was sold to patrons gathered around the bar or packaged to take home. This accessible, inexpensive drinking culture became popular with the working-class poor and was blamed for a myriad of social problems.

Figure 4.1: William Hogarth's Satirical Print *Gin Lane* (1751)

In response to the public disorder brought on by the gin craze and the general drunkenness of parts of the population, the British government eventually passed several Gin Acts. These new laws required a license in order to legally sell gin and also instituted taxation of the product; as a result, easy access to gin slowed. The "gin joints" were eventually licensed and expanded their range to include beer and wine, becoming the precursors to the modern-day pub or bar.

At this time, some producers began to produce higher-quality gins designed for drinking pleasure rather than just alcoholic consumption. Soon, with the invention of the continuous Coffey still in the mid-nineteenth century, the grain spirits used as the base distillate for gin greatly improved. Low-congener, high-proof neutral spirits shifted the flavor profile to the flavorings themselves and significantly reduced the need for sweetening to mask unpleasant flavors in the gin. In this way, the "London dry" style of gin came into vogue.

England's empire helped spread the taste for gin to all continents, especially the warm-climate colonies. Bitter quinine, used to control malaria, blended perfectly with gin to create the crisp, clean, and cold flavor of the Gin and Tonic. Gin was used in the original Martini and was the star of pre-Prohibition America's "cocktail culture."

Prohibition did little to curb America's demand for gin. English gin was smuggled into the United States from Canada, and "bathtub gin," a homemade compound gin, was produced by the tubful by blending botanical oils with neutral spirits.

Developed well over a century ago, the style of London dry gin has been copied worldwide and is today, by far, the world's favorite style of gin. However, interest in all things historical has brought renewed interest to genever, Steinhäger, Old Tom, and other historic juniper-flavored beverages, while new flavors and styles are being created as well.

Table 4.1: Top-Selling Gin Brands

TOP-SELLING GIN BRANDS (GLOBAL SALES)	
	Brand
1.	Ginebra San Miguel
2.	Gordon's
3.	Bombay
4.	Tanqueray
5.	Beefeater
6.	Seagram's
7.	Larios
8.	Hendrick's

Source: Drinks International (2018)

THE PRODUCTION OF GIN

Gin is produced by adding the flavor of juniper berries to a base spirit. Other botanical flavorings may be used as well, but the dominant flavor of this light-bodied spirit must be the juniper berry.

Gin may be produced using any type of neutral spirit as its base. A mash of cereal grains is most commonly used, but gin may be produced from a base of sugarcane, potatoes, sugar beets, or other agricultural products. The wash is distilled, generally to at least 190 proof, to create a neutral spirit.

Botanicals: The range of botanicals used in the flavoring of gin is quite diverse and includes a variety of seeds, herbs, barks, citrus peels, roots, and nuts. The most widely used botanicals can be categorized into six classifications, as shown in table 4.2.

Table 4.2: Botanical Classification of Gin Flavorings

BOTANICAL CLASSIFICATION OF GIN FLAVORINGS					
Seed/Bean	Herb	Bark	Citrus Peel	Root	Other
Aniseed	Angelica	Cassia	Grapefruit	Fennel	Almond
Caraway	Chamomile	Cinnamon	Lemon	Ginger	Calamus
Cardamom	Hyssop	Quinine	Lime	Licorice Root	Clove
Cocoa	Marjoram		Orange	Orris Root	Gentian
Coriander	Mint				
Juniper Berry	Rosemary				
Vanilla	Sage				

Juniper itself comes from the berries of an evergreen tree, imparting a fresh pine aroma to the spirit. Coriander seed, which is the second most widely used botanical, adds a peppery or spicy note, along with hints of citrus. Angelica root is used to add an earthy, wood-like character, while orris root provides floral aromas reminiscent of violets. Citrus peels are widely used to provide the aroma and flavor of the respective fruit. See table 4.3 for a definition and description of the botanicals most often used in the production of gin.

Aging: Most gins are bottled unaged, but aging is allowed. Barrel-aged gins are increasing in popularity, particularly among craft distillers. Some types of gin may be sweetened, although most modern gins are dry. Gins are differentiated primarily based on the types of mash from which the base spirits are distilled, the quality of the juniper berries, and the selection of botanicals used to flavor a specific gin.

Table 4.3: Description of Selected Gin Botanicals

DESCRIPTION OF SELECTED GIN BOTANICALS		
Name	**Description**	**Aromas/Flavors**
Angelica	A tall flowering herb native to the Northern Hemisphere. The stems and ribs are often candied and used as culinary decorations.	Earthy, wood-like, delicate aroma, somewhat reminiscent of celery.
Calamus	A semiaquatic flowering plant officially known as *Acorus calamus*; also known as sweet flag.	Often used as a substitute for ginger, cinnamon, or nutmeg.
Cardamom	An ancient spice; the seedpods of a variety of plants in the ginger family.	Smoky, mint, camphor, floral, resinous, grapefruit.
Cassia	The spice made from trees related to the "true" Sri Lanka cinnamon; marketed as cinnamon in North America.	Cinnamon, resin, pungent.
Citrus Peel	The dried peels of oranges, lemons, limes, or other citrus fruits.	Provides the aroma and flavor of the respective fruit.
Coriander Seed	The seed of the coriander plant, which is sometimes called cilantro or Chinese parsley.	Adds a peppery or spicy note, along with citrus.
Gentian	The root of a large family of small flowering plants producing trumpet-shaped flowers.	Very bitter and aromatic. Used in cocktail bitters.
Hyssop	An herb native to southern Europe and the Middle East. Used as a culinary herb and in herbal medicine.	Herbal, minty, and bitter.
Juniper Berry	Not a true berry, but the female seed cone of the juniper plant.	Must be the dominant flavor in gin. Lends a clean, pine-like aroma, as well as floral notes.
Orris Root	The dried root of the iris flower, used in herbal medicine and perfumery.	Floral, violet, raspberry. Often used to scent potpourri.
Quinine	A chemical that occurs naturally in the bark of the cinchona tree.	Bitter, clean, and medicinal. Used in tonic water and cocktail bitters.

DISTILLED GIN

The standards of the United States and the European Union both define distilled gin as a subcategory of gin. Distilled gin must be produced via *original distillation*, also known as *direct distillation*, or by *redistillation*.

It should be noted that while both the United States and the European Union recognize two distinct types of gin—distilled and compound—neither of these terms is required to be stated on the label; the term "gin" is considered sufficient for product identification. Some gins produced solely through distillation and/or redistillation will, however, use the term "distilled" on the label.

Original Distillation: In the original distillation method, a fermented mash is placed into a special still that contains a mesh tray and a basket or perforated rack known as a *gin head*. This type of still, invented in the nineteenth century, was originally known as a Carter head still. The gin head is filled with juniper berries and other botanicals, according to the distiller's formula. As the mash is distilled, the alcoholic vapors pass through the gin head, becoming impregnated with the aromatic oils of the botanicals. The resulting vapors come off the gin still at a high proof and then condense into gin.

Figure 4.2: Juniper Berries

Redistillation: The redistillation method is similar to original distillation; however, the mash is distilled into a neutral spirit before being flavored. To complete the flavoring, the neutral spirit is first cut with water. In some instances, the neutral spirit is then placed in the still and allowed to steep with the botanicals before redistillation; in other cases, distillation begins immediately after the botanicals are added to the still. If a specialized still is used, the botanicals are placed in a gin head allowing only the vapors to contact the flavorings. In some cases, a combination of the techniques may be used, with the more delicate botanicals placed in the gin head. Once the preparations are complete, the base spirit is distilled a second time in the presence of the juniper berries and other botanicals. As the vapors come off the still, only the heart of the run, which contains the ideal proportion of flavorings, is used to condense into gin.

A unique style of redistillation known as *cold distillation* or *vacuum distillation* is based on the fact that the boiling point of all beverages alters with air pressure. Basically, the lower the air pressure, the lower the boiling point. (This is why water boils at lower temperatures at higher elevations—the air pressure is lower at higher elevations.) When a low air pressure environment is used in the redistillation of gin, the neutral spirits can be macerated with juniper berries and other botanicals with no heat applied. Thus, the botanicals retain their structure, allowing for a more intense, fresher botanical flavor. The Sacred Spirits Company (the London-based producer of Sacred Gin) and a variety of vodka producers have begun to use vacuum distillation in the production of their spirits.

In 2007, a team from Bacardi Limited, led by food technologist Derek Greer, filed a patent for a unique method of cold distillation which allows distillation to take place at 23°F (−5°C). They began production of Oxley Cold Distilled London Dry Gin using the process in 2009; the patent was granted in 2010.

COMPOUND GIN

The standards of both the United States and the European Union also allow for gin to be flavored by mixing neutral spirits with naturally produced extracts and flavorings of juniper berries and other botanicals. No redistillation is required. This type of gin is known as compound gin and is considered to be of a lower quality than distilled gin. Compound gin may be produced via the *cold compounding* method or the *essential oils* method.

Cold Compounding: There are three basic methods of cold compounding. One involves a batch of crushed botanicals that are added to a base of neutral spirits and left to "soak" for a week or more. A second method follows basically the same procedure, except that the botanicals are enclosed in a mesh bag.

The third method, commonly called the circulatory method, is similar to a method often used in the production of liqueurs. The circulatory method entails suspending a mesh tray of botanicals in the top of a large tank containing the base spirit and pumping the alcohol repeatedly over the botanicals until the desired flavor is achieved. After any of the cold compounding procedures are complete, the spirit will be filtered and, if unaged, reduced to bottling strength and bottled.

Essential Oils: In the essential oils method, sometimes called the compounding essence procedure, a recipe of essential oils is added to a neutral spirit and thoroughly blended. The mixture is allowed to rest for a week, after which time it is filtered and, if unaged, reduced to bottling strength and bottled.

LEADING STYLES OF GIN

London Dry Gin

London dry gin is a type of distilled gin originally produced in nineteenth-century London. Despite its name, there are no geographical restrictions on the production of London dry gin.

The European Union defines London dry gin as having less than 0.1 gram of sugar per liter. As London dry gin is defined as a type of distilled gin, all of its flavoring must be created via original distillation or redistillation, with no flavoring or other additives (besides water) allowed to be added post-redistillation. The style is light, dry, and crisp, with a clean juniper berry flavor. These gins are ideal for Martinis or other cocktails, as well as for tall drinks such as the Gin and Tonic.

Figure 4.3: A Selection of London Dry Gins

The term *dry,* as in "dry gin," "extra-dry gin," or "very dry gin," is used for many gin products as a descriptor of the style. All of these terms indicate a lack of sweetness.

Leading brands of London dry gin include Beefeater London Dry Gin, Tanqueray London Dry Gin, Bombay Dry, Bombay Sapphire, No. 3 London Dry Gin, and Gordon's London Dry Gin.

Plymouth Gin

At the time when the London dry gin style became popular, distillers in other English cities developed their own styles of gin as well. Plymouth, Bristol, Warrington, and Norwich all had their unique styles. Plymouth gin, produced since 1793, is the only one of these historic gins still produced today.

The building which was to become the Plymouth Gin Distillery was originally a Dominican monastery inhabited by an order known as the Black Friars. In 1536, at the time of the Reformation, the monastery was dissolved, and the building was put to other uses. It was, over the years, used as a debtor's prison and a meeting place. Legend has it that the Plymouth pilgrims who sailed to America aboard the *Mayflower* spent their last night in England in this meeting place in 1620. The next morning, they made the short walk down to the harbor, ready to set sail to America, where they would found a "new" Plymouth. The *Mayflower* ship forms a part of Plymouth Gin's trademark label today.

In 1697, the building became the Black Friars Distillery. Part of the distillery is housed in what was once the rectory of the monastery and retains a hull-shaped timber roof built in 1431. This makes it one of the oldest buildings in Plymouth. As such, it is a protected national monument. With records of a "mault-house" on the premises dating to 1697, the distillery also claims to be the oldest working gin distillery in the world. The distinctive Plymouth gin began to be produced in 1793, not long after the business became known as Coates and Company.

In 1896, Plymouth gin was mentioned in what is considered to be the first documented recipe for the drink that would become known as the dry Martini. The recipe, under the name Marguerite Cocktail, appeared in a book—*Stuart's Fancy Drinks and How to Mix Them* by Thomas Stuart—published by the Excelsior Publishing House in New York. Plymouth gin is listed as the key ingredient, along with "French vermouth and a dash of orange bitters."

Figure 4.4: The Black Friars Distillery in Plymouth, England

The style of Plymouth gin is crystal clear in color and has a full-bodied texture, fruity aromas, and a very aromatic juniper berry profile.

Old Tom Gin

Old Tom gin, one of the predominant styles of gin in the mid-1800s, was popular in both England and America with the growing "cocktail culture." The slightly sweet Old Tom gin was the original gin used in the Tom Collins cocktail, as is evidenced by an 1891 recipe in one of the earliest cocktail books, *The Flowing Bowl: When and What to Drink,* by "The Only William" (also known as William Schmidt).

While history is not quite sure how the name "Old Tom" came to be, one of the better stories involves a London merchant named Dudley Bradstreet who sold gin illegally from his house. According to legend, Bradstreet placed a large sign in the shape of a black cat outside of his house. A pipe led from the cat's paw back inside the house. A passerby could deposit a coin in the cat's mouth, after which Bradstreet would pour a shot of gin through the tube, to be caught in the customer's mouth. Apparently, this business model soon became widespread throughout England, and "Old Tom" became a euphemism for gin.

Old Tom gin fell into obscurity for a while after the rise of the popularity of London dry gin. While it continued to be produced in England, its availability dwindled; reportedly, by the 1960s, it was produced by just one distillery. However, Old Tom gin is enjoying a resurgence in popularity and is now appreciated as a sipping drink and for use in craft cocktails. Hayman Distillery in England and Ransom Spirits in Oregon are among the many modern producers of Old Tom gin.

Gin de Mahón

Gin de Mahón is produced on the Spanish island of Menorca, one of the Balearic Islands located in the Mediterranean Sea. Gin production on Menorca (and in its capital city, Mahón) dates back to the eighteenth century when the island was occupied by the British. To produce Gin de Mahón, white wine is distilled into brandy and then redistilled in wood-fired copper pot stills along with aged juniper berries and other botanicals. The spirit is then aged in oak barrels for a period of time. This process creates gin with the distinct flavor of juniper, a smoky undertone, and a clean finish. Gin de Mahón has PGI status in the European Union and is produced solely by Xoriguer—a family business first established in 1784.

Vilnius Gin

Vilnius gin (Vilniaus Džinas), produced in Vilnius (the capital city of Lithuania), was award a protected geographical indication (PGI) by the European Union in 2008. The Vilniaus Degtinė Distillery—currently the only producer of Vilnius gin—has been making the spirit for over 30 years. In addition to juniper, Vilnius gin is flavored with coriander seed, dill seed, and orange peel. It is considered to be similar in style to London dry gin, although it is bottled at 45% abv—slightly higher than most dry gins.

Flavored Gins

US federal regulations specify flavored gins as those gins containing added natural flavoring materials, with or without the addition of sugar. These products must be bottled at a minimum of 30% alcohol by volume (60 proof) and must show the name of the dominant flavor on the bottle. While flavored gin has not yet reached the popularity of flavored vodka, styles of gin flavored (post-distillation) with a variety of flavors, including grapefruit, tarragon, ginger, coconut, and saffron, have made their way onto the market. Some of them are lightly sweetened.

JUNIPER-FLAVORED SPIRIT DRINKS

Steinhäger

Steinhäger, produced in the municipality of Steinhägen, is a classic German spirit that dates back over five hundred years. Legend has it that for centuries, the citizens of the area made spirits from grain and the fermented must of juniper shrubs picked in the nearby Teutoburg Forest. In 1688, Frederick "the Great Elector" William, ruler of Brandenburg-Prussia, was so impressed with the drink that he granted the citizens of Steinhägen the exclusive privilege to produce distilled spirits in the area.

Today, Steinhäger is produced using triple-distilled grain spirit, neutral spirits, and a juniper berry distillate. It is a mellow spirit with distinctive juniper flavor, packaged in bottles that resemble traditional stone crocks.

Today, only a few companies produce Steinhäger. The H. W. Schlichte Company, established in 1766, is the oldest producer and the one most likely to be found on store shelves outside of Germany. In 1989, Steinhäger was awarded a Protected Geographical Indication designation by the European Union.

Genever

Genever (alternately spelled "jenever" or "geniève") is a specific style of spirit originally produced using malted grain spirits flavored with juniper berry and other botanicals. Genever is considered to be the precursor of modern gin and is often referred to as genever gin, Holland gin, or Dutch gin. However, as it is often produced at lower proofs than required for gin, genever is not a "true" gin and is classified by the European Union as a juniper-flavored spirit drink. In the United States, it may be labeled as a "flavored grain spirit" or "flavored neutral spirit."

Figure 4.5: The Evolution of the Bols Genever Bottle

Genever is produced, at least in part, from a malted grain spirit. Malted barley, rye, wheat, corn, or other grains may be used. The fermented mixture is then typically distilled in a column still to 50% alcohol by volume and then reduced in strength to 25% alcohol by volume via the addition of distilled water. At least two additional distillations may be performed in pot stills to make the final distilled spirit. The finished malt spirit, which has been described as whiskey-like, may be infused with botanicals.

Table 4.4: PGI Categories of Genever

PGI CATEGORIES OF GENEVER	
Style	**Approved Regions of Origin**
Genever	Belgium, the Netherlands, France (Départements Nord and Pas-de-Calais), and Germany (Bundesländer, Nordrhein-Westfalen, and Niedersachsen)
Grain Genever (Graanjenever)	
Fruit Genever (Fruitjenever)	
Jonge Genever	Belgium and the Netherlands
Oude Genever	
Hasseltse Jenever	Hasselt, Zonhoven, and Diepenbeek, Belgium
Balegemse Jenever	Balegem, Belgium
O'de Flander-Oost-Vlaamse Graanjenever	Oost-Vlaanderen, Belgium
Genièvre Flandres Artois	Départements Nord and Pas-de-Calais, France

The malt spirit may next be combined with a low-proof neutral spirit that has been infused with botanicals, including juniper berries, anise, cloves, ginger, angelica root, licorice, and hops, and then redistilled. Genever is not required to be aged, but aging is allowed and is practiced by some producers.

Genever was traditionally marketed in a cylindrical stoneware crock. Due to high production costs, many products today are packaged in glass bottles that have been spray-coated to resemble stoneware. The traditional shape, however, is usually retained.

The two most widely distributed subcategories of genever, which have specific guidelines concerning their style and manner of production, are known as *oude* and *jonge*. Despite their names, the categories have nothing to do with aging requirements but rather refer to the "old" and "modern" styles of production:

- Oude ("Old"): The original style of genever, oude must contain a minimum of 15% malt spirit. This style is straw-colored and relatively sweet, with malty aromatics. It does not require any aging.
- Jonge ("Young"): The more modern style of genever, jonge genever is drier and lighter in body, and may not contain more than 15% malt spirit. It does not require any aging.

Genever was awarded a Protected Geographical Indication by the European Union in 2008. According to these standards, production is limited to the Netherlands, Belgium, two departments in France, and some areas in Germany. Since 2008, several subappellations of genever have been recognized, as shown in table 4.4.

The tradition in Amsterdam is to serve genever ice-cold in a tulip-shaped cordial glass. A bartender will set the glass on the bar and fill it nearly to overflowing. Those who are in-the-know then lean over the bar and, without using hands, take the first sip from the glass, following it with a glass of beer. It is the custom to serve these *kopstootjes* ("head-butts") with bar foods during the Amsterdam version of happy hour.

Wacholder
Wacholder is a classic German juniper-flavored spirit produced mainly in the German state of North Rhine-Westphalia. One of the oldest operating wacholder distilleries is the Brennerei Eversbusch (Eversbusch Distillery) in Hagen, which was founded in 1780 and has been operating out of the same facility since 1817. *Wacholder* is the German word for *juniper*. As such, it is often used in Germany as an umbrella term for all juniper-flavored spirits.

ANISE-FLAVORED SPIRITS
Anise-based spirits are produced throughout the Mediterranean Basin, where star anise was initially imported from its native China. Under EU law, anise-flavored spirits, many of which have attained Protected Geographical Indications, must derive their flavor from star anise, green anise, licorice root, fennel, or a similar plant that shares the same principal aromas. These plants all contain a flavor compound known as *anethole*, which imparts the unique, licorice-like aroma and flavor. While other flavorings are allowed, anise must be the dominant flavor. The spirit base is generally a neutral spirit to which the flavor is added through maceration, distillation, redistillation, the introduction of extracts, or a combination of these methods.

These beverages, given their intense flavor, are often consumed diluted with water. Dilution with water will cause a condition known as louching, also known as the louche effect, which makes the spirit appear cloudy. The cloudiness occurs because the botanical oils present in the beverage are readily dissolved in alcohol but are not so easily combined with water. Therefore, the oils fall out of emulsion. Louching commonly occurs with pastis, Pernod, absinthe, ouzo, raki, and Sambuca, among others.

Raki
Raki (pronounced *rucka*) is an unsweetened anise-flavored spirit produced in Turkey. Raki is widely consumed throughout the Balkan countries as an aperitif. It was originally produced from the pomace left over from winemaking. However, when pomace was in short supply, spirits were imported and processed with aniseed. During the First World War, when trade was restricted, raisins, dried figs, and mulberries were used in the production of raki. Today, high-quality raki is produced from sultana grapes, both fresh and dried. The grape must is fermented into wine and distilled in a column still to create a spirit base known as *suma*. The suma, which

may be mixed with a neutral spirit, is then redistilled with aniseed using an alembic still and allowed to rest for a minimum of thirty days. Raki is considered to be one of the highest-quality anise spirits.

Absinthe

Absinthe is a flavored spirit with a colorful past. Loosely defined, it is produced using anise, sweet fennel, and other culinary and medicinal herbs, in particular the flowers and leaves of *Artemisia absinthium,* also known as grand wormwood. Wormwood seems to have been known and used as a flavoring since antiquity; a wormwood-infused wine was known in ancient Greece.

Legends abound about the earliest use of a wormwood-flavored spirit. However, one widely held story dates to 1792, when Dr. Pierre Ordinarie, a French doctor living in Switzerland, produced a medicinal elixir flavored with wormwood, green anise, and fennel. Another version of the story dates to the same time and place but claims that the Henriod sisters made the first version. In either case, the story continues with a gentleman known as Major Henri Dubied, his son Marcelline, and his son-in-law Henry-Louis Pernod, who acquired the formula and, in 1797, opened the first absinthe distillery in Couvet, Switzerland.

In 1805, they built a second distillery in Pontarlier, France, under the name Maison Pernod Fils. Pernod Fils remained one of the most popular brands of absinthe up until 1914, when the drink was banned in France.

Figure 4.6: *L'Absinthe (The Glass of Absinthe)* by Edgar Degas (1875)

Absinthe was wildly popular in France in the late nineteenth and early twentieth centuries, particularly among Paris-based artists and writers. Ernest Hemingway, Charles Baudelaire, Henri de Toulouse-Lautrec, Vincent van Gogh, and Oscar Wilde were all known to enjoy absinthe. Because of its association with the bohemian lifestyle, absinthe was opposed by some social conservatives and came to be thought of as a dangerous and addictive drug that was often blamed for hallucinations and for provoking criminal activities.

The alleged harmful effects of absinthe were blamed on the chemical compound *thujone,* despite the fact that the spirit contains only trace amounts of the substance. By 1915, absinthe had been banned in the United States and in much of Europe, including France, the Netherlands, Belgium, and Switzerland.

It was eventually proven that absinthe was no more dangerous than any other spirit made with the same level of alcohol by volume. In the 1990s, realizing that the United Kingdom had never outlawed absinthe, Britain began to import Hill's Absinthe from the Czech Republic. This led to renewed interest in the once-maligned spirit. Soon, absinthe was brought back to life.

Beginning in 1998, one by one the countries of Europe legalized absinthe, subject to a maximum limit of 10 mg/L of thujone. Legend has it that historic versions of absinthe produced before the ban may have contained up to 260 mg/L of thujone, although this claim has been largely disproven using gas chromatography. After a ninety-year ban, the United States, in 2007, also legalized absinthe, subject to a limit of 10 ppm of thujone. The repeal of the ban has permitted the importation of European products into the US market. Now, several US producers are making artisanal absinthes.

Figure 4.7: Absinthe Fountain

Modern absinthe may be clear in color, but it is usually a natural clear green color, leading to its nickname "la fée verte" ("the green fairy"). Traditionally, absinthe is prepared in a reservoir glass. A specially designed slotted spoon is used to suspend a sugar cube over a glass that has been filled one-third full with absinthe. Ice water is then poured or dripped over the sugar cube into the absinthe until the drink contains one part absinthe to three-to-five parts water. The water will "release the green fairy," meaning that it will cause the beverage to louche, or turn milky in appearance, as well as allow for the "blossoming" of the spirit's aromas and flavors.

Pernod and Pastis
The ban on absinthe closed the Maison Pernod Fils Distillery in Pontarlier until 1928, when it relaunched with an eponymous anise spirit. Similar to absinthe but sweeter, lower in alcohol, and minus the wormwood, *Pernod* was instantly popular with the absinthe-starved French population. Four years later, twenty-three-year-old Paul Ricard discovered a formula for an anise-based spirit and developed pastis as a dry, anise-based spirit option. Ricard's formula contained fennel, licorice root, and forty-eight other botanicals in addition to anise. The two firms competed for many years before reaching an agreement to amicably merge and become Pernod Ricard in 1975.

Herbsaint
Herbsaint is an American anise liqueur created in New Orleans. It was first produced in 1934 as a substitute for Absinthe. Absinthe had been very popular in New Orleans before it was banned, and the city had been known for its establishments such as the Old Absinthe House bar on Bourbon Street, famous for both its selection and its ornate absinthe fountains.

Herbsaint's creators, J. Marion Legendre and Reginald Parker, had learned how to make absinthe while in France during World War I. Their liqueur was originally named "Legendre Absinthe" despite the fact that it never contained wormwood. However, not long after it was first offered for sale (after the repeal of Prohibition), the Federal Alcohol Administration objected to the use of the word "absinthe" in the product's name. The name was soon changed to *Legendre Herbsaint*— based on the term *Herbe sainte* (the French/Creole term for *Artemisia absinthium*; meaning "sacred herb"). The Sazerac Company (based in Metairie, Louisiana) bought J.M. Legendre & Co. in 1949 and now produces Herbsaint in a 90-proof version and the 100-proof *Herbsaint Original*.

Ouzo
The leading Greek aperitif *ouzo* has a long and legendary history. In one version, it was originally produced by a group of monks living in a monastery on Mount Athos during the fourteenth century. The monks produced a range of pomace brandies called *tsipouro*. The anise-flavored version was known as ouzo, which eventually became the spirit widely produced in Greece today. Ouzo first became popular at the beginning of the nineteenth century following Greek independence. After the ban on absinthe, it again rose in favor, as a "substitute for absinthe, minus the wormwood."

Modern ouzo is produced with a neutral base spirit that is flavored with anise and, sometimes, star anise, cloves, cinnamon, and other spices. While it is mainly known as a sweetened spirit, dry versions are produced as well.

OTHER FLAVORED SPIRITS

Pacharán

Pacharán (*patxaran* in the Basque language) is a traditional flavored spirit produced in the north of Spain. Pacharán is produced using sloe berries, the fruit of locally grown blackthorn bushes, which resemble small plums. To make pacharán, sloe berries, coffee beans, and vanilla beans are soaked in anise-flavored spirits for one to eight months. The resulting spirit is naturally a light mahogany red color; no coloring may be added. Pacharán is bottled at 25–30% alcohol by volume and may be dry or slightly sweet.

Pacharán is produced in Navarra, La Rioja, and the Spanish Basque Country; however, the version produced in Navarra has been granted a Protected Geographical Indication status and is known by the name Pacharán Navarro. Pacharán is much beloved by the locals, who enjoy it chilled or on ice as an aperitif.

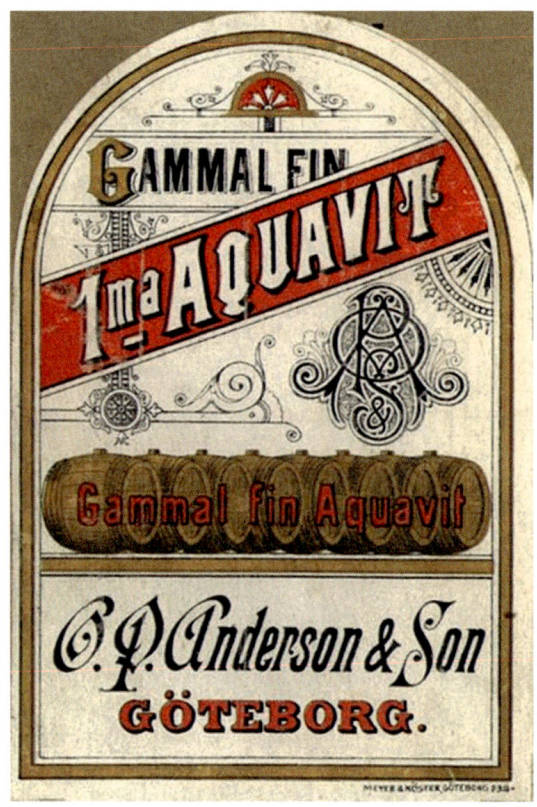

Figure 4.9: Original Label for O. P. Anderson Aquavit (Sweden, 1891)

Figure 4.8: A Bottle of Pacharán Navarro

Note: The product widely recognized in the United States as sloe gin is actually a sweetened liqueur, traditionally "homemade" in England by soaking sloe plums and sugar in gin. Most commercially produced sloe gin is made with neutral spirits.

Akvavit

Caraway-flavored spirits have been produced in Scandinavia since the fifteenth century and are enjoyed as a traditional aperitif (or digestif) throughout the region today. *Akvavit,* or aquavit, as it is often called, is made in a variety of styles throughout Scandinavia; however, it may be produced in other parts of the world as well.

Akvavit is generally based on a neutral spirit, distilled either from grain (as is common in Germany) or potatoes (as is common in Norway). Sweden and Denmark produce akvavit using grain and/or potatoes. After distillation, the base spirit is flavored with caraway and may be further flavored with herbs, spices, or fruit oil. Fennel, cardamom, cumin, dill, anise, lemon peel, orange peel, and even amber are used in some versions. Each brand has its own unique formula; however, caraway is typically the dominant flavor. (Note: In the United States, TTB regulations require that caraway be the dominant flavor in akvavit; however, in the EU, the dominant flavor may be either caraway or dill. While a few examples of EU akvavit use dill as their primary flavor, in practice almost all are caraway-dominant.)

Akvavit does not have an aging requirement, although some versions are aged. This allows for a wide range of colors, from water-white to deep amber. As is the case with many other spirits, the use of certain colorings is permitted, so color is not a reliable indicator of age. Clear akvavit may be known as *taffel akvavit*, which is typically not aged or else is aged for a short period of time in old casks.

Linje aquavit is unique to Norway. Linje aquavit is based on the tradition of aging aquavit in oak barrels by sending them in sailing ships from Norway to Australia and back again, thus passing the equator, or the "linje" (Norwegian for "line"), twice before being bottled. Legend has it that Arcus-Gruppen, Norway's largest distiller and a leading producer of aquavit, once tried to simulate the constant movement, humidity, and temperature fluctuation of an actual journey in its barrel-aging rooms, with unsatisfactory results. For this reason, boats loaded with linje aquavit still set sail from Norway to Australia, spending over nineteen weeks at sea. The company says that at any given time, there are more than a thousand barrels of aquavit making the ocean journey. Every bottle's travel itinerary is printed on the back label.

Akvavit is traditionally enjoyed neat from shot glasses or small tulip-shaped glasses. Taffel akvavit is generally served chilled, while richer, oak-aged versions are best at room temperature. As would be expected, the spirit is a natural match for Scandinavian foods like rye bread, pickled vegetables, and smoked fish. A traditional saying holds that aquavit "helps the fish swim down to the stomach."

Sweden has protected geographical indication (PGI) status for its *akvavit*, known locally as *Svensk Akvavit* or *Svensk Aquavit*.

TASTING AND SERVING GIN

Gin is one of the more uniquely flavored spirits and, therefore, tends to maintain its character more than some liquors when used in a cocktail or mixed drink. Gin blends well with juices, sodas, soda water, and, of course, tonic. Popular mixed drinks and cocktails made with gin include the classic dry Martini, the Gin and Tonic, the Tom Collins, the Pink Lady, and the Singapore Sling.

Figure 4.10: A Classic Gin and Tonic

There is no standard glass for the tasting or serving of gin, as it is rarely served straight—although many cocktail aficionados prefer their Martini ultra-dry, with only a drop (or a thought) of vermouth.

Most London dry gin, by far the most popular style, is colorless. However, botanicals used in the production process may leave behind traces of color as well as flavor, although you may really have to look while holding the glass up to a light to notice any. Aged styles of gin may be pale yellow to lightly golden. Flavored gins will likely reflect the natural hue of the flavoring.

High-quality gin will generally show faintly sweet aromas highlighted by juniper, which may be described as having a clear, sharp flavor of pine, resin, citrus, and herb. Harold McGee, in his book *On Food and Cooking,* describes the flavor of juniper as "green-fresh." Coriander, the second most widely used flavoring in gin, will lend a bit of spice. Other common aroma descriptors include floral, lemon zest, lime zest, grapefruit, pine, and mineral.

Gin is often described as clean and crisp on the palate, although, given their diversity, some brands may feel full-bodied or almost "oily." The juniper flavor should not last too long; it should fade before you are ready to take your next sip. Good gin will have a mild, clean, and lingering finish. In the best of all possible worlds, there will be little or no "bite" or harshness in the aftertaste.

Table 4.5: Tasting Gin – Typical Flavors and Aromas

_	TASTING GIN – TYPICAL FLAVORS AND AROMAS
Gin Resin	Juniper, Angelica
Herbal	Coriander, Mint, Chamomile, Pine, Rosemary, Sage, Verbena, Dried Herbs
Citrus	Lemon, Lemon Zest, Lime, Lime Zest, Orange, Grapefruit, Citrus Blend
Spice	Anise, Pepper, Cinnamon, Cardamom, Ginger, Coriander Seed, Cassia, Nutmeg, Vanilla
Floral	Orris, Violet, Lavender, Lilac
Vegetal	Cucumber, Fennel
Earthy	Forest Floor, Mineral
Solvent	Soapy, Linalool

Table 4.6: Tasting Gin – Typical Descriptors for Palate and Style

_	TASTING GIN – TYPICAL DESCRIPTORS FOR PALATE AND STYLE
Style	Light, Fresh, Aromatic, Flavorful, Pungent, Botanical
Palate	Clean, Crisp, Sweet, Dry, Spicy, Oily, Prickly
Other	Buttery, Solvent

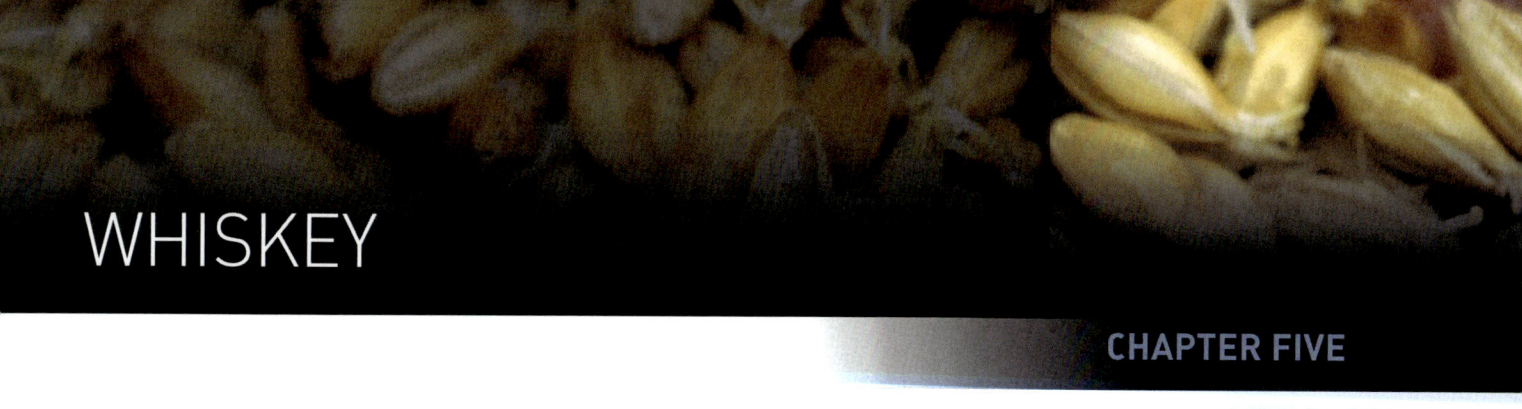

WHISKEY

CHAPTER FIVE

LEARNING OBJECTIVES

After studying this chapter, the candidate should be able to do the following:
- Define whiskey in terms of base materials, distillation processes, maturation, and other post-distillation procedures.
- Describe the various types of whiskey, including Scotch whisky, Irish whiskey, bourbon, Tennessee whiskey, Canadian whisky, and Japanese whisky.
- Identify and discuss the various types of American whiskey, including corn whiskey, rye whiskey, straight whiskey, and bottled-in-bond.
- Describe the product category known as white whiskeys.
- Discuss the sensory evaluation of whiskey and the typical procedures for the serving of whiskey and whiskey-based drinks.

Whiskey is a spirit produced from grains. These grains, as they are not readily fermentable, must first be modified in order to be converted to alcohol. Whiskey is produced throughout the world, and although the production of whiskey varies from country to country, there is worldwide agreement that the distilling proof cannot be so high that the distillate loses its unique flavor. Most whiskeys are also required to be aged in oak, although there are a few products exempt from the requirement. Given these parameters, whiskey is generally considered to be a beverage whose main flavor profile is derived from its grain-based raw materials and the time it spends in oak.

This chapter begins with an overview of whiskey, including a standard definition, history, and the basic production techniques used in the creation of whiskey. It then proceeds to describe the leading styles of European whiskeys, with an emphasis on Scotch whiskies and Irish whiskeys. It continues with a discussion of North American whiskeys, including bourbon, Tennessee whiskey, and Canadian whisky. The chapter concludes with a discussion of whiskeys from some of the newer and smaller producers of whiskey located around the world.

A Note on Spelling: Different countries use different spellings of the word *whiskey* or *whisky*. Traditionally, Scotland, Japan, and Canada have used the spelling *whisky* (without the *e*), and Ireland and the United States use the spelling *whiskey* (with the *e*). While either spelling is considered correct in the United States, this Study Guide will use the version with the *e* when referring to whiskey in general, and the spelling without the *e* when referring to the products of Scotland, Japan, and Canada. At all times, however, the spelling chosen by a particular producer will be honored.

DEFINITION OF WHISKEY

According to the US Standards of Identity, the category of whiskey is defined as:
- A distilled spirit produced from the fermented mash of grain
- Distilled at less than 95% alcohol by volume (190 proof)
- Produced in a manner such that the distillate possesses the taste, aroma, and characteristics generally attributed to whiskey
- Stored in oak containers (with the exception of corn whiskey)
- Bottled at no less than 40% alcohol by volume (80 proof)

According to the *Beverage Alcohol Manual—a Practical Guide to Basic Mandatory Labeling Information for Distilled Spirits* (as published by the TTB of the United States), a specific age statement is required on the label of any whiskey that is less than four years old.

The US Standards of Identity also define various subcategories of whiskey. These include the following:
- Bourbon whiskey is whiskey made in the United States, produced from a fermented mash of no less than 51% corn, distilled at an alcohol by volume not exceeding 80% (160 proof), and stored at no more than 125 proof in charred new oak containers.
- Rye whiskey, wheat whiskey, malt whiskey, and rye malt whiskey are whiskeys produced from a fermented mash of no less than 51% rye, wheat, malted barley, or malted rye grain, respectively. Such whiskeys must be distilled at an alcohol by volume not exceeding 80% (160 proof) and must be stored at no more than 125 proof in charred new oak containers.
- Corn whiskey must be produced from a fermented mash of no less than 80% corn and at an alcohol by volume not exceeding 80% (160 proof). There is no requirement for corn whiskey to be stored in oak containers, but if it is, it must be stored at no more than 125 proof in used or uncharred wood.
- Whiskey conforming to the definitions above—and which has been stored for a period of two years or more in the type of oak containers prescribed—may be called "straight" whiskey, such as "straight bourbon whiskey."
- "Grain spirits" are neutral spirits distilled from a fermented mash of grain and stored in oak containers.

Further definitions of these American whiskeys, as well as others, such as Tennessee whiskey, light whiskey, and bottled-in-bond whiskey, will be described later in this chapter.

The EU definition of whiskey has slightly different specifications:
- It must be produced by the distillation of a grain mash made from malted cereals. It may include unmalted grains.
- It must be distilled to less than 94.8% alcohol by volume (189.6 proof) so that the distillate has an aroma and taste reflective of the raw materials.
- It must be aged in wooden casks no larger than 700 liters (185 gallons) for at least three years.
- It must be bottled at a minimum strength of 40% alcohol by volume (80 proof).

The European Union further defines the following types of whiskey:
- Scotch whisky, which must be produced in Scotland from a mash of malted barley and other cereal grains and aged in oak casks in an approved warehouse in Scotland for a minimum of three years
- Irish whiskey, which must be produced in Ireland from a mash of cereals and aged in wooden casks in Ireland for no less than three years

Further definitions of these whiskeys, as well as other European whiskeys, are included later in this chapter.

HISTORY OF WHISKEY

It is generally believed that the Irish Celts were the first to produce a spirit from grains; it is believed that these early spirits were quite similar to the whiskeys presently made in Ireland. However, the first *written* evidence of a spirit produced from grain appears in the last decade of the fifteenth century in Scotland, as a transfer of malt to be made into aqua vitae, by order of the king, is recorded in the Exchequer Rolls of Scotland.

The present-day name "whiskey" is attributable to either the Scottish Celtic words *uisge beatha* or the Irish Celtic term *uisge baugh* (pronounced *whis-geh-BAW*), both of which mean "water of life" or, as some scholars believe, "lively water."

It is interesting to note that in early times, when alchemists were searching for extended and healthy lives, spirits were commonly (and interchangeably) called "water of life," "aqua vitae," and "uisge baugh." When the product was brought to England, the English found the Celtic word too difficult to pronounce, so it was anglicized to *whiskey*.

The history of American whiskey is discussed later in this chapter.

Figure 5.1: Barley Spikelets in the Field

THE PRODUCTION OF WHISKEY

Every whiskey, regardless of origin, is crafted using a five-step production procedure:
- Mash/Wort Preparation
- Fermentation
- Distillation
- Maturation
- Blending and Bottling

STEP ONE: MASH/WORT PREPARATION

The four primary grains used in the production of whiskey are barley, corn, rye, and wheat. The specific "recipe," or list of grain ingredients that will be fermented for use in a particular spirit, is known as the *mash bill* or *grain bill*.

As grains are primarily made up of starch, which is not directly fermentable, the grain must be prepared in order to allow saccharification—the conversion of its starch to simple, fermentable sugars. This conversion process is often initiated by *malting*—allowing the grain to sprout. The sprouting of the grain will cause the release of specific enzymes that, in turn, will help to convert the grain's starch to a fermentable form of sugar.

Of the four grains, barley is the most widely used, as it is the best source of these enzymes. A relatively small percentage of malted barley in a grain recipe is sufficient to convert the starch in any other grains present into fermentable sugar.

Figure 5.2: Green Malt (Barley)

Malting: To begin the malting stage, barley (or other grain) is soaked in water. This causes the grain to sprout, which releases two enzymes—alpha amylase and beta amylase (often called "diastase" in the beverage industry). These enzymes break down the carbohydrates in the grain into double or triple molecules, thereby producing maltose, a disaccharide. The maltose will then further break down into fermentable single-molecule sugars (*monosaccharides*). After sufficient germination, the malted barley is known as *green malt*.

Kilning: Next, the green malt is transferred to a heated kiln where the germination is stopped and malting is completed. At this stage, additional flavors may be introduced to the grain, depending on how the kilning is performed. For instance, *peat* (as is common in Scotland) may be used as a fuel source. The time and temperature of the heating process may be specified in order to caramelize the sugars in the malted grain to the degree the distillery desires.

Milling: The kilned (roasted) malt is next screened and ground into grist in the mill room.

Mashing: Simply put, mashing is a biochemical process where starches are converted to sugar. Mashing contains two basic steps: liquefaction (dissolving the starch in liquid) and saccharification (the actual conversion of starch into sugar via enzymatic activity).

To begin the process, the ground malt and any additional milled grains (if specified by the grain recipe) are mixed with hot water (heated to 135–170°F/57–78°C). The vessel used in this step is referred to as a *mash cooker* in the United States and a *mash tun* or *lauter tun* in Europe. The grain is soaked until the sugars are dissolved and most of the remaining starch is liquefied, and until the diastase completes the conversion process. It is at this point that the enzymes released in the malting step become fully activated (due to heat) and are able to convert the starch into sugar molecules.

Washing: In Scotland and Ireland, the sugary liquid is "washed" from the malt and drained off. This liquid is known as the *mash* or *wort*. This is often done in as many as four stages, with the term *sparging* used to refer to the final stage (or stages). The liquid from these final stages—the *sparge*—is sometimes retained for use in the next round of mashing rather than being passed on to the fermentation stage.

In the United States, the sugary liquid and ground grain particulates are generally allowed to remain together in the mixture. This thick slurry is called a cook or a mash.

The Importance of Water: Water plays a very important role throughout the entire whiskey production process. Of primary importance is that the water be iron-free, as the presence of iron would turn a matured whiskey's golden hue into an undesirable black tinge.

Another consideration is whether the water is *hard,* meaning that it contains minerals such as calcium, magnesium, or phosphates, or *soft,* meaning that it contains only sodium. As the presence of minerals (including sodium) in the water used in whiskey production can obviously impact the flavor of the finished spirit, a distillery's water source plays a key role in its whiskey's flavor profile.

As an example, Scotland's mountain streams provide soft water, which is ideal for steeping barley. On the other hand, the water found near the distilleries in the central United States contains dissolved limestone and minerals, which have been found to provide nutrients for the fermenting yeast. In both cases, the local water supply adds to the character of the resulting whiskey.

STEP TWO: FERMENTATION

Initiation of Fermentation: The mash or wort is next passed into the fermentation vats, and fermentation is initiated using either a cultivated proprietary yeast strain or a standard dry distiller's yeast. In Scotland, the fermentation occurs in large, closed containers known as *washbacks*. Washbacks, which may be as large as sixteen feet deep and may hold up to fifty thousand liters (13,209 gallons), may be made from wood or stainless steel. In North America, fermentation generally takes place in large, open fermenters, some of which hold up to twenty thousand gallons.

Figure 5.3: Washbacks at Glenfiddich Distillery

Completion of Fermentation: The fermentation process itself can take anywhere from forty to seventy-two hours. Fermentation is considered complete when the content changes from sweet to slightly acidic in taste, with an alcohol content of 5% to 10% alcohol by volume. The fermented mash is often termed *wash, distiller's beer,* or simply *beer*. In some cases, this beer or wash is strained or pressed to remove a portion of the solids before distillation begins.

STEP THREE: DISTILLATION

Choice of Still: Next, the beer or wash is put into either a pot still or a continuous column still. A continuous column still can produce a wide range of alcoholic strengths and is often used to create the lighter elements of a whiskey blend, which need to be distilled at a higher proof.

Pot stills usually require two separate distillations to bring the alcohol level up to the desired degree, although it will never reach the high level in proof that can be achieved with a column still.

When using a pot still, the first distillation of the fermented wash takes place in the *wash still* or *beer still*. This first distillate is of low alcoholic strength and is called *low wines*. The low wines pass into the second still, known as the *spirit still,* where they are redistilled to a higher alcoholic strength. The product that comes off the spirit still is referred to as *high wines* or *new-make spirit*.

Making the Cuts: During the process, the distiller will selectively return the foreshots and the feints to the next distillation cycle for further refinement, while being very careful to preserve only the heart (middle cut) of the distillation run. In some cases (particularly in Europe), this is accomplished by passing the spirit flow through a *spirit safe*, where it is analyzed, measured for alcoholic strength, and possibly classified (for many purposes, including customs duties and taxation).

Upon leaving the still house, the collected new-make spirit is generally diluted with water to reduce the strength to about 125 proof.

Figure 5.4: Spirit Safe at Glendronach Distillery

STEP FOUR: MATURATION

The Processes of Wood Aging: As the diluted new-make spirit is placed in the type of oak cask required by the regulations of the country where the whiskey is made, several different processes begin to occur.

- There is some interaction among the original components of the spirit and the barrel itself. As the outside temperature rises and warms the spirit, it expands and is forced into the barrel staves; as the outside temperature lowers, the spirit retracts into the barrel. The greater the diurnal change, the greater the effect of maturation.
- Evaporation: Both water and alcohol will evaporate through the pores of the barrel, resulting in a loss of volume. Depending on the ambient temperature and humidity levels, the alcohol percentage in the maturing spirit will either increase or decrease.
- Oxidation: Air drawn into the barrel during the evaporation process slowly oxidizes the spirit's components.
- Extraction: The spirit extracts aroma, flavor, and tannin from the staves of the oak.
- Coloration: Through contact with the "red layer" of the barrel, as well as through the process of oxidation, the spirit will darken and change color.
- Concentration: All of the chemical, physical, and extractive processes are concentrated in the decreasing volume of whiskey because of evaporation through, and soakage into, the wooden barrel.
- Filtration: If the barrel has been charred, then the interior of the barrel can act like an activated charcoal filter, absorbing some compounds and smoothing the spirit.

Barrel Parameters: The type and style of barrel used will impact the finished spirit. These parameters may include the following:
- The type of oak, either American or European
- By what method and for how long the oak was dried
- Whether or not the barrel was toasted or charred and, if so, to what levels
- Whether the barrel is new or used
- If used, what was previously held in the barrel

Physical Storage Conditions: The storage conditions under which maturation takes place will have a direct impact on the finished spirit. These conditions include:
- Whether the warehouse is made of brick, stone, or metal siding
- Whether the warehouse has windows
- Whether the warehouse is heated or naturally ventilated
- Whether the warehouse is a single-level or multilevel building
- Whether the barrels are stacked one atop another or stored in a single layer
- In a multi-level warehouse, where the barrel is located (low, middle, or high)

Maturation Time: The length of time the spirit stays in the barrel has a decided effect on the whiskey's flavor profile, yet the impact of the time spent in barrel is not the same from location to location. The geographic location of a distillery's warehouse, and its resulting climate, humidity, and seasonal temperature swings, can increase or decrease the rate of maturation, as can the physical layout of the warehouse itself.

Figure 5.5: Recently Filled Barrels of Bourbon Outside the Woodford Reserve Rackhouse in Woodford County, Kentucky

Thus, comparing the age statement on a whiskey's label with that of whiskeys from different countries and climates can be misleading. In general, most northern European whiskey requires a longer maturation period than do whiskeys matured in the southern US climates of Kentucky or Tennessee. Some experts estimate that for every year of aging in Kentucky or Tennessee, it takes well over three years of aging in the climate of Scotland or Ireland to achieve the same results. There are several reasons for this variation, which are discussed below.

In northern Europe, the following tends to be true:
- The climate is cooler.
- The maturation warehouses are generally one-story stone buildings, which evens out external temperature variations.
- Casks are usually closely stacked on top of each other in a cool, damp environment with little air circulation.
- Maturation is primarily conducted in used barrels that have saturated pores.

In contrast, the following tends to be true about the southern United States:
- The climate is warmer.
- The maturation warehouses, also called *rackhouses,* are typically several stories high, with wide temperature fluctuations between the top and bottom floors.
- Casks are generally not stacked on top of one another, which permits more air circulation.
- Producers use new American oak, which has less saturated pores.

In light of all of these variables, it should be easy to understand why the old master distiller's adage applies: "With whiskey, don't confuse age and maturity."

STEP FIVE: BLENDING AND BOTTLING

When discussing the blending stage of whiskey production, most people assume that the term applies to the creation of "blended whiskey" products, as discussed below. However, with few exceptions, such as in the case of single-barrel bottlings, almost all whiskey is actually a blend of sorts, crafted from multiple barrels of similar product.

Once the whiskey has matured and is ready for bottling, barrels of similarly flavored products are selected and then disgorged into large vats for blending. Purified water is often added to the whiskey at this stage to bring it to the desired proof before it is bottled. This "barrel mingling" is part of the art and craft of the master distiller, and is intended to produce a consistent product that conforms to the overall style of the distillery.

Blended Whiskey: Globally, blended whiskey is by far the largest category. It is most often made up of blends of whiskeys from different distilleries and of different classifications. In some categories, other spirit types and non-whiskey blending elements may be used as well.

Single-Barrel Bottlings: In some cases, a selected single barrel is first diluted with water until it is at bottling strength, which may be 80 proof or higher, and is then bottled without blending it with other barrels.

Cask-Strength or Barrel-Proof Bottlings: In the case of *cask-strength* or *barrel-proof* bottlings, no water is added to the whiskey before bottling.

SCOTCH WHISKY

With its long history and commercial success, Scotland leads all countries in the number of distilleries producing whisky, with over 130 presently in operation. The whisky produced in Scotland under precise regulations is called Scotch. This name may not be used for any other whisky.

Scotch whisky has protected geographical indication (PGI) status in the EU, and as such is highly defined. The 2009 Scotch Whisky Regulations clearly stipulate the following standards:

- Scotch whisky must be produced from a mixture of water, malted barley, and other whole cereal grains.
- It must be distilled at no more than 94.8% alcohol by volume (189.6 proof).
- Fermentation and distillation must occur at the same location in Scotland.
- Water and caramel coloring are the only allowed additives.
- All Scotch whisky must be aged in oak casks in Scotland, at a licensee's excise warehouse, for a minimum of three years. Oak casks must have a maximum capacity of 700 liters (185 gallons).

The following five categories of Scotch whisky are produced. As of 2011 and onward, one of these categories must be stated on the label. The five categories, and their definitions, are as follows:

Single Malt Scotch Whisky: A *single malt Scotch whisky* is generally considered to be a premium product. It is required to be distilled at a single distillery by batch distillation in a pot still, and it must be made solely with malted barley and no other grains.

Single Grain Scotch Whisky: A *single grain Scotch whisky* is any Scotch whisky distilled at a single distillery and produced from other malted or unmalted grains (generally, wheat or corn) in addition to malted barley. (All Scotch must contain at least some malted barley.) "Single grain" does not mean that the whisky was made from a single type of grain; rather, the word *single* refers to the use of a single distillery. There are no specific requirements as to the type of distillation used in the production of single grain Scotch whisky; however, most are continuously distilled in order to produce a lighter style of whisky.

Blended Malt Scotch Whisky: A *blended malt Scotch whisky* is a blend of two or more single malt Scotch whiskies that have been produced at more than one distillery. (Note that the terms *pure malt* and *vatted malt* are no longer authorized as synonyms for blended malt.)

Blended Grain Scotch Whisky: A *blended grain Scotch whisky* is a blend of two or more single grain Scotch whiskies that have been produced at more than one distillery.

Blended Scotch Whisky: *Blended Scotch whisky* is a blend of one or more single malt Scotch whiskies with one or more single grain Scotch whiskies. Today, blended Scotch whisky accounts for about 90% of the Scotch whisky consumed worldwide. Producers combine the various malt and grain whiskies to create a less expensive and more palatable product, both smoother and more distinctive than any of the blend's components would have been on its own. Blending also ensures uniformity of a given brand, providing consumers with a consistent product that can be expected to exhibit the color, aroma, flavor, and quality of the particular brand.

Typically, a Scotch whisky blend is the result of a combination of as many as thirty or more malt whiskies, together with five or more continuous still grain whiskies, with the malt whisky making up 20–50% of the blend. Moreover, many Scotches are a blend of whiskies from a variety of different distilleries. Well-known brands of blended Scotch whisky include the Famous Grouse, Johnnie Walker, Cutty Sark, J&B, Ballantine's, Dewar's White Label, and Chivas Regal. Blended Scotch whisky may carry an age statement (as in Chivas Regal 12 Year Old), but most do not do so.

Table 5.1: Top-Selling Scotch Whisky Brands

\multicolumn{2}{c}{TOP-SELLING SCOTCH WHISKY BRANDS (Global Sales)}	
Rank	Brand
1.	Johnnie Walker
2.	Ballantine's
3.	Grant's
4.	Chivas Regal
5.	J&B
6.	William Lawson's
7.	William Peel
8.	Dewar's
9.	Label 5
10.	Black & White

Source: Drinks International (2018)

THE FLAVOR OF SCOTCH

Scotch whisky is renowned for its unique flavor profile, which, aside from the blend, is partially derived from the aspects of its terroir, base materials, and production methods.

Use of Peat: During the kilning process, the kilns may be heated with peat, a compacted, vegetative form of carbon. The smoke from the burning peat is often allowed to come into contact with the grain through a *peat box* and permeate it with the aromas of smoke, seaweed, and tar, as well as what some describe as a slightly medicinal flavor. The peat deposited around Scotland varies with the region, and the final flavor of a Scotch whisky depends on the region's available peat as well as the amount of *peat reek* (or peatiness) allowed into the grain. There is a common misconception that all Scotch whisky has a heavy peat flavor, but in reality, most Scotch whiskies have only a mild "peat reek" influence. A few are even completely peat-free.

Figure 5.6: Peat Stacks on Lewis and Harris Island, Scotland

Fermentation Processes: If some solids are allowed to remain in the wort from the milling and mashing stages and carried forward to fermentation, then a more malty-flavored spirit will result. In general, the wort is fermented to 7–10% alcohol by volume. The length of time the wort is allowed to ferment can also impact the whisky's flavor. A short fermentation can add to the "malty" flavor, while a long fermentation allows for the development of more congeners.

Distillation Processes: Distillation of the malt wash generally takes place in copper pot stills. The malt wash undergoes at least two distillations before the new-make begins its aging regimen. The first distillation brings the wash to 21–28% alcohol by volume, while the final alcohol level from the second run will depend on the distiller's cut points. The second distillation, which takes place in a spirit still, generally produces a spirit at 70% alcohol by volume, but in any case the spirit will not exceed 94.8% alcohol by volume, due to regulations. As is the case with other spirits, the distillation in pot stills for malt-based whisky creates a spirit that is quite flavorful.

Scotch producers also make a grain-based whisky that can be bottled as such; however, most grain whisky is made as a light-to-neutral whisky to be blended with the heavier malt whisky. These grain-based whiskies are distilled in a column still instead of the copper pot still used for the malt-based wash. The resulting spirit is less flavorful but not quite neutral in character. The product of this distillation is also legally prohibited from reaching 94.8% alcohol by volume.

Aging Processes: After distillation, both malt whisky and grain whisky are aged separately in wood. Malt whiskies are generally placed into used barrels for at least the three-year minimum, but many malts remain in cask for five years—and much longer if the initial distilled spirit is distilled at a lower proof, which leaves more congeners in the distillate. The specific choice of barrel also impacts the final spirit. Some distillers age their malt whisky in barrels previously used for maturing bourbon, sherry, port, or Madeira (particularly in the final stages of aging, in a practice known as *wood finishing*) to differentiate their product and/or enhance certain flavors.

The type of oak used also impacts the whisky, since bourbon will have been matured in American oak whereas sherry will have been aged in European oak. Conversely, grain whisky is generally aged in new American oak barrels. Regardless of the type of barrel used, neither malt nor grain whisky may be aged in a cask larger than 700 liters (185 gallons).

GEOGRAPHICAL INDICATIONS OF SCOTCH WHISKY

In addition to the differences among Scotch blends, there is also great diversity among products due to the varied locations of the distilleries found throughout Scotland. There are currently five recognized Geographical Indications for Scotch whisky. Each region, and each distillery, varies in its water source, has its own style, and produces whisky of a distinctive character. The five Geographical Indications are described below.

The Highlands: The Highland region, which includes the islands of Mull, Jura, Lewis, Skye, and Arran as well as the Orkney Islands, is a geographically large area that produces a wide range of Scotch whiskies. Many of them are considered excellent "entry-level" whiskies with a sweet, soft finish and perhaps not quite as much of the robust complexity of other versions. There are over thirty distilleries currently operating throughout the Highland area (including the islands), the best known of which include the Dalmore, Glenmorangie, and Dalwhinnie.

The Lowlands: Traditionally, *Lowland* Scotch is triple-distilled, although this is not required and is not true of all of them. However, it is true enough that the region has a reputation for a triple-distilled, lighter style of whisky. Other typical attributes of Lowland Scotch are an overall subtlety, grassy notes, notes of citrus, and a light, dry finish. The region has five currently producing distilleries, Ailsa Bay, Auchentoshan, Bladnoch, Cameronbridge, and Glenkinchie, along with several new distilleries whose products are not yet ready to be bottled.

Speyside: *Speyside* was formerly considered part of the Highland region (at which time the Highland region was by far the largest Scotch-producing region, both in terms of geography and number of distilleries). However, as of the 2009 Scotch Whisky Regulations, Speyside was declared a separate region. With over forty distilleries, it now has the largest number of operating distilleries of the five regions. Located in the Spey River region, Speyside is recognized as an area that produces a complex, smooth style of malt Scotch, such as those produced by the Macallan, as well as the lighter styles produced by Glenfiddich and the Glenlivet.

Whisky-Producing Regions of Scotland

Figure 5.7: Map of the Whisky-Producing Regions of Scotland

Note: Speyside is technically a subregion of the Highlands and as such, whiskey produced in Speyside may use the Highland designation on the label.

Islay: The island of *Islay* (pronounced *eye-luh*) produces a distinctive style of whisky. Most of these have a medium to heavy peat character due to the abundance of peat on the island. Islay is the southernmost of Scotland's Western Isles and boasts a sunnier climate than many of the other Scotch-producing regions. Furthermore, the distilleries are located close to the sea, which imparts briny seaweed aromas and flavors. There are currently nine distilleries in Islay, with one scheduled to open in 2015. Classic examples are Lagavulin, Ardbeg, and Laphroaig.

Campbeltown: There were once over thirty distilleries operating in *Campbeltown,* located on the Kintyre Peninsula in western Scotland. However, this number has markedly declined. For a time, this area even lost its Geographical Indication (GI) status for lack of production. There are now three distilleries active in the area (with several more in the works); therefore, Campbeltown's GI status has been reinstated. Campbeltown is known for a slight saltiness in its whiskies, brought about by the "mists rolling in from the sea." One Campbeltown distillery that is particularly highly regarded is the Springbank Distillery, known for producing rich, complex single malt whiskies.

AGE STATEMENTS ON SCOTCH WHISKY

Scotch whisky may be labeled with age statements, which must always reflect the age of the youngest component in the product. The year of distillation may be included on the label, but only if the year of bottling and the age (in years) of the whisky are also included.

Table 5.2: Scotch Distilleries by Region

Region	Distilleries
SCOTCH DISTILLERIES BY REGION (AS OF 2018)	
The Highlands	Aberfeldy
	Arbikie
	Ardmore
	Ardnamurchan
	Balblair
	Ben Nevis
	Blair Athol
	Clynelish
	Dalmore
	Dalwhinnie
	Deanston
	Edradour
	Fettercairn
	Glencadam
	Glen Garioch
	Glengoyne
	Glenmorangie
	Glen Ord
	Glenturret
	Loch Lomond
	Lochnagar
	Oban
	Pulteney
	Teaninich
	Tomatin
	Tullibardine
	Wolfburn
The Islands (technically part of the Highlands)	Abhainn Dearg (also known as Red River)
	Arran
	Highland Park (Orkney Islands)
	Isle of Harris
	Isle of Jura
	Scapa
	Talisker
	Tobermory
The Lowlands	Ailsa Bay
	Annandale
	Auchentoshan
	Bladnoch
	Cameronbridge
	Daftmill
	Glenkinchie

Table 5.2: Scotch Distilleries by Region (continued)

SCOTCH DISTILLERIES BY REGION (AS OF 2018)	
Region	**Distilleries**
The Lowlands	Kingsbarns
Speyside	Aberlour
	Allt-à-Bhainne
	Auchroisk
	Aultmore
	Ballindalloch
	Balmenach
	Balvenie
	BenRiach
	Benrinnes
	Benromach
	Brackia
	Braeval
	Cardhu
	Cragganmore
	Craigellachie
	Dailuaine
	Dufftown
	Glenallachie
	Glenburgie
	Glendronach
	Glendullan
	Glen Elgin
	Glen Grant
	Glenfarclas
	Glenfiddich
	Glenglassaugh
	Glen Keith
	The Glenlivet
	Glenlossie
	Glen Moray
	Glenrothes
	Glen Spey
	Glentauchers
	Inchgower
	Kininvie Distillery
	Knockando
	Knockdhu
	Linkwood
	Longmorn
	The Macallan

SCOTCH DISTILLERIES BY REGION (AS OF 2018)

Region	Distilleries
Speyside (continued)	Macduff
	Mannochmore
	Miltonduff
	Mortlach
	Roseisle
	Speyburn
	The Speyside
	Strathisla
	Strathmill
	Tamdhu
	Tamnavulin
	Tomintoul
	Tormore
Islay	Ardbeg
	Bowmore
	Bruichladdich
	Bunnahabhain
	Caol Ila
	Gartbreck
	Kilchoman
	Lagavulin
	Laphroaig
	Port Charlotte
Campbeltown	Glengyle
	Glen Scotia
	Springbank

IRISH WHISKEY

Irish whiskey, traditionally known as *Uisce Beatha Eireannach*, is defined according to the Irish Whiskey Act of 1980 as a distilled spirit that must:
- Be distilled in Ireland from a mash of cereal grains
- Be distilled to an alcoholic strength of less than 94.8% alcohol by volume (189.6 proof)
- Be distilled so that the distillate has an aroma and flavor derived from the materials used
- Contain no additives except for water and caramel coloring
- Be stored in wooden casks (not to exceed 700 liters [185 gallons] in capacity) in Ireland for no less than three years

As of October 2015, a new set of technical standards was implemented in accordance with the European Union requirements for the PGI status of Irish whiskey. These standards expand upon the Irish Whiskey Act of 1980 and include the following regulations:
- Irish whiskey must be bottled in Ireland or, if not bottled in Ireland, it must be shipped off the island in inert bulk containers and subject to company controls and strict verification to ensure the safety and integrity of the product.
- Irish whiskey is not allowed to be exported from Ireland in any type of wooden container.

These new standards also provide definitions for the following types of Irish whiskey:

Irish Malt Whiskey: Irish malt whiskey must be made from 100% malted barley, with the wort separated from the solids before fermentation, and must be distilled in pot stills. The traditional practice is to use smaller pot stills in order to encourage complex flavors and a full, oily texture; however, there are no requirements as to the size of the still. Irish malt whiskey is traditionally triple-distilled, although double distillation may be used. Examples include Bushmills Single Malt, the Irishman Single Malt, and Tyrconnell Single Malt.

Irish Grain Whiskey: Irish grain whiskey is produced from a mash containing a maximum of 30% malted barley. The remainder is made up of unmalted cereal grains—typically maize, wheat, or barley. The mash typically does not undergo any separation of the solids from the liquids before distillation. This type of whiskey is continuously distilled using column stills. Irish grain whiskey may have either a light or a full flavor profile, depending on the cut points and other techniques employed by the distiller. Irish grain whiskey is typically used in blends; however, a unique single-grain, small-batch Irish whiskey known as Greenore Single Grain Irish Whiskey is produced by Cooley Distillery.

Irish Pot Still Whiskey: Irish pot still whiskey is required to be produced using a mash containing a minimum of 30% malted barley and a minimum of 30% unmalted barley. The remainder of the mash may be malted or unmalted barley, and may include up to 5% other unmalted cereal grains (usually oats or rye). The wort is separated from the solids before fermentation. This type of whiskey must be batch distilled in pot stills. The traditional practice is triple distillation in large pot stills, although double distillation may also be employed. There are no requirements as to the size of the still.

Irish pot still whiskey is a unique Irish product that was first produced as a result of an excise tax on Irish malt introduced in the 1600s. In order to avoid paying the full tax on their whiskey, distillers began to include a portion of unmalted barley in the mash bill.

Up until 2011, this style of whiskey was sometimes referred to as pure pot still whiskey. However, the name "Irish pot still whiskey" is reflective of the fact that term "pure" is no longer authorized for use (other than to refer to a specific ingredient or as part of a company name) on spirit labels in the United States.

Irish pot still whiskey is a traditional product only produced by a few distilleries. Examples include Redbreast, Green Spot, and Jameson 15-Year-Old Pure Pot Still Whiskey.

Blended Irish Whiskey: Blended Irish whiskey is a blend of two or more different whiskey types, which must be made in accordance with the standards stated above, and which may include Irish malt whiskey, Irish grain whiskey, and/or Irish pot still whiskey. The whiskeys that make up the blend may also be chosen from different distilleries, ages, types of cask finish, and flavor profiles in order to achieve

Figure 5.8: Wash still and spirit still at the Jameson Whiskey Heritage Center

the desired flavor and consistency. Blended Irish whiskey tends to be smooth and mellow with a range of flavors, and a light, silky mouth feel.

As with Scotch, Irish blends are the most popular whiskeys in the category. Jameson, produced at the Midleton Distillery, is one of the top sellers, along with Black Bush, Bushmills, Paddy, and Tullamore D.E.W.

THE FLAVOR OF IRISH WHISKEY

Irish whiskey and Scotch whisky are often compared and contrasted in terms of production techniques and their resulting flavors. Being the leading whiskies of Europe and similar in some ways—such as the fact that both products are distilled from a fermented mash of grains, namely malted barley, unmalted barley, corn, rye, wheat, and oats—this is perhaps inevitable. However, the production of Irish whiskey is unique in several ways, leading to its own distinct styles and flavors. Some of these factors are discussed below.

Non-Peated Malt: Most notable, perhaps, is the use of non-peated malt. While both Scotch whiskies and Irish whiskeys allow for the use of either peated or non-peated malt, in accordance with tradition, most producers of Irish whiskey use non-peated malt. As a result, Irish whiskey is generally considered to be smoother and less "smoky" than Scotch. There are, of course, some exceptions to this rule. One example is Connemara Peated Single Malt Irish Whiskey, produced by the Cooley Distillery.

Grain Recipe: With the exception of Irish malt whiskey, Irish whiskey is produced using a combination of malted and unmalted barley—as well as other unmalted grains—in its grain recipe. The use of unmalted barley gives many Irish whiskeys a unique "leathery" flavor.

Distillation: While tradition holds that Irish whiskey is triple distilled, modern rule of law does not have this requirement. Two styles of Irish whiskey—Irish malt whiskey and Irish pot still whiskey—must be distilled in pot stills but may utilize either double or triple distillation. Irish grain whiskey is required to be distilled in column stills. However, for all types of Irish whiskey, there are no requirements as to the shape of still, the size of the still, cut points, or other operational techniques, thus leaving a good deal of discretion to the individual distilleries.

Maturation: Irish whiskey is required to be aged in Ireland, in wooden casks, for at least three years. Many are matured for as long as seven to eight years before being bottled and shipped. The distillery may choose to use either new or used wooden casks, although used casks are the traditional choice. The new standards for Irish whiskey mention that the use of casks that were "previously used to store Madeira, Sherry, Port, or Bourbon" will produce a more complex and balanced spirit that will not be "overpowered by wood extracts and tannins."

Figure 5.9: The Jameson Whiskey Heritage Center in Midleton, Cork

Table 5.3: Whiskey Distilleries Operating in Ireland

SELECTED WHISKEY DISTILLERIES OPERATING IN IRELAND (AS OF 2018)

Distillery	Year Established	Brands/Notes
Kilbeggan Distillery	1757	The distillery ceased operations in 1957 but was reopened in 2007. Produces Kilbeggan, Locke's Blend, and Locke's Malt.
Old Bushmills Distillery	1784	Produces Old Bushmills, Black Bush 1608, and Bushmills single malt. Some accounts date the distillery from 1608, when a license to distill in the area was first granted by King James I.
New Midleton Distillery	1975	Produces Jameson, Powers, Paddy, Midleton, Redbreast, and Green Spot.
Cooley Distillery	1987	Converted from a potato-based alcohol plant in 1987; produces Connemara, Tyrconnell, and others.
West Cork Distillers	2008	Produces West Cork Irish whiskey, Cavanagh Irish whiskey, and several other related products, including aged and unaged grain spirits.
Glendalough Distillery	2011	Now operating out of a new distillery in Wicklow, Glendalough Distillery products include Double Barrel Single Grain Whiskey, aged in American ex-bourbon barrels and finished in ex-sherry casks, and several styles of poitín
Alltech Craft Distillery	2012	In late 2014, Alltech Craft Distillery began the process of converting a centuries-old Anglican church located along a historic walking trail in Dublin into a boutique distillery.
Dingle Distillery	2012	The first batch of Dingle whiskey—a triple-distilled single malt aged in ex-Bourbon casks, was released in November of 2016.
Echlinville Distillery	2013	The first distillery to be granted a license in Northern Ireland in over 130 years, Echlinville Distillery has just started its production.
Tullamore D.E.W. Distillery	2014	Tullamore D.E.W. opened their new distillery in Tullamore (County Offaly), in September of 2014.
Nephin Whiskey	2014	Located in the small village of Lahardaun (County Mayo), this distillery is creating peated, single malt whiskeys using locally grown barley, triple-distillation and traditional copper pot stills.
Teeling Distillery	2015	A revival of Walter Teeling's Dublin-based whiskey tradition dating from 1782, the Teeling Distillery is the first new distillery to be established in the city of Dublin for over 125 years.
Connacht Distillery	2015	Located in County Mayo on the west coast of Ireland, the Connacht Distillery opened in 2015 with three custom-designed copper pot stills. The new distillery is producing several spirits, including Connacht Irish Whiskey, Spade & Bushel Irish Whiskey, and Straw Boys Poitín.
Boann Distillery	2016	Located in County Louth, the family-owned Boann Whiskey Distillery opened in 2016. The Boann Distillery will produce Irish malt and pot still whiskeys, and is currently marketing a line of products under the brand "The Whistler."
Walsh Whiskey	2016	Established in County Carlow, the Walsh Whiskey Distillery began production in 2016 and will produce a range of whiskeys, including the Writer's Tears and The Irishman Irish whiskey brands (formerly outsourced).

While once there were several thousand little distilleries sprinkled all over Ireland, at present there are closer to twenty distilleries in operation. However, with several new distillery projects in the works and rumors of even more planned for the near future, this number is sure to increase soon.

A list of selected distilleries currently operating in Ireland may be found in table 5.3.

IRISH POITÍN

Long a part of Irish folklore, poitín (sometimes spelled "poteen") was traditionally produced in rural areas away from the interference of the law—in other words, it was a typically Irish version of "moonshine." However, poitín is now produced legally and was awarded protected geographical indication (PGI) status in 2008. As an often-unaged product with a number of permitted base materials (in addition to grains), it does not meet the EU or American standards for whiskey and is therefore technically classified as a "spirit drink."

According to the technical standards for poitín, the allowed base materials include grain, sugar beet molasses, and potatoes. Poitín (aside from the flavored version) is further defined as a clear, clean spirit with a minimum 40% abv—but some products bottled as high as 90% abv.

Flavored styles of poitín are produced via infusion or maceration using fruits, spices, berries, herbs, or natural flavorings. Most poitín is unaged; however, there are some styles—such as those that are produced using more than 50% non-grain base materials—that may be aged in wood for up to ten weeks. Irish Poitín is produced by several Irish whiskey distilleries, and is enjoying a resurgence in popularity as a traditional, craft spirit.

WHISKEY IN THE UNITED STATES

THE HISTORY OF AMERICAN WHISKEY

The story of whiskey in the United States dates to the late 1700s, with the founding of the original American colonies. During this period, Scottish, Irish, and German immigrants crossed the Atlantic to escape economic hardship and religious persecution, coming to America with the dream of farming their own property.

The vast territories of western Pennsylvania and Virginia were ideal locations for the production of whiskey. Rye grain grew exceedingly well in Pennsylvania's soil, while maize, a variety of corn, grew well in Virginia. These grains became widely cultivated, but as they were both perishable and expensive to transport, distilling them into whiskey became a profitable way to utilize the crops. Almost every farmer made whiskey, which was widely traded for other goods. Soon, a thriving market for whiskey had been established.

The Revolutionary War (1775–83) had helped to found a new nation, but it also left behind a huge debt. This, in turn, led to the Whiskey Excise Tax of 1791, stipulating that farmers who produced whiskey had to pay a new tax. This angered the farmers, most of whom were Revolutionary War veterans themselves. Many refused to pay the tax. Eventually, the people organized an uprising known as the Whiskey Rebellion, which was quickly suppressed once the government called out the militia. While the incident proved that the new government had the ability to enforce laws, the whiskey tax remained difficult to collect and was eventually repealed during Thomas Jefferson's presidency.

Figure 5.10: *The Whiskey Rebellion* (1795) (artist unknown; attributed to Frederick Kemmelmeyer)

Eager to avoid the tax, many farmers chose to move their whiskey making into the wilderness, where it remained outside of federal jurisdiction. Here, corn grew plentifully, and the limestone-filtered waters were ideal for producing what would ultimately become bourbon whiskey. This area eventually became the states of Kentucky, Indiana, and Tennessee. Bourbon County, Kentucky, which was named in honor of the French Bourbon royal family who had helped to finance American soldiers during the Revolutionary War, became the center of whiskey production.

By the 1800s, a high percentage of whiskey made in the United States was unaged and often unpalatable, leading producers to add ingredients of various kinds to improve the taste of the product or to stretch production. Furthermore, there were no trademark or brand name protection laws at the time.

However, the quality and reputation of some American whiskeys soon began to improve. In 1870, George Garvin Brown, a pharmaceutical salesman (whiskey was sold in pharmacies in those days), created a glass-bottled, sealed, labeled, and signed bourbon with a "quality guarantee." The product was named for Dr. William Forrester, a respected Union Army Surgeon. Eventually, the name was altered to "Forester," and the product became known as "Old Forester." It is believed that Old Forester was the first bourbon whiskey to be sold exclusively in sealed glass bottles. This type of packaging and endorsement soon became the standard practice, which in turn helped to establish the distinct brands and producers that American whiskey is known for today.

A few years later, E. H. Taylor, the mayor of Frankfort, Kentucky, and later a US senator, created the Bottled-in-Bond Act of 1897. The law was passed, ostensibly, to ensure the authenticity of bourbon whiskey. The act mandated that to be considered bonded and labeled as such, the maturing whiskey had to be kept in a locked (bonded) warehouse for four years; be the product of one distillery from one distilling season; and be bottled at 100 proof. This law provided the government with its tax revenues (which, at the time, accounted for over half of all government income) and ensured the authenticity of the whiskey.

Although the mandate did not directly address the issue of quality, the assurance of authenticity with controls was sufficient for the consumer to regard bonded whiskey as quality merchandise. The terms "bonded whiskey" and "bottled-in-bond," while considered to be quite old-fashioned, are still in use today.

Table 5.4: Top-Selling North American Whiskey Brands

\multicolumn{2}{c}{TOP-SELLING NORTH AMERICAN WHISKEY BRANDS (GLOBAL SALES)}	
Rank	Brand
1.	Jack Daniel's
2.	Jim Beam
3.	Crown Royal
4.	Evan Williams
5.	Canadian Club
6.	Black Velvet
7.	Maker's Mark
8.	Seagram's 7 Crown
9.	Wild Turkey
10.	Canadian Mist

Source: Drinks International (2018)

BOURBON WHISKEY

While bourbon whiskey is thought to have been named for Bourbon County, Kentucky (although there are some who claim that it was actually named for Bourbon Street in New Orleans), its production is not limited to Kentucky. It may be made anywhere in the United States. A 1964 resolution of the Congress of the United States declared bourbon to be a "distinctive product of the United States." The US Standards of Identity further define bourbon whiskey in the following manner:

- It must be made with at least 51% corn.
- It must be distilled at an alcohol by volume not exceeding 160 proof.
- It must be stored at no more than 125 proof in charred new oak containers.
- It must be bottled (like all other American whiskeys) at a minimum of 40% alcohol by volume (80 proof).

The Mash Bill: While bourbon is required to be made from at least 51% corn, many high-quality bourbons may use as much as 70% corn. The balance may be rye, malted barley, or wheat. Most versions include at least a small percentage of malted barley in order to facilitate the conversion process.

Sour Mashing: During the distillation process, some of the residue from the first distillation run, known as *backset,* is placed back in the fermenter for use in the next fermentation batch. The backset is quite acidic and is important in the fermentation process, as much of the local water used in bourbon production has a high alkaline content, which would otherwise interfere with the yeast. Using backset in this way is called *sour mashing*. The sour mashing process assists in creating a consistent product from one batch to another.

Distillation: While not required by law, most bourbon is double-distilled; some may be triple-distilled, in either pot or column stills. The first distillation generally takes place in pot or single column stills composed of copper or stainless steel, known as *beer stills*.

The second distillation takes place in a *doubler* or a *thumper.* A doubler is an addition to a pot still that continuously receives the condensed low wines from the first distillation. The newly condensed low wine is received into the doubler and driven to a chamber that contains heated liquid, causing an interaction that both concentrates (doubles) the alcohol and refines unwanted congeners.

A thumper is a type of doubler that receives the vapors from the first distillation run before they have been cooled and condensed. As the vapors enter the thumper, they are driven into a layer of hot water located in the base of the thumper. The water is kept at a temperature above the boiling point of ethanol, but below that of water, so the ethanol vapor continues on through the water for condensation as high wine or new-make spirit. In this process, heavier alcohols (the tails) are captured by the water and are drained off at the end of a run. The thumper is named as such because the bubbling of the vapors into the still causes a thumping sound.

Figure 5.11: The Jim Beam Distillery in Clermont, Kentucky

Aging: It is interesting to note that while the US regulations require bourbon to be "stored at not more than 125 proof in charred new oak containers," there is no legally mandated minimum aging requirement. Some bourbons are bottled after a very short period of aging, perhaps two or three months. However, it is typical for high-quality bourbon to be aged for two years or more; these may carry the designation "straight bourbon." (See the definition for straight bourbon that follows.)

A few years of aging in new charred oak barrels gives the whiskey its typical vanilla, sweet toast, and caramel flavors. The time spent in wood is solely responsible for the whiskey's color, as nothing may be added to the spirit (with the exception of bourbons labeled as blends, which are discussed below). The continental climate, with its wide temperature variations, impacts the maturation process, aging the spirit faster than it would age in a cooler climate.

The type of building used for aging the bourbon, and the resultant storage conditions, can also have an impact on the final product. In general, two different types of facilities are used. Some distillers use metal rackhouses, while others use warehouses made of brick. These buildings are typically several stories high, meaning that the spirit develops differently on the ground floor than it does on the top floor. Consistency is achieved through barrel rotation or blending. In some cases, the best barrels (traditionally known as *honey barrels*) may be separated out to be bottled as single-barrel bourbon.

Bottling: After aging, most bourbon is diluted with water and bottled at 80 proof. Other common proofs are 86°, 90°, 94°, 100°, and 107°, although bourbon (and other whiskeys) may be bottled at higher proofs. Many of the higher-proof bottlings are products that have been taken straight from the barrel and not diluted (or just slightly diluted). These are labeled as *barrel proof*. Bourbon (with the exception of blended bourbon) is not allowed to contain caramel or other forms of coloring materials.

Straight Bourbon: Bourbon is one of the six specific types of American whiskey that may be labeled as *straight*. (The others are rye, wheat, malt, rye malt, and corn.) To be labeled as straight bourbon, the spirit must have aged in charred new oak containers for at least two years. If the straight bourbon has been aged for four years or longer, then a statement of age is optional; however, if it has been aged less than four years, then the age (in years) must be stated on the label and, if a blend, must reflect the youngest age.

Blended Bourbon: Bourbon that is labeled as "blended" or "a blend" may contain coloring, flavoring, or other spirits (such as unaged grain neutral spirit), but it must be at least 51% straight bourbon.

Bourbon Heritage in the United States: On August 2, 2007, the United States Senate passed a resolution declaring September 2007 as National Bourbon Heritage Month to celebrate the history of bourbon whiskey as a unique part of the American heritage.

Bourbon is currently being produced in California, Colorado, Kansas, Iowa, Missouri, New York, Ohio, Pennsylvania, Texas, and Virginia, among other states. However, 95% of all bourbon is produced in Kentucky, which is home to the Four Roses Distillery, Jim Beam, Maker's Mark, Wild Turkey, Buffalo Trace, and Woodford Reserve, as well as other established and craft distilleries. It has been estimated that there are currently almost five million barrels of bourbon aging in Kentucky—a number that exceeds the state's *human* population. Bourbon that has been produced and aged (for at least one year) in the state of Kentucky may be labeled as "Kentucky Bourbon."

TENNESSEE WHISKEY

Tennessee whiskey is technically a type of bourbon whiskey, but you would be wise not to mention that in Tennessee. While the basic parameters of bourbon whiskey apply—the spirit must be made with a minimum of 51% corn, distilled at an alcohol by volume not exceeding 160 proof, stored in charred new oak containers, and bottled at a minimum of 40% alcohol by volume—there are other requirements as well.

According to the laws of the state of Tennessee, in addition to the standards for bourbon whiskey, Tennessee whiskey must also be:
- Produced in the state of Tennessee
- Filtered through maple charcoal—a production technique known as the *Lincoln County Process*—prior to aging

The Lincoln County Process uses a deep bed of sugar maple charcoal to remove some of the whiskey's lighter aldehydic congeners, giving the remaining spirit a smooth texture and a full, robust flavor. While the exact parameters of the procedure can vary, in many cases the bed of charcoal is more than 10 feet (3 m) deep, and the process takes a week (or even several weeks) to complete. The procedure is somewhat unique in that it is required to be performed using the new-make spirit before it goes into the barrels to age; in the case of many other styles of whiskey, filtration is accomplished after aging is complete.

The process—which harkens backs to the days when a good deal of American whiskey was sold unaged—is named for Lincoln County, Tennessee. Lincoln County was the original home county of Jack Daniel's Lynchburg distillery, although the county lines have since been re-drawn and the distillery is now within the confines of Moore County.

Figure 5.12: The Rickyard at the Jack Daniel's Distillery in Lynchburg, Tennessee (The distillery produces its own charcoal from stacks of 2" × 2" sugar maple timbers called *ricks*.)

The requirement for the use of the Lincoln County Process, as specified in Tennessee House Bill 1084, was signed into law on May 13, 2013, by Tennessee Governor Bill Haslam. One exception—to Benjamin Prichard's Distillery—was granted. At the time of its passage, the bill was contested by some distilleries, whose representatives argued that it imposes prohibitive costs, with the counterargument being that it maintains the essential and traditional nature of Tennessee whiskey as it currently exists in fact. While the argument remains volatile and unsettled, the law remains in effect at the time of this publication.

There are relatively few producers of Tennessee whiskey today, which is the result of a statewide prohibition that lasted longer than the nation's de facto Prohibition era. Even today, many counties in Tennessee prohibit the sale of alcohol. Until quite recently, only three of Tennessee's 95 counties (namely, Lincoln, Moore, and Coffee) permitted the distillation of spirit alcohol. A law passed by the Tennessee General Assembly in 2009 granted permission to 41 additional counties.

Producers of Tennessee whiskey include Jack Daniel's, George Dickel, Collier and McKeel, and Benjamin Prichard's. Typical flavors of Tennessee whiskey include maple syrup, vanilla, caramel, and smoke.

AMERICAN RYE WHISKEY

American *rye whiskey* is made from a mash of at least 51% rye. The remainder of the mash bill is generally corn and malted barley. Rye whiskey must adhere to the typical production standards of bourbon. If aged for at least two years, it may be designated as straight rye whiskey. In the late 1700s, rye was the prevalent whiskey of the northeastern United States, particularly around Pennsylvania and Maryland. However, it largely disappeared after Prohibition. One brand, Old Overholt, founded in 1810, survived. Today, along with the revival of many classic drinks and cocktails, rye is enjoying a newfound popularity. Versions of rye whiskey are now being produced by Heaven Hill, Sazerac/Buffalo Trace, Jim Beam, and Wild Turkey, among others.

AMERICAN CORN WHISKEY

American *corn whiskey,* sometimes called corn liquor, is made from a mash of at least 80% corn. Many modern versions are marketed based on the connection between corn mash and the tradition of illicit (and illegal) moonshine, as corn (perhaps along with sugar) was often used as the base material for illegal whiskey production.

However, there is nothing illegal about the corn whiskey produced today, which is actually enjoying a renewed popularity. Corn whiskey follows all of the typical production standards for American whiskey, except that it is often unaged. If it is aged, then it must be done in used or uncharred oak barrels. The high proportion of corn in the mash bill lends a smooth mouthfeel to the spirit and a slightly sweet corn note. Well-known producers of corn whiskey include Heaven Hill and Buffalo Trace. One version is packaged in a mason jar and is known as Shine On Georgia Moon, produced by the Johnson Distilling Company of Kentucky. (It should be noted that corn whiskeys are not to be confused with some brands that contain the word *moonshine* on the label, which may be flavored spirits and may not qualify as corn whiskey.)

Figure 5.13: A Jug of Platte Valley Corn Whiskey, Produced in Weston, Missouri

AMERICAN STRAIGHT WHISKEYS

More restrictive than basic whiskey, the *straight whiskey* category is built upon hundreds of years of American whiskey tradition. To be considered a straight whiskey, the spirit must be matured in charred, new oak barrels for a minimum of two years (with the exception of corn whiskey, which requires the use of uncharred or previously-used barrels). While many styles of American whiskey are permitted to contain caramel coloring, all forms of straight whiskey (with the exception of blended straights, as discussed later in this chapter) are specifically excluded from the allowance and are therefore not allowed to contain colorings.

The grain bills allowed for particular straight whiskeys are as follows:
- At least 51% corn for straight bourbon whiskey
- At least 51% rye for straight rye whiskey
- At least 51% wheat for straight wheat whiskey
- At least 51% malted barley for straight malt whiskey
- At least 51% malted rye for straight rye malt whiskey
- At least 80% corn for straight corn whiskey

Additionally, a whiskey produced from less than 51% of any single type of grain, appropriately aged, may be labeled as simply "straight whiskey."

As is the case with straight bourbon (discussed earlier in this chapter), if a straight whiskey has been aged for four years or longer, then a statement of age on the label is optional. However, if it has been aged less than four years, then the age (in years) must be stated on the label—and, if a blend, it must reflect the youngest age. Note that without the two-year cask-aging requirement, straights revert to just bourbon, rye, wheat, and corn whiskeys, with all other requirements remaining the same.

BOTTLED-IN-BOND WHISKEYS

A spirit that is labeled as *bottled-in-bond* or *bonded* must be produced, aged, and bottled in accordance with the United States Bottled-in-Bond Act of 1897, which was originally passed in order to guarantee the authenticity of a spirit. While the regulation technically applies to any American-made spirit, most bonded spirits are whiskeys. In order to be labeled as "bottled-in-bond," the act requires that a spirit:

- Be a product of one distillation season, defined as a sixth-month period from January to June or July to December
- Be a product of one distiller at one distillery
- Has been aged in a federally bonded warehouse under US government supervision for a minimum of four years
- Be bottled at 100 proof
- Be labeled in such a way that identifies the distillery and (if different) the location where it was bottled.

AMERICAN BLENDED WHISKEYS

In the United States, blended whiskeys (whiskey—a blend) are allowed to contain a straight whiskey (or whiskeys) combined with light whiskey or neutral spirits, as well as small amounts of certain coloring and flavoring materials (such as caramel and sugar).
- Blended bourbon, which must contain no less than 51% straight bourbon whiskey
- Blended rye, which must contain no less than 51% straight rye whiskey
- Blended wheat, which must contain no less than 51% straight wheat whiskey
- Blended whiskey, which must contain a blend of straight whiskeys (to make up not less than 20% of the alcohol content on a proof gallon basis) with whiskey or neutral spirits

AMERICAN LIGHT WHISKEYS

The category of American *light whiskey* was first introduced in the 1960s, as large spirits producers noticed the robust market for Scotch whiskies and Irish whiskies, which are required to be distilled to a higher proof than American whiskeys. Light whiskeys were a commercial failure with consumers, and most were taken off the market; however, light whiskeys are still made for blending purposes.

American light whiskey must be distilled to a higher proof than standard American whiskeys. The regulations require light whiskey to be distilled at higher than 160 proof but lower than 190 proof, as the product would then be classified as a grain neutral spirit. The whiskey is still required to be stored in oak, which must be either used or uncharred new oak barrels. This procedure produces a spirit with limited "whiskey character" that still retains the whiskey name.

SPIRIT WHISKEY

Although rarely seen, another "lighter" version of whiskey is technically classified in the United States as *spirit whiskey*. The US Standards of Identity define spirit whiskey as a mixture of neutral spirits (defined as a product distilled at or above 190 proof) and no less than 5% (on a proof gallon basis) of whiskey or straight whiskey, as long as the straight whiskey component stays below 20% (also on a proof gallon basis).

FLAVORED WHISKEY

Flavored spirits continue to be popular in the United States, and the whiskey category is no exception. US spirits regulations allow for the production of flavored whiskeys which may be bottled at a minimum of 30% abv (as is allowed in other spirit categories as well). Cinnamon-flavored whiskeys—such as Fireball (produced by the Sazerac Company), Jim Beam Kentucky Fire, and Jack Daniels Tennessee Fire—were among the first American flavored whiskey products to be released and continue to be widely distributed. Other popular flavors include cherry, apple, blackberry, peach, maple, honey, and vanilla. Some flavored whiskey products contain sugar or liqueurs, or are themselves (technically) classified as liqueurs.

WHITE WHISKEYS

A type of clear spirit whiskey has recently begun to enjoy renewed popularity. These products may technically be an unaged corn whiskey, a light whiskey, a whiskey that has been briefly aged, or a whiskey that has been filtered to remove any traces of coloration. In addition, such products may fall under the category of a grain spirit, a spirit whiskey, neutral spirit, or distilled spirit—specialty. These products are sometimes called *white dog* or *new-make spirit*; if the product does indeed meet all of the US requirements for actual whiskey, the name *whiskey* may be used on the label. These products often boast a variety of creative names, such as Rogue Distillery's Dead Guy Whiskey and Corsair Distillery's Wry Moon.

Although perfectly legal, these products draw on the mystique and tradition of moonshine. In general, they are meant to taste like exactly what they are—young, raw, and (perhaps) rough—although producers are using terms like *flamboyant* and *bright*.

A favorite of craft distillers, white-style whiskey is also being produced by large distilleries these days. Some examples include Unaged Tennessee Rye produced by Jack Daniel's and Jacob's Ghost by Jim Beam.

It should be noted that "white whiskey" is not a legally-defined category of spirits in the United States, but is rather an informal term used to describe a certain style.

CANADIAN WHISKIES

Eastern Canadian territory was perfect for growing rye and barley. Early Canadian distillers created Canada's fledgling distillation industry in the 1790s. As Canadian settlers extended their farms further west in the seventeenth and eighteenth centuries, corn and wheat became part of the grain blends used in distillation as well.

Canadian whisky was very popular in the United States by the early 1900s. During American Prohibition, enormous amounts of Canadian whisky were smuggled into the United States, including a great deal from Hiram Walker's Distillery located in Windsor, Ontario, directly across the Detroit River from Michigan. After the repeal of Prohibition, this popularity continued, and large quantities of Canadian whisky continued to be (legally) imported to the United States.

Figure 5.14: Walkerville Distillery (1905-15) (The model town of Walkerville [now part of Windsor, Ontario] was founded by Hiram Walker, the producer of Canadian Club whisky.)

The laws regulating Canadian whisky, via the Food and Drug Regulations of Canada, specify that Canadian whisky must:
- Be made from a mash of fermented cereal grains
- Be aged in small wood containers for no less than three years
- Possess the aroma, taste, and character generally attributed to Canadian whisky
- Be mashed, distilled, and aged in Canada
- Be bottled at no less than 40% alcohol by volume.

Further, the regulation states that Canadian whisky may be labeled with the terms "Canadian whisky," "Canadian rye whisky," or "rye whisky." These terms may be used interchangeably and without regard to the ingredients used. This is a big point of difference between American rye whiskeys, which must be made from a minimum of 51% rye, and Canadian rye whisky, which may contain far more corn than rye and may even contain no rye whatsoever.

The use of the term *rye* to refer to Canadian whisky in general is a throwback to several hundred years ago, when rye was the most plentiful grain in Canada. Canadian distillers would add small amounts of rye to their mostly corn-based whisky, thus producing a spicy, flavorful whisky. People started demanding this rye-flavored whisky, often referring to whisky in general as simply "rye." As such, the terminology (and, perhaps, the confusion) continues to this day.

The following types of whisky are produced in Canada:

Grain Whisky: The largest production of whisky distilled in Canada is *grain whisky,* sometimes referred to as *base whisky.* This product is much like the light whiskey distilled in the United States; however, its main ingredients are likely to be corn or wheat. Its distillation procedure is not specified by law, but in general, it is column distilled at 185–189 proof. The whisky is aged for the legally mandated minimum of three years, generally in used barrels. Canadian grain whisky is rarely sold or labeled as such, but it is used in Canadian blended whisky.

Flavoring Whisky: These whiskies are typically made with a high percentage of a single grain, are stored in charred oak barrels, or are otherwise produced in a particular style (similar to American bourbon or straight rye). Like Canadian grain whisky, flavoring whiskies are not usually labeled as such, but they are most often used in Canadian blended whisky.

Canadian Blended Whisky: Most Canadian whiskies are marketed as blends and are comprised of a base grain whisky and a flavoring whisky. The base whisky, usually made from corn, is very light in flavor and is blended with a small amount of flavoring whisky, which may contain a high rye content or be produced in some other manner to provide a certain flavor profile to the finished blend. The law also allows for added ingredients in an amount of up to 9.09% of the total product. These ingredients often include sherry, sweetener, caramel coloring, wine, or even non-Canadian whiskey or brandies added to the finished blend in order to produce a distinctive flavor.

Figure 5.15: Glenora Distillery in Nova Scotia

Specialty Whiskies: Specialty distilleries producing unique whiskies can certainly be found in Canada. For instance, Glenora Distillery, located in Nova Scotia and billed as North America's first single malt distillery, produces a single malt Canadian whisky distilled from just water and malted barley. Likewise, the Still Waters Distillery in Ontario has recently released a single-barrel bottling of Stalk and Barrel single malt whisky, which is distilled in a copper pot still and produced from 100% Canadian two-row malted barley. Other unique Canadian whiskies include Crown Royal's extra-rare whisky series, Hiram Walker's Lot 40 single copper pot still Canadian whisky, and Alberta Premium's thirty-year-old Canadian whisky. It is important to note, however, that terms such as *single malt* and *extra rare* are not specifically defined per Canadian law.

JAPANESE WHISKY

Whisky production in Japan began in the late 1870s, with the first commercial distillery in Japan, Suntory, opening in 1923. The original Suntory Distillery is located in Yamazaki, a suburb of Kyoto. The location was chosen for the excellence of its water; the quality of the water was so renowned that the legendary tea master Sen no Rikyū built his tearoom there.

Suntory's founder, Shinjiro Torii, was a successful wholesaler who had become wealthy selling wine and pharmaceuticals. Torii hired Masataka Taketsuru, who had trained at Hazelburn Distillery in Campbeltown, Scotland (now closed), as his first distiller.

Suntory initially set out to make a Scotch-style whisky. Their first whisky, known as Shirofuda White Label, was released in 1929. It was rich in flavors of peat and smoke. As such, it was not overwhelmingly accepted in Japan, so this style has been modified over the years. Today, Suntory operates three distilleries: the original Suntory Distillery located in Yamazaki (near Osaka), the Hakushu Distillery located in the Yamanashi Prefecture (near Hokuto), and the Chita Distillery (on the Chita Peninsula). Especially in recent years, Suntory has enjoyed an excellent reputation and wide acclaim for its diverse range of whiskies.

Figure 5.16: Suntory Yamazaki Single Malt Whisky

Suntory's founding distiller, Masataka Taketsuru, opened his own whisky house, known as Nikka, in 1934. Nikka currently operates two distilleries: Yoichi Distillery, on the northern island of Hokkaidō, and Miyagikyo, located in the city of Sendai, on the island of Honshu. The Yoichi Distillery produces rich, peaty malt whisky using a traditional direct-heat-style distillation in which the pot stills are heated with finely powdered natural coal. The Nikka Distillery, now widely recognized for its consistently excellent products, produces single malt, blended malt, and grain whiskies in addition to blends.

In many ways, the production process of Japanese whisky continues to be similar in style to the production of Scotch; even the barley—and, when necessary, the peat—is imported from Scotland. However, while the original goal was to duplicate Scotch whisky, Japan has now established its own style of quality whisky.

One practice unique to Japanese whisky is the emphasis on clear, almost transparent worts. This style of wort is produced by using a long fermentation time and a carefully selected strain of yeast. Another point of differentiation is that Japanese distillers do not often sell their whiskies to other distillers. When a Japanese whisky house produces a blend, it will most often be created using a variety of whiskies from the distiller's own company.

INDIAN WHISKY

India is a large consumer and producer of whisky. Many of the best-selling whisky brands in the world are produced and, for the most part, consumed in India. However, the definition and regulations concerning whisky in India are not the same as those used by the United States or the European Union. As such, much of the "whisky" produced in India is at least partially made with molasses-based neutral spirits.

These molasses-based "whiskies" are classified in India as "Indian-made foreign liquor" (IMFL). This term is used to refer to all of the distilled spirits produced in India other than traditional beverages such as arrack and feni (a beverage distilled from cashew fruit). It is estimated that 90% of the spirits consumed in India that are labeled as whisky are actually these molasses-based products, which would not qualify as "true whisky" based on the standards of the United States or the European Union. The best-selling brands of these whiskies include Officer's Choice, McDowell's No. 1, Royal Stag, and Imperial Blue.

Indian-made foreign liquor may be flavored and may be blended with small amounts of other spirits, which often include imported Scotch whisky. These flavored products may be imported into the European Union under the category "blended whisky," and into the United States under the category "spirit whiskey." This practice is widespread and legal, although not without controversy from an international trade perspective.

However, true whisky produced from grains and following standards equal to those employed by the United States and the European Union is produced in India and exported throughout the world.

The first producer to make a true grain-based whisky in India was Amrut Distilleries. The company, located in Bangalore, was founded in 1948 by Neelakanta Jagdale. After producing spirits based on a combination of grains and molasses for several decades, they released a single malt whisky in 2004. Known simply as Amrut, it was first distributed locally in Bangalore, and, after a positive response, was ceremoniously released in Glasgow, Scotland. This was followed by releases throughout much of Europe as well as Australia, North America, South Africa, and Asia.

The name Amrut comes from a Sanskrit word which may be translated as "nectar of the gods" or, as the company translates it, "elixir of life." Amrut single malt whisky quickly became famous after being reviewed well by several well-known and respected whisky critics and publications.

Amrut Distilleries has continued to evolve in terms of production techniques and maturation regimes. Now produced at the company's main distillery in Kambipura, Amrut is made from 100% barley, including some peated barley imported from Scotland. The whisky is double-distilled in large pot stills before being diluted to 125 proof and aged in oak barrels for four years or longer. Surinder Kumar, the master blender at Amrut Distilleries, has estimated that because of climate differences, one year of barrel aging in India is equal to three years of aging in Scotland.

Amrut single malt whisky is now released in over 10 styles, including those aged in ex-sherry barrels, those aged in ex-bourbon barrels, peated versions, non-peated versions, cask-strength bottlings, and single barrel bottlings. The distillery currently produces 4 million cases of liquor a year, including approximately 10,000 cases of Amrut single malt.

John Distilleries, founded in 1992 and located in Bangalore, also produces high quality grain-based whisky. The company, one of the largest distilleries in India, produces a wide range of products, including Original Choice blended (molasses-based) whisky. Original Choice is one of the best-selling whisky brands in the world, with annual sales of over 5 million cases.

In 2007, John Distilleries opened a new location in Goa and began to produce "true" Indian whisky. Its first 100% grain-based product, Paul John Single Cask 161 Whisky, was named after Mr. Paul P. John, the founder of the company, and was successfully launched in London in 2012. Paul John Single Cask 161 is made using 100% Indian barley. It is double-distilled in traditional copper pot stills and aged for three to five years in American oak barrels. The Goa distillery now produces several quality whisky products, including Paul John Single Malt Whisky, Paul John Single Malt Select Cask Peated Whisky, and a version aged in ex-bourbon barrels known as Brilliance.

WHISKEYS FROM AROUND THE WORLD

Aside from the main whiskey-producing countries, there are some large successful distilleries located throughout the world.

In Europe, the Czech Republic, building on its base of fine malted brews, has a few distilleries producing malt whiskeys. One in particular, known as Pradlo Distillery, a producer of single malts, became nationalized in the 1980s. In 1989, with the fall of communism, the distillery was largely forgotten, and a large stash of whiskey became lost. It was just recently found and was named Hammer Head, after the hammer mill used to grind the grain. Recently, this unique twenty-year-old Czech single malt whiskey was put on the market.

Turkey, which has been producing whiskey for many years, is steadily increasing its production, while England, which was originally one of the first places to produce whiskey, only has a few distilleries still in production. In Spain, Destilerías y Crianza del Whisky S.A. (otherwise known as Whisky DYC) has a production of over two million cases of whisky per year, enough to supply all of Spain with very fine malt, grain, and blended whiskies.

In the Southern Hemisphere, both New Zealand and Australia originally set about to copy Scotland's methods and now have several successful distilleries providing products for their respective home markets. An Australian whisky, Sullivans Cove Single Cask Malt Whisky produced by Tasmania Distillery, was even named the best single malt whisky out of a field of over three hundred entrants at the prestigious World Whisky Awards in 2014. It was the first time that a Tasmanian distillery won the award, which is typically bestowed on Scotland or Japan.

Table 5.5: Top-Selling Global Whiskey Brands

Rank	Brand
1.	Officer's Choice (India)
2.	McDowell's No.1 (India)
3.	Imperial Blue (India)
4.	Royal Stag (India)
5.	Johnnie Walker (Scotland)
6.	Jack Daniel's (United States)
7.	Original Choice (India)
8.	Haywards Fine (India)
9.	Old Tavern (India)
10.	Jim Beam (United States)
11.	8 PM (India)
12.	Crown Royal (Canada)
13.	Ballantine's (Scotland)
14.	Jameson (Ireland)
15.	Bagpiper (India)

Source: Drinks International (2018)

Southern Distilleries, located in New Zealand's South Canterbury District, bills itself as "the world's most southern distillery" and produces single malt and blended malt whiskeys, as well as Hokonui Moonshine. Hokonui Moonshine is based on a bit of local lore concerning Mary McRae, a widow from Scotland, who, along with her seven children, supplied a good part of southern New Zealand with illegal whiskey in the Hokonui Hills from 1872 until the mid-1950s. Their story is told at the Hokonui Moonshine Museum and celebrated each year with a food and whiskey festival.

TASTING AND SERVING WHISKEY

There are almost as many ways to taste and enjoy whiskey as there are whiskeys themselves. Whiskey is typically served in a stemless glass or tumbler as wide as it is short, with room for ice or a splash of water for those who prefer it. Of course, a wide variety of specialty whiskey-tasting glasses are available, and every aficionado may have his or her favorite.

Figure 5.17: Whiskey Neat

Whiskey is a diverse category of spirits. Interesting experiences can be had by tasting a flight of spirits from a similar category, such as Scotch whisky, Irish whiskey, Tennessee whiskey, or bourbon. Interesting tastings can also be arranged across styles, such as single malts, single grains, and blends. Or one may engage in a vertical tasting across various aging classifications.

Start by observing your whiskey for color and clarity. A good whiskey should have a warm glow to it and be devoid of any free-floating particles or turbidity. The color of the beverage, from light golden beige to dark brown, should be an indication of its age, except in the case of those spirits that are permitted to use caramel coloring (which are, for the most part, blends). Swirl the whiskey in the glass and note the character of the legs; richer, more full-bodied whiskeys will have noticeable tears.

Whiskey can show a complex array of aromas, with certain forward notes to be expected based on the type and style. In general, Scotch whisky will have a graininess, woodiness, smokiness, and peat note in the initial aroma. Irish whiskey is similar but will be overall lighter than Scotch and have a distinctive "leathery" aroma. Bourbon and Tennessee whiskeys will smell more of corn, vanilla, caramel, and smoke, perhaps with a suggestion of sweetness. Canadian whiskies and blended whiskeys are expected to exhibit subtle aromatics.

The best whiskeys will seem smooth and warm on the palate. Stronger-proof whiskey may seem to have a slight "burn" on the attack. If one finds this to be overwhelming or unpleasant, then one may dilute the whiskey with a few drops of water. A good whiskey should be lingering, mellow, and warm on the finish.

While whiskey is served in a variety of ways, most consumers prefer to take their whiskey neat, or with a single ice cube as an aperitif or after-dinner drink. Some people like to dilute their whiskey with a bit of water; for other people, this would be a travesty. Lighter, blended whiskeys are often enjoyed long, over ice, and with soda water, ginger ale, or cola. Classic whiskey-based cocktails, such as the Manhattan, the Rob Roy, the Old-Fashioned, and the Mint Julep, are popular as well.

Table 5.6: Tasting Bourbon – Typical Flavors and Aromas

TASTING BOURBON – TYPICAL FLAVORS AND AROMAS	
Grain	Corn, Rye, Barley, Wheat
Malt	Cereal, Cocoa, Malted Barley
Sweet Aromatics	Vanilla, Caramel, Maple Syrup, Butterscotch, Honey, White Chocolate, Dark Chocolate
Brown Spices	Black Pepper, Clove, Cinnamon, Coffee, Tobacco Leaf
Savory Spices	Spearmint, Anise, Herbs
Fruit	Apple, Green Grape, Pear, Cherry, Orange, Coconut, Lemon, Tropical Fruit, Blueberry, Blackberry, Raspberry, Cooked Peach, Cooked Apricot
Floral	Rose Petal, Geranium
Oak	Green Oak, Smoked Oak, Toasted Oak
Wood	Pine, Cedar
Nut	Walnut, Almond, Pecan

Table 5.7: Tasting Scotch Whisky and Irish Whiskey – Typical Flavors and Aromas

TASTING SCOTCH WHISKY AND IRISH WHISKEY – TYPICAL FLAVORS AND AROMAS	
Grain/Cereal	Bran, Biscuit, Corn Husk, Tobacco, Barley, Malted Barley
Mash	Cooked Corn, Porridge
Sweet Aromatics	Vanilla, Caramel, Maple Syrup, Butterscotch, Honey, Chocolate
Brown Spices	Black Pepper, Clove, Cinnamon, Coffee, Tobacco Leaf
Savory Spices	Spearmint, Anise, Herbs
Fruit	Cherry, Orange, Blackberry, Cooked Peach, Cooked Apricot
Floral	Heather, Rose Petal, Lavender, Carnation, Violet
Oak	Oak Resin, Oak Polish
Cedar	Sawdust, Pencil
Nut	Marzipan, Walnut, Almond, Coconut, Hazelnut
Burnt/Peat	Tar, Soot, Ash
Smoky/Peat	Kippery, Wood Smoke, Smoked Bacon
Medicinal/Peat	TCP (Antiseptic), Hospital, Iodine

Table 5.8: Tasting Whiskey – Typical Descriptors for Palate and Style

TASTING WHISKEY – TYPICAL DESCRIPTORS FOR PALATE AND STYLE	
Style	Light, Full, Rustic, Flavorful, Shows Flavor of Dominant Grain(s)
Palate	Round, Delicate, Pungent, Full-Bodied, Rich, Balanced
Other	Mellow, Complex, Layered, Warm, Lingering

CHAPTER SIX BRANDY AND OTHER FRUIT-BASED SPIRITS

BRANDY AND OTHER FRUIT-BASED SPIRITS

CHAPTER SIX

LEARNING OBJECTIVES

After studying this chapter, the candidate should be able to do the following:
- Define brandy in terms of base materials, distillation processes, maturation, and other post-distillation procedures.
- Describe the various types of grape-based brandy, including cognac, armagnac, brandy de Jerez, pisco, and other grape brandies produced throughout the world.
- Identify and discuss the various types of pomace brandy, including grappa and marc.
- Discuss the various types of apple- and pear-based brandy, including calvados and applejack.
- Identify and define other fruit-based brandies, fruit-based spirits, and flavored brandies.
- Discuss the sensory evaluation of brandy and the typical procedures for the serving of brandy and brandy-based drinks.

Brandy is a class of spirits distilled from fruit. More specifically, brandy is produced from grape wine, the pomace left after winemaking, or the fermented juice of other fruits. Cognac and armagnac, arguably the most famous of all brandies, are distilled from grape wine and produced in specified regions of France. Grape-based brandy is also made in many places around the world, and most wine-producing regions have their own brandy traditions. Brandy is also made from apples and pears, such as the French apple-and-pear brandy calvados and the historic American product known as applejack. Brandy is also produced around the world from cherries, plums, apricots, berries, and other fruits.

Most brandies made from grapes and apples are "brown spirits" due to barrel aging or the addition of caramel to imitate barrel aging, whereas pomace and fruit brandies are generally unaged and remain clear.

This chapter begins with an overview of brandy, including a standard definition, history, and basic production techniques. It then proceeds to a discussion of grape brandies, beginning with cognac, armagnac, brandy de Jerez, pisco, and other leading grape brandies of the world. It continues with sections on pomace brandies, such as grappa and marc, as well as apple and pear brandies, such as France's calvados and the United States' historic apple brandy called applejack. Sections on fruit brandy, such as eaux-de-vie, kirschwasser, and framboise, follow—and the chapter ends with a short discussion of the sensory evaluation and service of brandy.

DEFINITION OF BRANDY

According to the US Standards of Identity, the category of brandy is defined as follows:
- A distilled spirit produced using the fermented juice, mash, or wine of fruit (or the residue thereof)
- Distilled at less than 95% alcohol by volume (190 proof)
- Produced in a manner such that the distillate possesses the taste, aroma, and characteristics of the base ingredient
- Bottled at no less than 40% alcohol by volume (80 proof)

The US Standards of Identity also define various subcategories of brandy, such as the following:
- Grape brandy, which is produced using the juice or wine of grapes, with a maximum of 30% (by volume) grape pomace or lees. Grape brandy is the only type of brandy that can be labeled with the term *brandy* without a qualifier naming the base ingredients, such as "apricot brandy" or "pomace brandy." The term *immature* or *unaged* must precede the term *brandy* on the label of any

grape brandy product that has not undergone two years of oak aging, with the exception of neutral brandy and pomace brandy.
- Fruit brandy, which must be made from fruit, fruit juice, or fruit wine, with a maximum of 30% (by volume) fruit pomace or lees. Fruit brandy not derived from grapes must be labeled with the name of the fruit it is produced from, such as "apple brandy" or "pear brandy." Apple brandy may also be called applejack. If made from more than one type of fruit, then the product may be labeled as "fruit brandy," accompanied by a truthful statement of composition.
- Pomace brandy, which is produced from the leftover skins and pulps of fruit used in winemaking.
- Neutral brandy, which is distilled at more than 170 proof.

The European Union defines several types of fruit-based spirits, such as brandy made from grapes (the only product that is truly a brandy, according to the EU standards), fruit spirits, and wine spirits.

The EU definition of brandy has the following specifications:
- It must be a spirit distilled from grape wine. (Other wine spirits can be added.)
- It must come off the still at a maximum of 94.8% alcohol by volume (189.6 proof).
- The finished product after maturation cannot exceed 47.4% alcohol by volume (94.8 proof) before bottling.
- It must be matured for at least one year in any type of oak container, or for no less than six months in small oak barrels.
- It must be bottled at no less than 36% alcohol by volume (72 proof).
- It may not be flavored, except for in certain traditional production methods, but it may contain caramel coloring.
- The term *weinbrand* is considered synonymous with *brandy*.

The EU definition of fruit spirits includes products commonly known as fruit brandy. A fruit spirit has the following specifications:
- It must be made from fruit besides grapes, which may include plums, apples, pears, raspberries, blackberries, apricots, peaches, cherries, or other fruits.
- It does not need to be aged.
- It must be distilled at less than 86% alcohol by volume (172 proof) so that the distillate has an aroma and taste derived from the raw materials.
- It may not be flavored.
- It must be bottled at a minimum of 37.5% alcohol by volume (75 proof).
- It may be called *wasser,* along with the name of the fruit (kirschwasser, for example).
- In some cases, the name of the fruit may replace the word *spirit* on a label. Some of the products that may be so labeled include mirabelle, quetsch, and Williams (which may only be used for pear spirits produced using the Williams, or Bartlett, variety).

EU regulations further define unaged grape brandy under the term *wine spirits.* EU pomace brandy, which also does not need to be aged, is defined as "grape marc spirit" or "fruit marc spirit."

In this guide, the term *brandy* will be, at times, used to refer to all fruit-based spirits, as is commonly done in many parts of the world.

HISTORY OF BRANDY

The art of distillation, it is believed, was first applied to wine (at least in a commercial sense) in the sixteenth century, building upon the existing brisk trade in wine between the port of La Rochelle, on the Charente River in France, and Holland.

All of this trade was conducted by sea. As casks of wine obviously take up a lot of space on small sailing vessels, it was eventually discovered that the wine could be "concentrated" by eliminating the water content and transporting the spirit, or the "soul," of the wine to Holland. Upon its arrival, water would be added, thereby reconstituting the wine. Concentrating the wine had the added benefit of reducing the tax burden on the shipment, as taxes were based on volume.

As the first shipments of "concentrated wine" arrived in Holland, it was discovered that the concentrate had a unique, pleasing flavor of its own. It became apparent that after being shipped in wooden casks, the product was better than the original wine. The Dutch called the new product brandewijn ("burnt wine"), and eventually, the term was anglicized to form the present-day word, *brandy*. The term *weinbrand*, "burnt wine," remains the German word for brandy and, throughout the European Union, is an acceptable synonym for *brandy*.

Figure 6.1: *Plum Brandy* by Édouard Manet (1877)

THE PRODUCTION OF BRANDY

Every brandy, despite its origin of production or its base material, is produced according to the following general process.

Base Material: Brandies are made from either a wine or fruit base. Many regions in various countries specify the particular grapes and fruits that can be used in the brandy that carries the name of that region. Certainly, the choice of a particular grape to make the wine that will be distilled into a brandy will have a distinct influence on the brandy's style and flavor. Also, a particular fruit flavor, such as apple or raspberry, will carry over into the resulting brandy.

Fermentation: Fermentation may or may not be performed by the producing distillery. Many brandy producers who use grape wine as their distillate base purchase the wine. Conversely, many non-grape brandy producers press and ferment their own fruit or purchase fruit juice, which they ferment to their own specifications.

Distillation: In brandy production, as in all spirits production, the choice of still type impacts the final product. More complex, fuller-bodied brandies are produced in pot stills, while lighter, simpler styles are made in column stills. In this regard, many non-grape brandies are produced in column stills to create a cleaner, purer spirit.

Pot stills for brandy production are usually constructed from copper or stainless steel. Copper is easier to manipulate into the complex traditional still shapes used in various countries. Furthermore, copper, during the vapor stage, promotes chemical reactions that produce new aroma components. Stainless steel is harder to fabricate into a still, but it lasts much longer and provides a cleaner, more consistent distillate.

A typical batch process carried out in a pot still begins with a base of fermented wine or fruit juice. The base ferment is generally 6–10% alcohol by volume at the beginning of the process. As the base ferment is heated, the resulting vapors are condensed and collected. This first distillate has an alcohol concentration of approximately 30% alcohol by volume.

This is followed by a second distillation, resulting in a spirit of approximately 70–80% alcohol by volume in concentration. In the second distillation, the "heart" of the run is collected separately from the start and end of the distillation run. Both the start, or "heads" (products that come off at a low boiling point), and the end, or "tails" (those products that have a high boiling point), of the distillation run may be added back to the wash of a new distillation or returned to the still with the product of the first distillation.

Maturation: After distillation is complete, some brandies are ready for bottling, while others require maturation. Most fruit and pomace brandies are not aged and are deliberately kept out of wood to ensure that the full flavor of the base material shines through. This absence of wood contact also keeps them colorless.

Figure 6.2: Brandy Aging in the Cellars at Koöperatieve Wijnbouwers Vereniging (KWV) in Worcester, South Africa

Brandies that are matured in wood are most frequently aged in a single cask over the full specified time period. They are then bottled on their own or are blended with other brandies that have been aged in the same manner in order to produce a product with a consistent flavor profile. However, some brandies are vintage-dated or marketed as "single barrel aged." In these instances, the contents of a given barrel are kept separate in order to maintain the provenance of the stored brandy and qualify it for vintage dating and "single barrel" status on the bottle's label.

The *solera system,* in a process similar to the unique aging method of sherry, is used by some brandy producers to store and age the product. In this process, a series of rows of barrels are hypothetically stacked on top of each other, with the barrels in the bottom row containing the oldest brandies and the barrels on the top row containing the youngest. Each year, a portion of brandy is removed from these bottom-level barrels, blended together, and then bottled. The bottom row is then topped off with brandy from the row just above, and so on, until all of the barrels have been filled. The newly made spirit is placed in the top row of barrels. In this way, the brandy is progressively aged and blended over time.

Vintage-dated brandies are not produced via the solera method; however, an age statement on the label of a solera brandy is permitted, establishing the minimum age of the final blend. For example, in a solera consisting of ten rows—in which brandy from each row is transferred annually to the barrel just beneath it—the minimum age would be ten years. In reality, as some of the brandy remains in the casks for many years, the average age is quite older than the age stated on the label.

Blending: After the maturation process, some brandies are blended to create a finished product, whereas others are bottled on their own. Based upon the length of their maturation period, brandies may qualify for a designated quality level. The traditional stars, alphabetic abbreviations, and unique nomenclature used to label cognac (discussed later in this chapter) are often employed for brandies produced elsewhere. These and other typical classifications used for various types of brandy are discussed in the sections that follow.

GRAPE BRANDY

As delineated in the definition section above, the various types of brandy include grape brandies, fruit brandies, and pomace brandies. Grape brandies are the most prevalent type of brandy and are produced in many regions and countries.

Cognac

Among the best-known and most highly regarded are the brandies from the *Cognac* region in southwestern France. The region is located just north of the Bordeaux region around the town of Cognac. The full, official name for cognac is *eau-de-vie de Cognac* or *eau-de-vie des Charentes,* but, with time, the shortened version of the title has become so widely used that the term *cognac* has become the accepted name in use, even on bottle labels.

Figure 6.3: On the Grounds of the House of Martell

Chief among the qualifications for the cognac designation is that cognac must be distilled from wine made of grapes grown within the legally defined area of the Charente and Charente-Maritime departments of France. The entire Cognac region was delimited by law in 1909. In 1936, the Cognac region was among the very first to be granted an appellation d'origine contrôlée (AOC) when the INAO (Institut National de l'Origine et de la Qualité, formerly known as the Institut National des Appellations d'Origine) was created in the mid-1930s.

The Crus: The Cognac AOC is divided into six *crus*—officially recognized districts that may be used on labels to indicate geographic origin. If the name of a cru appears on a label of cognac, then 100% of the grapes must have been grown in the named region.

In order from most prestigious to least renowned, the crus are *Grande Champagne, Petite Champagne, Borderies, Fins Bois, Bons Bois,* and *Bois Ordinaires.* The term *Fine Champagne* may be used to indicate a cognac produced with a combination of grapes from the Grande Champagne and Petite Champagne areas, with at least 50% of them grown within Grande Champagne.

The overall subsoil in Cognac is chalky. Varying amounts of chalk are found throughout the region. The two growing districts considered highest in quality, Grande Champagne and Petite Champagne, contain the highest amounts of chalk.

The use of the term *Champagne* in the context of cognac often leads to confusion. However, it is helpful to know that the French term *champ* originally referred to a wide-open plain or meadow, and once upon a time it was an apt description for the pastoral landscape of the Champagne region, which now produces the famous sparkling wine. The term *bois* refers to a forest, and *Borderies* describes the sharecroppers' farms that used to be located in this area.

The attributes of each of the six crus include the following:

- **Grande Champagne:** Cognac from the Grande Champagne region is considered to be the highest quality and may take twenty to thirty years to mature. Grande Champagne cognac has been described as both intense and elegant, with fruity and floral aromas. The area contains a good deal of chalk soil, layered over limestone and sandstone bedrock, and has a maritime climate. The Grande Champagne area, despite its name, is less than half the size of the Petite Champagne area, although it produces nearly as much cognac each year.
- **Petite Champagne:** The soil and terroir of the Petite Champagne region, while similar to that of the Grand Champagne region, has a lower concentration of limestone and contains other soil types. Petite Champagne produces brandies that, while highly desirable, are not considered to match the finesse of the Grand Champagne cognacs.
- **Borderies:** Outside the Champagne area, the chalky layer of the soil becomes shallower while the earthy top layer becomes deeper. The smallest subregion, Borderies, has a predominantly clay soil and more sun exposure, which causes the grapes to ripen more quickly than the grapes in the other growth areas. This causes the resulting brandy to mature faster. Spirits produced here provide weight and floral notes when added to a blend.
- **Fins Bois:** The Fins Bois, which surrounds the first three areas in a concentric circle, is by far the largest of the six crus and annually produces more than three times the volume of its neighbor, the Bons Bois. The Fins Bois, with a wide diversity of soils and a maritime climate, produces brandies that are fruity and well-balanced and that will mature within fifteen years—quite a bit earlier than the higher-quality cognacs.

The Cognac Region

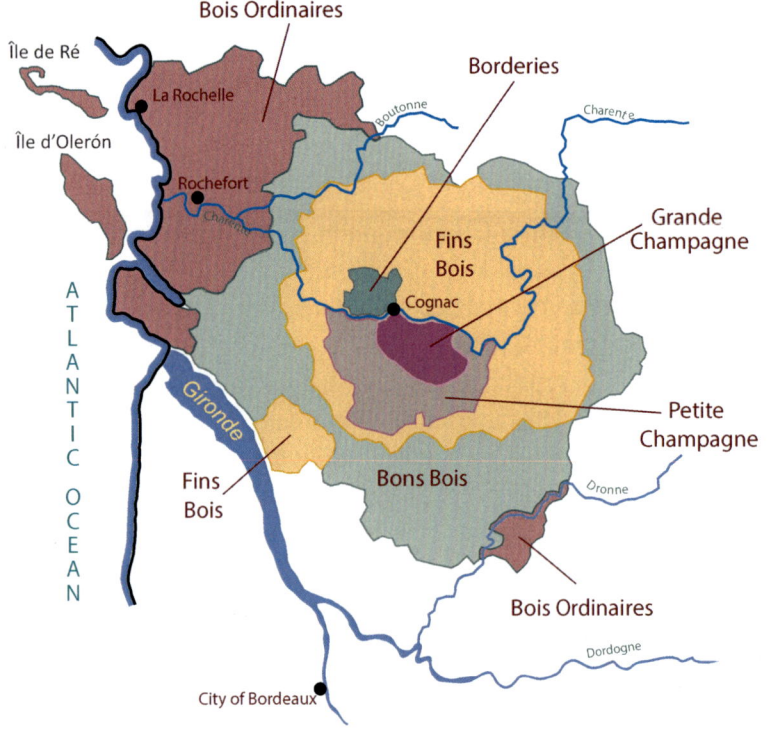

Figure 6.4: Map of the Cognac Region

The Grapes: Cognac is produced from white grape varieties, with Ugni Blanc (locally known as Saint Émilion, and known as Trebbiano Toscano in Italy) being the leading variety. The standard base wine for cognac is produced using 90% Ugni Blanc, Folle Blanche, and/or Colombard. Other permitted grape varieties include Montils, Sémillon, and Folignan (a Folle Blanche X Ugni Blanc cross). Folignan is legally limited to a maximum of 10% of all plantings.

Other minor grapes used in cognac include Jurançon Blanc, Meslier-Saint-François, and Sélect. However, these are currently allowed only if planted prior to September 18, 2005. The regulation permitting these grape varieties is scheduled to expire after the 2020 harvest.

In reality, Ugni Blanc is the sole grape variety used in most versions of cognac, as it is prized in the area for its disease resistance and neutral flavors. The grapes are normally harvested in October and November, pressed immediately, and fermented into a thin wine with low alcohol and high acidity. This uninteresting, neutral base wine will be concentrated in flavor and character as it is distilled and aged into cognac.

Micro-distillation: A new development in Cognac is now widely used, that of putting samples of the wine through a quick "micro-distillation" prior to full distillation in order to "preview" the characteristics of the vintage and predict the nature and style of the resulting brandy. This allows distillers and blenders to consider how they will proceed and what decisions they will make to achieve the desired product.

- **Bon Bois:** The Bon Bois surrounds the Fins Bois in a large loop. It consists mostly of heavy clay soils, although there are some patches of chalk and limestone, particularly in the regions closest to the Petite Champagne region. This is a large region in terms of geographic size; however, only 5% of the area is planted to grapes for use in cognac. The Bon Bois is considered to produce grapes that are not as "ordinary" as the Bois Ordinaires and not quite as "fine" as the Fins Bois.
- **Bois Ordinaires:** The vineyards of the Bois Ordinaires, occupying the westernmost portion of the Cognac AOC, which includes two islands as well as a small section on the eastern edge, are made up of mostly sandy soil and are more heavily influenced by the maritime climate on the Atlantic coast. This area produces brandies that are, in comparison to those of the other regions, heavier, coarser, and less preferred for creating quality cognac.

The Distillation Process: Distillation takes place in a traditional alembic or pot still, referred to as a Charentais still in this region. Cognac distillation is a two-stage process known as *à repasse*. The still must be made of copper, directly heated, and limited in size. The first stage of distillation, known as the *première chauffe*, produces a distillate with an alcohol volume of 28–32% known as *brouillis*. When enough brouillis is collected, the product is sent through the second stage of the distillation.

To perform the second-stage distillation, known as the *bonne chauffe*, the brouillis is returned to the boiler for a second heating. The heart of the run, coming off as a clear distillate at about 60% alcohol by volume, will be matured into cognac. A portion of the heads, or *têtes*, and *secondes* (that portion of the tails that are considered worthy) may be collected and redistilled with either the base wine or the brouillis of a subsequent batch.

Figure 6.5: Charentais Still Manufactured by Chalvignac Prulho Distillation

During the distillation process, the distiller may use several optional processes to impact the character of the final spirit. For instance, the lees left over after fermentation may be left in the wash, which is transferred to the still. In the *Martell Method,* the lees are discarded, which creates lighter, earlier-maturing spirits that are less likely to develop "rancio" flavors. In contrast, the *Rémy Martin Method* uses the lees in order to impart a richer character to the spirit and also allow for longer aging potential, which can add complexity and a *rancio* character to the finished product.

The distiller must also decide what to do with the têtes and secondes from the bonne chauffe distillation run. Adding the secondes back into the base wine will result in a lighter style of spirit, as this will raise the alcohol level of the base wine significantly. With the higher alcoholic concentration in the base wine, the resulting distillate will be less concentrated with congeners and will produce a lighter-flavored spirit. This method is favored by the Martell Cognac House. Adding têtes and secondes to the brouillis will result in a deeper, richer spirit. The Hennessey Cognac House equally divides the secondes and adds half to the base wine and half to the brouillis, producing a spirit somewhere between the "light" style of Martell and the richer style of Rémy.

During the distillation season, which starts in November and lasts for three to five months, the Charentais stills work continuously, twenty-four hours a day, seven days a week. All distillation must be completed by March 31 of the year after harvest. Because no sulfuring of the wine is allowed, this limited time frame ensures that the nature of the wines does not change—and also that the wines will not age prior to distillation.

Aging and Maturation: After distillation is complete, the newly created brandy is put into oak barrels to age. These are sealed and stored in a well-ventilated aboveground warehouse known as a *chai*. Barrels are typically made of Limousin oak obtained from the nearby forest of Limoges; however, oak from Alliers or Tronçais may also be used. Limousin oak is preferred because of its porosity, which allows for a slow oxidation of the brandy. Also, it is low in harsh tannins.

The porous nature of the barrels, as well as Cognac's maritime climate, causes the alcohol in the spirit to evaporate more rapidly than the water and other constituents do. Thus, in addition to the typical 3–4% annual loss in volume, there is a corresponding diminution in alcoholic strength, averaging around 2% alcohol by volume per year. Cognac that has matured for many years in the barrel will eventually reach 40% alcohol by volume, the minimum alcohol percentage allowed for bottling. These very old cognacs are often transferred into large glass containers known as *demijohns,* where they maintain their alcohol level and are used for blending into prestige cognacs.

Figure 6.6: Cognac Aging at Martell

Cognac is matured for a minimum of two years in oak, but some versions are aged for much longer. The age of cognac is calculated from April 1, following the vintage. Traditional maturation cellars are near the Charente River, originally for ease of shipping; these cellars tend to be cool and damp, which provides for a slow maturation. Newer cellars are now built on surrounding hilltops; these cellars are much drier and warmer and lead to more rapid and pronounced maturity.

Most cognac is blended after maturation is complete in order to achieve a particular character and also to ensure that a consistent house style is maintained from year to year. The various ages and qualities of cognacs may be labeled with stars, alphabetic letters, or other designations. In order to use a particular designation, it must refer to the youngest component in the blend. Inventory and age control of cognac is overseen by the Bureau National Interprofessionnel du Cognac (BNIC).

Single variety and single vintage/age-dated cognac may be released, but these are comparatively rare. Most cognacs are carefully created blends by experienced master blenders. Blanche, or "white cognac," is not allowed by the AOC regulations.

Table 6.1: Cognac Labeling Terms

COGNAC LABELING TERMS	
*** (three stars) / VS (Very Special)	Minimum of 2 years of wood aging
Supérieur	Minimum of 3 years of wood aging
VSOP (Very Superior Old Pale) / Réserve	Minimum of 4 years of wood aging
VVSOP / Grande Réserve	Minimum of 5 years of wood aging
Napoléon	Minimum of 6 years of wood aging
Extra	Minimum of 6 years of wood aging (equal to Napoléon, but often marketed as "higher" in quality/price than a producer's Napoléon)
Vieille Réserve	Minimum of 6 years of wood aging; must be at least as old as Extra, but is usually much older and marketed as "higher" in quality/price than Extra
Hors d'Âge ("Beyond Age")	Minimum of 6 years of wood aging; required to be at least as old as Vieille Réserve in terms of minimum age, but is usually marketed as "higher" in quality/price than Vieille Réserve
XO (Extra-Old)	Minimum of 10 years of wood aging

Note: The aging standard of XO Cognac was raised from a minimum of six years to a minimum of ten years effective April 1, 2018. Spirits bottled as XO Cognac under the previous minimum of six years will be allowed to be sold through March 31, 2019.

The Cognac Industry: In reality, the cognac industry is dominated by four major houses: Hennessy, Martell, Rémy Martin, and Courvoisier. However, within Cognac, there are various types of producers. Beginning with the small farmer who grows grapes and makes the wine, there are several choices:

- If the farmer owns a still, then he or she can make cognac, age it, and sell it under his or her own name.
- Alternately, if the farmer owns a still, then he or she can produce the spirit and then sell it to one of the small firms that will age, blend, and bottle the cognac under its own label.
- If the farmer does not own a still, then he or she can sell the wine to a local distilling cooperative that distills and ages the cognac and eventually sells it under the co-op's brand name.
- The farmer can sell his or her wine to one of the large cognac houses that do not have sufficient vineyards to supply its own needs. These houses distill, age, blend, and bottle the cognac under their own labels.

Whoever produces the final product must obtain AOC approval before shipping. Every consignment of cognac must also be accompanied by an *Acquit Régional Jaune d'Or* ("golden certificate") issued by the local tax office. This certificate warrants that the product has been produced and distilled in Cognac. The requirement of the Acquit Régional Jaune d'Or was created in 1929 as part of a regional effort to protect the name and origin of cognac.

Armagnac

Although armagnac production significantly predates cognac, the region's more landlocked position in the department of Gers, southeast of Bordeaux in the heart of the Gascony region, meant that the spirit did not achieve the early export popularity enjoyed by cognac. Armagnac is sometimes described as more rustic than cognac. It may be distinguished by its fuller aroma and flavor, plus its rounder texture. It also ages more quickly and thus requires a shorter initial period of maturation.

The Crus: The AOC region of Armagnac consists of three subregions, as defined in 1936:

- *Bas-Armagnac,* the most westerly area, is considered the highest quality and is the largest producer of grapes among the three crus. Here, a unique topsoil known as *boulbènes*—consisting of a combination of sand, chalk, clay, and stones—helps to produce the most elegant spirits.
- *Ténarèze,* the central growing area, possesses a higher quantity of chalk and is associated with producing spirits that are round and complex.
- *Haut-Armagnac,* the most easterly, is the least prized and creates the lightest style of spirits. This area grows only a small amount of grapes for armagnac, as much of its vineyards are dedicated to producing wine under the *Vin de Pays Côtes de Gascogne* and a vin de liqueur under the *Floc de Gascogne AOC*.

The Armagnac Region

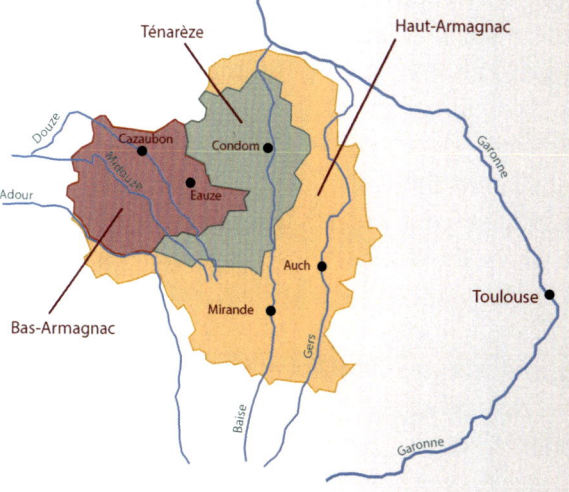

Table 6.2: Top-Selling Cognac Brands

Rank	Brand
1.	Hennessy
2.	Martell
3.	Rémy Martin
4.	Courvoisier

Source: The Spirits Business (2018)

Figure 6.7: Map of the Armagnac Region

The Grapes: Ten grape varieties are allowed to be used in the production of armagnac. Of these, four are considered the most important:

- Ugni Blanc, known here sometimes as Saint-Émilion, is the most widely planted, accounting for nearly 60% of all grapes used. It is responsible for armagnac's floral character and good acidity.
- Baco Blanc, also known as Baco 22a, is a hybrid grape produced from the American Noah grape X Folle Blanche. Baco Blanc, which accounts for just over 30% of all plantings, provides fruitiness, earthiness, and weight to the blend.
- Folle Blanche provides added subtlety and floral aromas. Plantings of Folle Blanche in the Armagnac region were heavily damaged by phylloxera in the 1890s. Today, they account for a mere 1% of the total vine area.
- Colombard provides a spicy, peppery edge, as well as fruitiness and aroma. Colombard grapes bound for armagnac are generally picked early to retain their fresh, lively, fruity flavors.

Six other varieties, sometimes known as the phantom varieties, are also allowed and are scattered throughout the region in small amounts. These include Clairette de Gascogne (Blanc Dame), Meslier Saint-François, Plant de Graisse, Jurancon Blanc, Mauzac Blanc, and Mauzac Rosé.

The Distillation Process: Armagnac is generally distilled using only a single distillation via an armagnac still, which is an early, small-scale version of a continuous still. (Double distillation using a pot still is also permitted but is used only by a few distillers.) The spirit is taken off the still at 52-72% alcohol by volume; in practice, most distillers aim for a strength close to 60%. This is lower than the typical alcohol strength of cognac at this point of production, which means that there are more congeners in the distillate, resulting in armagnac's fuller flavor.

Aging and Maturation: After distillation, young armagnac may be aged for three months in inert containers and released as a clear spirit labeled as "blanche" armagnac. However, most armagnac is aged.

Maturation generally occurs in casks made of black oak from the nearby Monlezun Forest, although Limousin barrels are also permitted. The local oak has high tannin content, which further contributes to armagnac's strong flavor and color and also accounts for a surprisingly smooth taste. In practice, the producers generally use the Monlezun black oak for the first year, and then transfer the brandy to other barrels so as not to impart too much tannic astringency to the maturing spirit. Newer barrels are used for shorter aging periods, while older oak is selected for lengthier maturation.

As of 2013, armagnac may be released after spending a minimum of only one year in wood. Most armagnac is, however, aged for much longer, and, as with most brandies, is often blended during and after aging. Armagnac may also be bottled as a vintage spirit, with a minimum of ten years of age. These vintage brandies may be bottled and sold at cask proof. Single variety bottlings are also allowed.

As with cognac, the various ages and qualities of armagnac may be labeled with stars, alphabetic letters, or other designations; however, the terms and their corresponding minimum and average aging periods have different meanings when applied to armagnac.

Brandy de Jerez

Spain produces a unique, highly regarded brandy known as *brandy de Jerez*. Despite its name and its origination in Jerez, or the sherry region, most of the grapes sourced for the production of this brandy come from the region of La Mancha. Some distillation can take place in La Mancha as well.

The Grapes: The grapes used are 95% Airén. The remaining 5% are Palomino. The hot, dry climate of La Mancha produces grapes high in sugar content and low in acid, meaning that the base wine for brandy de Jerez is higher in alcohol and lower in acidity than the base wines used, for instance, in cognac or armagnac.

The Region of Origin: Brandy de Jerez has PGI (protected geographical indication) status and must be aged within the "Sherry Triangle" defined by the towns of Jerez de la Frontera, Sanlúcar de Barrameda, and El Puerto de Santa María.

Brandy has been a tradition in this area since the eighteenth century, when Jerez winemakers began producing unaged eaux-de-vie for use in the distinct

Table 6.3: Armagnac Labeling Terms

ARMAGNAC LABELING TERMS	
Blanche d'Armagnac	Requires no aging beyond 3 months in inert containers
*** (three stars) / VS	Minimum of 1 year of wood aging (generally represents 1–3 years)
VSOP	Minimum of 4 years of wood aging (generally represents 4–9 years)
XO	Minimum of 10 years of wood aging (generally represents 10–19 years)
XO Premium	Minimum of 20 years of wood aging
Hors d'Âge	Represents the highest-quality armagnacs. The term means "without age" or "age unknown" and has often been described as "beyond age." Minimum of at least 10 years of wood aging, although most in this category have been aged for much longer.
Vintage	Vintage armagnac, produced with the grapes of a single-year's harvest, is dated for the year of harvest. Many vintage armagnacs are aged for 20 years or more.

fortified wines of the region. The excess was sold to Dutch traders, who shipped it back to Holland to use in the production of liqueurs. These unaged spirits were known as *holandas*, or Dutch spirits. When the winemakers began to age these holandas in their own cellars, the tradition of brandy de Jerez was born.

The Distillation Process: Distillation can take place in either pot stills or column stills, with column stills being the most prevalent. The resulting spirits are divided into three categories:
- **Holandas:** up to 70% alcohol by volume
- **Aguardiente:** up to 80% alcohol by volume
- **Destilado,** which has two strengths: the first, up to 85% alcohol by volume, and then the second, which reaches up to 94.8% alcohol by volume

Higher-quality brandies are produced in pot stills known as *alquitaras,* which results in premium holandas. Appellation law dictates that spirits below 86% alcohol by volume make up at least half of the final blend. The variety of heavier and lighter spirits presents the blender with a wide selection of components from which to choose.

Aging and Maturation: Brandy de Jerez is unique in that it is aged using the solera system, which was originally developed for the aging of the famous wines of the region. The barrels used for aging the brandy must have previously held sherry for at least three years. Barrels may be either ex-fino barrels (American oak) or ex-oloroso barrels (European oak), both of which can impart unique flavors to the spirit. Minimum aging periods are prescribed and correspond with regulated labeling terms. The use of the solera method, which promotes oxidation, coupled with the warm climate in which the barrels are matured, adds to the rich, sweet, and softer style of these brandies.

Table 6.4: Brandy de Jerez Labeling Terms

BRANDY DE JEREZ LABELING TERMS	
Solera	Minimum of 6 months of solera aging in wood
Solera Reserva	Minimum of 1 year of solera aging in wood
Solera Gran Reserva	Minimum of 3 years of solera aging in wood; must be 100% holandas

Pisco

Pisco has been produced in South America since at least as early as the 1700s. It is thought to have originated with Spanish settlers, who brought their technology and traditions of wine production to the New World. Brandy is widely produced in South America, although Chile and Peru are the only two countries permitted to use the term *pisco*.

The birthplace of pisco, the origin of the name pisco, and even the right to use the term as the name of a beverage is a subject that has long been, and continues to be, hotly debated between Peru, Chile, and other South American countries. As of May 16, 2013, the TTB (Alcohol and Tobacco Tax and Trade Bureau) of the United States recognized Pisco Perú as a distinctive product of Peru, and Pisco Chileno as a distinctive product of Chile. Within the European Union, both Chile and Peru have the right to use the name pisco. However, as of 2013, the European Union recognized the Peruvian province of Pisco as the geographical origin of the drink, and Peru was granted the sole privilege of using the term as a Geographical Indication.

The Pisco Sour: While the debate rages on, one thing that both countries seem to agree on is this: an excellent way to drink pisco is in the popular cocktail known as the Pisco Sour. The Pisco Sour is considered the "national drink" of both Chile and Peru; both countries even have a national holiday on which to celebrate it. Both countries claim to be the birthplace of the cocktail and, as with pisco itself, have their own versions. The Peruvian Pisco Sour is made by mixing Peruvian pisco with lime juice, simple syrup, and egg white, shaking it and serving it over ice, garnished with a dash of Angostura bitters. The Chilean version is made with Chilean pisco, the juice of pica limes (similar to key limes or Mexican limes), and sugar, shaken and served over ice.

Figure 6.8: Peruvian Pisco Sour

Chilean Pisco: The main grapes used for making Chilean pisco include Moscatel (Muscat of Alexandria), Moscatel Rosado (Pink Muscat), Pedro Jiménez, Moscatel de Austria (Torrontés Sanjuanino), and Torontel (Moscatel Amarillo, a descendant of a País X Muscat of Alexandria cross). The Elqui Valley subregion of Coquimbo has emerged as the premier Chilean pisco zone. The government-based *Pisco Chile* trade group was formed in 2009 and has set new standards for Chilean pisco.

While Chilean pisco may be produced as a pomace brandy, many versions are produced using wine. Chilean pisco is generally double-distilled via pot stills to a maximum strength of 73% alcohol by volume. All Chilean pisco must rest for a minimum of sixty days before bottling. Unlike Peruvian pisco, Chilean pisco is sometimes aged in wood.

Chilean pisco is sometimes diluted with water or cut with neutral spirits to alter the final alcohol content by volume. The products are categorized based on minimum alcohol strength by volume, as follows:
- Pisco Corriente or Tradicional (minimum 30% alcohol by volume)
- Pisco Especial (minimum 35% alcohol by volume)

- Pisco Reservado (minimum 40% alcohol by volume)
- Gran Pisco (minimum 43% alcohol by volume)

The minimum alcohol by volume is 40% for those products exported to the United States.

Chilean pisco is often labeled with the term *transparent pisco*. These products are aged for the required sixty days, generally in glass, stainless steel, ceramic, or inactive wood in order to retain their water-white appearance.

The following styles of wood-aged pisco are also produced in Chile:
- Pisco de guarda: Aged in active French or American oak for a minimum of 180 days
- Pisco envejecido ("aged pisco"): Aged in active French or American oak for one year, though most producers age for two or more

Peruvian Pisco: According to the Denominación de Origen, pisco may be produced in the Peruvian departments of Lima, Ica, Arequipa, and Moquegua, as well as in the valleys of Locumba, Sama, and Caplina in the department of Tacna. The grape varieties authorized for use are categorized as "aromatic" and "nonaromatic." The aromatic varieties are Italia, Moscatel, Albilla, and Torontel. The nonaromatic varieties include Quebranta, Criolla Negra, and Mollar. While it is often assumed that pisco is a pomace brandy, Pisco Perú is made from fermented grape must.

Peruvian pisco is produced via pot still distillation. This spirit is unique in that it must be bottled at the same level of alcohol as when it was produced. Additives of any kind—including water and neutral spirits—are prohibited, so the distillation must be precise. Per the regulations of the governing body, the Comisión Nacional del Pisco (CONAPISCO), the alcohol percentage must be between 38 and 48.

Peruvian pisco is not permitted to be aged in wood, but it is required to be aged for a minimum of three months in vessels made of copper, glass, stainless steel, clay, or some other inert material.

There are several styles of Peruvian pisco, including the following:
- Pisco puro (pure pisco), made from a single grape variety
- Pisco acholado (blended pisco), produced with more than one grape variety, generally referring to a blend of aromatic and nonaromatic varieties or a product made with several different types of pisco blended together
- Pisco mosto verde (green must pisco), produced via the distillation of partially fermented grape must distilled while the must still contains some residual sugar
- Pisco aromático (aromatic pisco), produced using just the aromatic grape varieties

GRAPE BRANDY AROUND THE WORLD

France: Aside from cognac and armagnac, substantial quantities of good grape brandy are distilled in various regions of France. The term *fine brandy* is usually applied to a high-quality local brandy and is often indicated with its local designation, such as the following:
- Fine de Bordeaux, produced from grapes originating from the Bordeaux area
- Fine de Bourgogne, produced from Burgundy grapes
- Fine de la Marne, produced using grapes from the Champagne wine region

When requesting a brandy at a French bar, ordering a "fine" (pronounced *feen*) will get you a good local product that is much less costly than a cognac.

Table 6.5: Top-Selling Grape Brandy Brands

TOP-SELLING GRAPE BRANDY BRANDS (GLOBAL SALES)	
	Brand
1.	Emperador
2.	McDowell's No.1
3.	Honey Bee
4.	Dreher
5.	Old Admiral
6.	Paul Masson Grande Amber
7.	Torres
8.	Old Kenigsberg

Source: Drinks International (2018)

The United States: US brandy production is centered in California, which produces more than 90% of the brandy made in the United States. While Spanish missionaries began the tradition of brandy distillation along with wine production, California brandy began on a large scale in the 1860s when Almaden Vineyards began to make brandy.

California brandy must be made using grapes grown in California, but the varieties are not regulated. Nevertheless, the majority of grapes used are Thompson Seedless and Ugni Blanc, with some Colombard and Folle Blanche also in the blend. These grapes are grown almost exclusively in the San Joaquin Valley, from Lodi to Fresno.

The prime method of distillation is via continuous column still, which yields a clean distillate of uniform quality and consistency. It is also highly energy-efficient. Artisanal producers frequently opt for pot still distillation, emulating the cognac tradition.

California grape brandy, with the exception of those products labeled as "immature brandy," must be aged for a minimum of two years in oak containers. Some producers age their brandy for a longer period, such as four to eight years. Varietal designations, particularly Chardonnay and Pinot Noir, have begun to appear on labels of California brandy as well.

South Africa: South Africa has a long history of brandy production. The first brandy in South Africa was made in 1672 aboard a Dutch ship anchored in Table Bay Harbor. There are records of the ship's assistant cook's having succeeded in transforming "two leaguers [1,164 liters] of Cape wine into three ankers [126 liters] of delicious brandy."

South Africa continues to produce large quantities of brandy, mostly in the regions of Robertson and Worcester. South African law allows for the production of three types of brandy:

- **Pot Still Brandy:** As of 2014, South African pot still brandies, which previously could contain a maximum of 10% unmatured wine spirits, must now be 100% pot still brandy. South African pot still brandy must be aged for a minimum of three years in oak barrels.
- **Blended Brandy:** South African blended brandy must be made up of a minimum of 30% pot still brandy, with unmatured wine spirits permitted to be used up to a maximum of 70% of the blend. This style of brandy is much lighter in character because of the reduced requirement for aged pot still brandy.
- **Vintage Brandy:** South African vintage brandy is produced from a minimum of 30% pot still distillate that must have been aged for a minimum of eight years in oak barrels. Column still spirits, which must also have been matured for at least eight years, may make up a maximum of 60% of the blend. Any remaining balance (to a maximum of 10%) may be unmatured wine spirit.

Germany: The majority of German brandy is distilled from imported wine, as the high cost of producing wine using German-grown grapes limits the use of local product. Most of the wine used in German brandy comes from Spain. These wines are generally distilled in column stills to a high strength. German brandy producers categorize their spirits by age:
- German brandies labeled with the term *Alter,* as in Alter Weinbrand, must be aged for a minimum of six months in wood.

- German brandies labeled with the term *Uralt,* as in Weinbrand Uralt, must be aged for a minimum of twelve months in wood.

Asbach Uralt, produced by the company Asbach GmbH, is one of the most widely distributed German brandies.

Greece: A significant quantity of brandy is distilled in Greece, and much of it is exported. The most famous brand, Metaxa, is made in small pot stills, aged in Limousin oak for three to thirty years, and infused with rose petals and herbs. Before bottling, Metaxa is blended with Muscat wine to give the finished product a touch of smoothness and sweetness. Given its level of sweetening and flavorings, Metaxa could technically be categorized as a liqueur.

Figure 6.9: Metaxa

Mexico: Mexico is a large producer of brandy. El Presidente Brandy, a Mexican brandy aged for three years in white oak, is one of the best-selling brandies in the world. The principal grapes used are Thompson Seedless and Perlette.

Bolivia: Bolivia produces a distinctive brandy known as *singani*. Singani has been legally defined since 1992, when the Bolivian government established a set of regulations regarding the spirit's production as well as a protected denomination of origin for singani. Foremost among these standards is the requirement that it be produced using only Muscat of Alexandria grapes grown at an elevation of 1,600 meters (5,250 feet) above sea level or higher. Singani is a clear spirit that is aged for a short period of time (typically six months) in stainless steel before bottling.

Australia: Australia's brandies are usually distilled from wines made with grape varieties such as Ugni Blanc, Pedro Ximénez, Palomino, and Sultana. This wide selection of grapes allows distillers to produce a broad range of styles and flavors of brandy. Both pot and continuous stills are used. If blending of the spirits from the two distillation processes is done, then the label of the brandy will state, "Australian Blended Brandy." The length of maturation of a given brandy is labeled as follows:
- Matured: minimum of two years in wood
- Old: minimum of five years in wood
- Very Old: minimum of ten years in wood

Portugal: Many of Portugal's wine-producing regions also produce grape spirits—much of which is used to fortify Port wine. However, several areas have historically crafted brandy—known as *aguardente*—as a fine, aged spirit. The most well-known brandy of Portugal is undoubtedly *Aguardente de Vinho Lourinhã*, produced in the Oeste region of Portugal. The production area is located on the Atlantic coast about 40 miles (65 km) north/northwest of Lisbon. A number of grapes are permitted to be used in Aguardente de Vinho Lourinhã; however, the recommended varieties of Alicante, Alvadurão, Boal Espinho, Marquinhas, Malvasia Rei, Talia, and Cabinda are the most widely used. These grapes are made into a wine of no more than 10% alcohol by volume before being distilled in either a continuous still (to a maximum of 78% alcohol by volume), or a pot still (to a maximum of 72% alcohol by volume). The spirit is then aged in oak barrels for a minimum of twenty-four months before being blended and bottled. Aguardente de Vinho Lourinhã has had DOC status in the European Union since 1992.

The following Portuguese brandies have protected geographical indication (PGI) status through the EU:
- Aguardente de Vinho Alentejo
- Aguardente de Vinho Douro
- Aguardente de Vinho Ribatejo
- Aguardente de Vinho da Região dos Vinhos Verdes

Note: The term aguardente (or aguardiente) is used in many areas to refer to various types of distilled spirits. It is loosely translated as "fire-water."

Other Countries: Other countries producing grape brandy include Armenia, Brazil, Bulgaria, Canada, China, Croatia, the Czech Republic, Georgia, Holland, Hungary, India, Israel, Japan, Lithuania, New Zealand, Poland, Slovakia, Taiwan, and Ukraine.

POMACE BRANDY

While still technically a grape brandy, pomace brandy is made from the grape skins, seeds, and stems left over after wine production. This practice came about during the feudal period when the peasants working the land made the wine but had to turn it over to the landowner. They were, however, able to keep the pomace. Making do with what they had, they used the pomace to make a distilled spirit.

To produce pomace brandy, the skins, pulp, and seeds are lightly pressed or steamed to release the remaining juice, to which water may be added before the mixture is fermented and distilled. The pomace must be kept fresh to avoid spoilage or oxidation, if one is to produce a high-quality product. This type of brandy is produced throughout the winemaking world, although most is consumed locally. *Marc* (produced in France) and *grappa* (produced in Italy) are two types of pomace brandy that are distributed internationally.

Grappa

Some people believe that the name *grappa* is based on the Italian town of Bassano del Grappa, located in Italy's Veneto region. Others say it is based on the fact that the word *grappa* literally means "grape stalk" in Italian.

Figure 6.10: Distilleria Marzadro in Trentino, Italy

We may never know exactly where the word came from or where grappa was first made, but we do know that grappa has been produced as a by-product of Italian winemaking since the Middle Ages. Itinerant distillers used to travel from vineyard to vineyard, distilling the fresh pomace (called *vinaccia* in Italian) on the spot, and providing the vineyard workers with a raw, potent spirit to ward off the cold.

The tradition of vineyard distillation is no longer practiced, as current Italian law does not allow distillation to take place at the winery. Laws concerning the production of grappa were tightened due to the fact that the stems often present in pomace tend to produce a small amount of toxic methanol, which must be carefully removed during distillation. In order to abide by current laws, winemakers must bring their pomace to a distiller or else run their own distillation operations separate from the winery premises. This updated law has actually helped to improve the reputation of grappa from the moonshine of yesterday to the artisanal spirit of today.

Modern grappa is produced in column stills and pot stills or by traditional steam distillation. Grappa is generally bottled at 40–45% alcohol by volume and may be produced from a single variety or, more commonly, from a mixed batch. Grappa produced from a single grape variety may be known as a *monovitigno*. The single-grape variety style of grappa was pioneered by the Nonino Distillery of Friuli in 1973, with the production of a grappa made with 100% Picolit grapes.

After distillation, grappa may be aged for several months in glass or other inert containers before distribution as a clear, unaged spirit. Some unique grappas are aged in barrels made of oak, ash, chestnut, or other types of wood. If wood-aged, grappa may be labeled with one of the following terms:
- Vecchia or Invecchiata: aged for a minimum of twelve months in wood
- Riserva or Stravecchia: aged for a minimum of eighteen months in wood

Grappa is often served as a digestif or as a *caffè corretto* ("corrected coffee") with a shot of espresso. A variation of this is the *resentin* ("little rinser"), where the espresso is consumed first, followed by a swirl of grappa served in the same cup.

Figure 6.11: Monovitigno Grappa

In the European Union, the term grappa is a PGI reserved for products made in Italy. Several specific grappa-producing areas within Italy have also been awarded specific PGIs—these include Grappa di Barolo, Grappa del Piemonte, and Grappa del Veneto (among others). Outside of the EU, modern craft distillers in the United States and elsewhere, such as the Cedar Ridge Winery and Distillery and the Clear Creek Distillery, are also making artisanal pomace brandies labeled with the term *grappa*.

Marc

French brandies distilled from grape pomace are called *eaux-de-vie de marc* (the last is pronounced *mar*) and are produced in small quantities in more than thirty of the wine-producing areas of France. Several of the most notable marc-producing regions, including Burgundy (Bourgogne), Champagne, Côtes-du-Rhône, Languedoc, and Provence, have PGI status for their eaux-de-vie de marc. *Eau-de-vie de marc de Bourgogne* is considered to be one of the highest-quality examples. It is generally produced using a Charente-type pot still. Other regions, including Champagne, still use portable stills that are taken from vineyard to vineyard.

Orujo

Orujo is a traditional pomace brandy made throughout Spain. Orujo has a special significance in the north of Spain, and *Orujo de Galicia* has been awarded PGI status. Like most pomace brandies, orujo is typically produced as an unaged spirit. However, a style known as *orjuo envejecido* (aged orujo) is oak-aged for a minimum of one year in barrels of 500-liter capacity or smaller (or two years in larger barrels).

Orujo de Galicia is used in a regional beverage known as *queimada*. Queimada is made with orujo, sugar, lemon peel, cinnamon, and coffee beans. The ingredients are poured into a clay pot, set aflame, and stirred until the blue flames die out. The communal sharing of queimada—which may include the recitation of an incantation and other aspects of ceremony—is based on Celtic lore and considered a part of Galician tradition.

Bagaceira

Portugal has its own version of pomace brandy, known as *aguardente bagaceira*—also referred to as *destilação do bagaço* or simply *bagaço*. Bagaceira is made throughout Portugal's wine producing areas, and several regions have earned protected geographical indication (PGI) status for their bagaceira. These include Aguardente Bagaceira Alentejo, Aguardente Bagaceira Bairrada, and Aguardente Bagaceira da Região dos Vinhos Verdes. Portuguese bagaceira may be bottled as a clear, unaged (or briefly-aged) spirit; however, many of the finest versions are aged for at least two years in oak and labeled with the term *velha*.

APPLE AND PEAR BRANDY

Calvados

Calvados is an apple brandy (which, in the European Union, would technically be classified as a fruit spirit) produced in the French area of Normandy (Normandie). The climate here is a bit too cold for the successful farming of grapes, but the region is home to vast apple and pear orchards, as well as a thriving cider and fruit spirits industry.

Calvados is distilled from cider made from specially grown and selected apples. Some versions, such as *Calvados Domfrontais,* use pears in addition to apples. All fruit used in the production of calvados must be grown within the delineated Calvados region.

The production of calvados begins with the juice of cider apples produced from a combination of more than forty permitted varieties. The apples used in the production of calvados, which resemble small crabapples rather than large apples intended for eating, are divided into four categories: sweet, bitter, bittersweet, and acidic/sour. Each of these types of apples lends a particular characteristic to the finished product.

- Acidic/sour apple varieties acidify and stabilize the cider and add to its freshness.
- Bitter apples provide tannin and help fix the aroma.
- Sweet apples provide the sugar necessary for fermentation.
- Bittersweet apples add tannin and, along with sweet apples, provide sugar.

Figure 6.12: Apple Orchards in Calvados Pays d'Auge

A typical blend consists of 10% acidic/sour, 20% bitter, 50% bittersweet, and 20% sweet apples.

After harvest, the fruit is crushed to a pulp and further pressed to release the juice. The juice, which is not allowed to be adjusted with sugar, sulfur dioxide, or manufactured yeast, is allowed to ferment for at least a month at a low temperature until there is no sugar left, resulting in a dry cider with an alcoholic strength of approximately 6% alcohol by volume. Cider produced for the more premium (and more geographically restricted) AOC *Calvados du Pays d'Auge* undergoes a slower fermentation of six to eight weeks. Distillation techniques vary depending on the type of calvados being produced.

Calvados is traditionally aged in large oak barrels known as *foudres,* which range in size from 250 gallons to 2,500 gallons (950 to 9,500 liters). Foudres are traditionally kept in use for many decades in order to allow the spirit to slowly oxidize while limiting the "oak" flavor influence. Some modern producers age their spirits in small or new oak barrels for a short period of time before transferring them to the foudres for the remainder of the aging period. The minimum required aging period for calvados varies according to the specific AOCs.

Apple and pear brandy from the region around Calvados have been protected under an appellation d'origine since 1942, with the regulations updated and revised in 1984. There are currently three separate AOCs for calvados. They are as follows:

- **Calvados AOC:** Calvados AOC is considered to be "basic" calvados and may be produced anywhere within the designated region. This type of calvados makes up over 70% of the total production. While double distillation is permitted, most of these products are produced using single column distillation. Calvados AOC also requires a minimum of two years of aging in oak barrels.

- **Calvados Pays d'Auge AOC:** Considered to be the highest quality, the production area for Calvados Pays d'Auge is limited to the east end of the département of Calvados and a few adjoining districts. Apples are dominant here; pears are limited by regulation to no more than 30% of the blend. This style of calvados requires a minimum of two years of aging in oak barrels and double distillation in an alembic pot still. Calvados Pays d'Auge AOC is often matured extensively. It may be aged up to forty years, acquiring the finesse of cognac.

Table 6.6: Calvados Labeling Terms

CALVADOS LABELING TERMS	
*** (three stars) / Fine / VS	Minimum of 2 years of aging (does not apply to Calvados Domfrontais)
Vieux / Réserve	Minimum of 3 years of aging
VO / VSOP / Vieille Réserve	Minimum of 4 years of aging
XO / Extra / Napoléon / Hors d'Âge	Minimum of 6 years of aging, although many products are aged longer

- **Calvados Domfrontais AOC:** Calvados Domfrontais requires the use of a minimum of 30% pear cider, reflecting the long tradition of pear orchards in the area. Many versions of Calvados Domfrontais actually use between 70% and 80% pears in their production. This style of calvados is distilled in a continuous reflux column still. Calvados Domfrontais must be aged in oak for a minimum of three years. It has a minimum requirement for "heavier alcohols," which impart the aroma and flavor of pears.

The term *Calvados Fermier*, sometimes written as *Produit Fermier*, on the label indicates a farmer-produced spirit that is made using traditional agricultural methods. Many high-quality products within the Calvados Pays d'Auge AOC region are produced in this manner.

A related spirit known as *pommeau* is made by mixing two parts unfermented apple juice with one part one-year-old calvados. The resulting mixture, which has 16–18% alcohol by volume, is then aged in oak barrels for a minimum of 14 months. Being a mixture of unfermented juice with a distilled spirit, pommeau is technically a mistelle (the French term for fruit juice whose fermentation has been halted by the addition of spirits; typically served as an aperitif). *Pommeau de Normandie* was granted its own AOC in 1991.

APPLEJACK

Applejack, a type of brandy made from apple cider, was one of the most popular beverages in colonial America. Applejack was historically made by a traditional method known as *freeze distillation* (congelation), which involved leaving apple cider outside to freeze and chipping off chunks of ice in order to concentrate the alcohol content. The term *applejack* derives from the term *jacking*, meaning "freeze distillation."

In 1780, soon after the American Revolution, the new nation's first distillery permit—US License #1—was granted to a producer of apple brandy, Laird's Distillery of Scobeyville, New Jersey. Laird's had been producing its proprietary AppleJack since the late 1600s and supplied brandy to George Washington's troops during the Revolutionary War. Laird's AppleJack was later used as currency to pay road construction crews during the colonial period. In 1933, Laird and Company was granted a federal license under the Prohibition Act to produce apple brandy for "medicinal purposes," allowing the company to resume operations prior to repeal.

AppleJack is still produced by Laird's Distillery, albeit using modern distillation methods. The distillery is now located in Virginia near the source of Laird's apples, but the historic New Jersey site is still maintained for use in maturing and bottling the spirits. The company produces AppleJack, Blended AppleJack, Old Apple Brandy (aged for seven and a half years), twelve-year-old rare apple brandy, and Laird's Bottled-in-Bond Straight Apple Brandy (100 proof). For many years, Laird's was the only producer of apple brandy in America. However, several other craft distillers in the United States, notably Clear Creek in Oregon and Germain-Robin distillery in California, are now producing apple brandy.

Figure 6.13: The Evolution of the Laird's AppleJack Bottle

The terms *applejack* and *apple brandy* are now permitted to be used synonymously in the United States. The US Standards of Identity also recognize "blended applejack," which is defined as a mixture that contains at least 20% apple brandy (applejack) that has been stored in oak containers for no less than two years, combined with no more than 80% of neutral spirits (which, by definition, do not require aging).

Demand for apple brandy declined in the 1960s, but the spirit is seeing a renewed interest among mixologists and consumers. The classic cocktail made with applejack is the Jack Rose, a blend of applejack, lemon juice, and grenadine.

PEAR BRANDY

Pear brandy, more formally called *eau-de-vie de poire,* is generally unaged, colorless, and produced in such a way as to preserve the distinctive aroma of ripe pear. Pear brandies are produced from the Williams Bon-Chrétien variety of pear in France, Switzerland, Austria, the United States, and parts of Italy. Thus, many pear-based brandies (even those produced outside of France) are labeled as *Poire William.* The Williams Bon-Chrétien variety is known as the Bartlett pear in the United States.

Poire William is sometimes sold with a whole pear "trapped" inside its glass bottle; this is accomplished by hanging bottles on pear trees and allowing the budding fruit to grow inside. France's Boisset Family Estates produces one such product cleverly known as *Le Captive.* Other producers use the French term *poire prisonnière.*

Note that pear brandy is a dry, unsweetened spirit, not to be confused with pear liqueur. Pear liqueur, often based on brandy, cognac, or neutral spirits, is a widely produced sweetened spirit product.

CHERRY BRANDY

Cherry brandy is believed to have originated in the Black Forest of Germany. It is traditionally made from the double distillation of the fermented juice of the black morello cherry. Known as *kirsch* or *kirschwasser* (German for "cherry water"), this style of cherry brandy is now made in Alsace, Switzerland, and the United States. Other varieties of cherries, in addition to the black morello, are also used today.

Kirsch is a clear and colorless fruit spirit. It is generally unaged, although it may be aged for a short period of time in stainless steel, earthenware, or paraffin-lined ash barrels. Kirsch can be produced using just the fruit or the fruit and the pits. Using just the fruit gives the resulting brandy a good deal of cherry flavor. When fermented "complete," meaning including the liquid, pulp, and pits, the pits release a small amount of hydrocyanic acid, which lends a bitter-almond or marzipan-like flavor to the brandy.

The best kirschwassers have a refined taste with subtle flavors of cherry and a slight bitter-almond aftertaste. Kirsch is generally served neat as either an aperitif or a digestif and is used in recipes such as Swiss fondue and Black Forest cake.

APRICOT BRANDY

True apricot brandy (technically a fruit spirit), as opposed to the sweetened liqueur that often goes by the name apricot-flavored brandy, is hard to find. One such product is Hungary's *Barack Pálinka* (the first word is pronounced *baratsk*). The term *pálinka* has been used historically to refer to a wide variety of fruit spirits produced throughout Central and Eastern Europe; however, since the 2008 passage of the Hungarian Pálinka Law, it can only be used for products produced in Hungary, and for apricot-based spirits produced in four specific regions of Austria. The term *barack* is a collective term for both apricot (literally, "yellow-peach") and peach (literally, "autumn-peach") in Hungarian.

Another type of true apricot brandy, this one produced in the Wachau region of Austria, is known as *marillenschnaps* or *marillenbrand* and may also go by the name of *marillen apricot eau-de-vie*. *Marillen* is the Austrian term for apricots, which are known as *aprikosen* in other German-speaking nations. Marillenschnaps is clear and should have a strong, clean apricot aroma.

Figure 6.14: Bottles of Slivovitz

PLUM BRANDY

Plum brandies are produced in many regions around the world. They are particularly popular in traditional forms in Central Europe, where they are known as *slivovitz*. Many brands of slivovitz are commercially produced and widely available in the United States.

Slivovitz, which has many traditional spellings and many home countries, is produced in Serbia, Slovenia, Croatia, Bosnia, the Czech Republic, Slovakia, Poland, Hungary, and Bulgaria, as well as in other countries. The name is derived from the Slavic word for *plum* ("slíva") and the suffix *–vitsa,* meaning "vice."

Slivovitz is traditionally made from crushed black damson plums that are fermented with their skins, seeds, and pulp. There may be one or several distillation stages, and the brandy may be aged or unaged, depending on the desired final product or the region of production.

France produces plum brandy, as well. French plum brandy made from yellow plums is known as *mirabelle*. A plum brandy known as *quetsch,* made using black plums, is produced in Alsace. Plum brandy, sometimes known as *pflümli* or simply *plum eau-de-vie,* is also produced in Switzerland and the United States.

SOFT FRUIT AND MIXED FRUIT BRANDY

Berries and other soft fruits are sometimes used in the production of fruit-based distilled spirits. France produces eaux-de-vie from raspberries, known as *framboise*, and from strawberries, known as *fraise*. Producers elsewhere, such as Bonny Doon and St. George's Spirits, both located in California, are producing artisanal brandies from soft fruits.

Fruit spirits produced from a mixture of fruit—often containing apples, pears, apricots, cherries, plums, berries, or wild fruit—are known in the EU as *obstler* or *obstbrand*. These clear spirits are traditional to Austria, Switzerland, and southern Germany—where they are often referred to as *schnaps*.

However, soft fruits such as strawberries and raspberries are low in sugar compared to most fruits; therefore, they are not always fermented into wine to be distilled into brandy. Rather, they can be macerated in neutral alcohol to impart their flavor, and the resulting infused liquid can then be distilled. In the European Union, this type of spirit may be referred to as *geist*. One well-known example is *himbeergeist*, a raspberry-infused spirit produced mainly in Germany and Austria. *Schwarzwälder Himbeergeist*—a clear spirit created by macerating fresh raspberries in neutral spirits for several weeks before diluting and distilling the mixture—has protected geographical indication (PGI) status as a product of Germany. Geist may also be produced using other flavorings such as flowers, vegetables, or spices. (Note: the term is a specific usage of the

German noun *Geist*—which is often used in the philosophical context to refer to the "spirit/mind" or "intellect" of a person or thing.)

FLAVORED BRANDY

In the United States, flavored brandies must be made with natural flavorings. They must be bottled at a minimum of 30% alcohol by volume (60 proof). If there is a predominant flavor, then the name of the flavor must appear on the label, such as "blackberry-flavored brandy" or "apricot-flavored brandy." Most flavored brandies are sweetened, some to such an extent that they can also be classified as liqueurs.

TASTING AND SERVING BRANDY

Tulip-shaped glasses are recommended for brandy tasting. Those marketed as brandy snifters will do just fine, but many experts stress that a smaller snifter or tulip-shaped wineglass or tasting glass is preferred for serious tasting exercises, as these help to concentrate the aromas.

Figure 6.15: Brandy in a Small Brandy Snifter

Brandy is a diverse category of spirits. Interesting tastings can be arranged by sampling a flight of spirits from a similar category, such as cognac, armagnac, calvados, or California brandy. Other ideas include a tasting of various apple-based or fruit-based brandies or pomace brandies; a selection of unaged brandies/grape spirits; and a vertical tasting across various aging classifications.

Observe your brandy for its color, clarity, and legs. Brandy, even if amber or golden in hue, should display a see-through level of clarity. A good brandy might even have a nice "glow" or "shine" to it. Sediment or impurities are uncommon and are often a result of problems in clarification or filtration.

Grape brandies should have a complex array of aromas, with nutty/sweet/caramel aromas as well as fruity aromas such as apple, pear, and dried apricot. Note whether your brandy reminds you of "sweet aromatics," and remind yourself not to be shocked when the liquid is dry on the palate. Eaux-de-vie and other fruit brandies should have a simpler flavor indicative of the base fruit without the nut/caramel overtones of aged brandy.

Cognac has its own tasting vocabulary. The *montant* aroma is the first aroma that hits the nose, while the next is known as the *second nose*. Frequent descriptors used for the montant of a cognac include vanilla, nuts, flowers, and caramel. Some aficionados claim that the aromas of cognac pass through four "ages": the first is fruit, the second is flowers, the third is spice, and the fourth is rancio.

Brandy should have a warm, lingering finish. Any harshness, shortness of finish, or bitterness on the finish may be indicative of a low-quality brandy.

For most consumers, the traditional way to serve brandy—as an unadorned after-dinner drink in a short-stemmed glass—is the best. This is undoubtedly the ideal choice for particularly fine aged cognac, armagnac, and the like. However, in many parts of Europe, it is common to serve a simpler brandy as a long drink with soda or fruit juice as an aperitif. Others prefer their brandy on ice. Classic cocktails based on brandy, such as the Sidecar, the Stinger, and the Brandy Alexander, are popular as well.

Table 6.7: Tasting Brandy – Typical Flavors and Aromas

TASTING BRANDY – TYPICAL FLAVORS AND AROMAS	
Fruit	Apple, Bitter Apple, Baked Apple, Orange, Pear, Cherry, Peach, Apricot, Dried Apricot, Plum, Fig, Prune, Citrus, Synthetic Fruit, Base Fruit (if eau-de-vie style)
Muscat	Grape, Muscat (Moscato) Wine, Raisin
Floral	Rose, Dried Roses, Potpourri
Wood	Oak, Cedar, Cigar Box, Resin, Dusty Wood
Toasted	Coffee, Smoky
Nutty	Walnut, Hazelnut, Pecan, Almond
Spice	Cinnamon, Clove, Nutmeg, Baking Spices
Herbal	Tea, Hay, Straw, Grass, Mint, Eucalyptus, Tobacco
Sweet Aromatics	Vanilla, Caramel, Maple, Molasses, Toffee, Sweet Sherry, Honey, Chocolate, Baked Apple, Baking Spices
Rancio	Earthy, Nutty

Table 6.8: Tasting Brandy – Typical Descriptors for Palate and Style

TASTING BRANDY – TYPICAL DESCRIPTORS FOR PALATE AND STYLE	
Style	Smooth, Supple, Clean, Rich, Soft, Delicate
Palate	Sweet (from added caramel or sugar), Balanced, Creamy, Dense, Mouth-Filling, Silky
Other	Mellow, Complex, Layered, Warm, Hot (from alcohol)

CHAPTER SEVEN RUM AND OTHER SUGARCANE-BASED SPIRITS

RUM AND OTHER SUGARCANE-BASED SPIRITS

LEARNING OBJECTIVES

After studying this chapter, the candidate should be able to do the following:
- Define rum in terms of base materials, distillation processes, maturation, and other post-distillation procedures.
- Compare and contrast "agricultural" rum and "industrial" rum.
- Describe the types of rum produced in the various rum-producing regions of the world.
- Identify and discuss the different styles of rum in light of flavor profile and aging regimen.
- Discuss the various other types of sugar- and sugarcane-based spirits available, including Ronmiel de Canarias, batavia arrack, Seco Herrerano, and tuzemák.
- Discuss the sensory evaluation of rum and the typical procedures for the serving of rum and rum-based drinks.

Rum is a large classification of spirits produced from sugarcane. Rum may be produced from sugarcane syrup, the by-products of sugar production (such as molasses), or directly from sugarcane juice. The majority of the world's rum production occurs in the Caribbean and Latin America, with rum playing a large part in the culture of most islands of the West Indies.

As there is no specified geographical region for the production of rum, it is also produced in Spain, Australia, New Zealand, Fiji, Mexico, the Philippines, India, South Africa, Taiwan, Japan, the United States, and Canada, among other locations. While not required, if a geographical name such as Barbados or Puerto Rico is included on the label, the rum is required to have been produced in the respective country.

Rum has a colorful history, including famous associations with the British Royal Navy—where a rum-based drink known as *grog* was considered part of a sailor's rations—and with piracy, from where we get the legend of drinks called Bumbo and the Traitor.

This chapter begins with an overview of rum, including a standard definition and a short history of rum. It then proceeds to a discussion of basic production techniques, the leading rum-producing regions of the world, and the various types and styles of rum. The chapter concludes with a discussion of some other sugarcane-based spirits, many of them very similar to rum and produced around the world, as well as a short discussion on the tasting and service of rum.

DEFINITION OF RUM

According to the United States Standards of Identity, rum is defined as the following:
- A spirit distilled from the fermented juice of sugarcane, sugarcane syrup, sugarcane molasses, or other sugarcane by-products
- Distilled at less than 190 proof
- Bottled at no less than 40% alcohol by volume (80 proof)
- Produced in such a manner to possess the taste, aroma, and characteristics attributed to rum

The EU definition of rum has slightly different specifications:
- It must be a spirit produced by the fermentation and distillation of molasses, syrup produced in the manufacture of cane sugar, or sugarcane juice itself.
- It must be distilled at less than 192 proof.
- It must be bottled at no less than 37.5% alcohol by volume (75 proof).

- It must retain the discernible organoleptic characteristics of rum.
- Agricultural rum, or "rhum agricole," is a defined subcategory of EU rum for rum produced using raw sugarcane juice. In the EU, the use of the term *rum* (or *rhum*) *agricole* is limited to certain approved production areas primarily located in the French Overseas Departments.

HISTORY OF RUM

The history of rum is intimately connected to the sources of sugarcane. Historically, it is believed that sugarcane originated in New Guinea and, from there, was taken to China and India. The plant continued to be transported westward through Asia and then to the eastern shores of the Mediterranean Sea. Finally, it was introduced into Europe by the Arabs after the seventh century CE, where it was grown in the warm climates of Spain, Portugal, and Northern Africa.

Christopher Columbus brought sugarcane cuttings from the Canary Islands off the coast of Africa to the New World during his 1493 arrival in the West Indies. Sugarcane flourished in the climate of the Caribbean. Soon, sugar was shipped to Europe to supplement the sugar processed there from the sugar beet.

European settlers in the West Indies soon found that the molasses residue from sugar production was easily fermented, so they began to distill the ferment, which led to the spirit we now know as rum. It is believed that New World rum was first produced on the British island of Barbados and the French island of Martinique, although fermented varieties of sugarcane juice had been known in ancient India and China. From Barbados and Martinique, rum production spread to Haiti, Jamaica, and Cuba.

It was in Cuba, in the mid-1800s, that the family of Don Facundo Bacardi began to produce rum on a large scale in a truly industrialized fashion. The Bacardi family isolated a proprietary strain of yeast that enabled them to produce a light, clean style of rum that is still among the world's top sellers to this day.

Figure 7.1: The Old Bacardi Building in Havana, Cuba (note the bat logo on the top)

There are a number of theories about the derivation of the word *rum*. The most probable source is the Latin word for *sugar, saccharum,* shortened to simply "rum." Another theory states that the source is the word *rumbullion,* which means "a great tempest." Whatever the original source, throughout history there were many words with the term *rum* in them, and most of these denoted an inclination toward the powerful effect of the consumption of rum. *Kill-Devil,* also known as rumbullion, was a synonym for the first rums made in Barbados. *Rombustion,* meaning "a strong liquid," was another slang expression for the effects of the spirit. Any of these terms may have been corrupted into the modern term *rum*.

The development of the rum industry grew as more and more sugarcane plantations sprang up in the West Indies. Sugarcane, harvested by hand with a machete, was extremely labor-intensive, requiring many workers. The need for cheap labor was met by importing slaves from Africa. Slave labor allowed the plantations to thrive and spread throughout the West Indies and southern America by the seventeenth century.

A tragic by-product of the rum trade was the import/export market known as the Triangle Trade. A ship filled with slaves would sail from Africa, bound for the West Indies. There, the slaves would be exchanged for molasses, which would fill the ship's hold as ballast. The ship would then sail northward to New England, where the molasses would be traded for rum made in the distilleries of that region. Finally, the ship would carry its cargo of rum to Western Africa, where it would once again take on slaves. Each step along the triangular path resulted in profits for the ship's owner. The route was continuously retraced until it was finally abandoned in the early 1800s, under pressure from England's Royal Navy embargo of the transoceanic slave trade.

Rum production was also part of the early history of the United States. Dozens of distilleries were established in the colonies. By 1775, twelve million gallons (45 million liters) of rum made with imported Caribbean molasses were being consumed by American colonists—about four gallons (15 liters) per person annually.

In light of this fact, there are those who claim that the American Revolution was not about tea and taxation but was, in fact, about rum and taxation, since the British law of 1763 was designed to force the colonists to abandon the purchase of West Indies rums and buy only the more expensive British rums. Accordingly, rum may have been the actual spark that started the Revolutionary War. The American love of rum continued throughout the Revolutionary War and into the next century, waning only after the dissolution of the Triangle Trade, when the popularity of rum declined as that of whiskey rose.

The first legal definition of rum was created in 1909 when the British Royal Commission on Whiskey declared that "rum is a spirit distilled directly from sugarcane products, in sugar-growing countries." Today, rum is produced in over one hundred countries worldwide and is consumed in virtually every nation of the world.

THE PRODUCTION OF RUM

Rum is a large and diverse spirit category, and as such it has very few universal requirements aside from the mandated use of sugarcane as the fermentable source. This does not mean, however, that rum is largely unregulated—but rather that many of the requirements concerning specific types and styles of rum are prescribed at the regional or national level (as will be discussed later in this chapter). However, nearly every type of rum is made using a similar set of production procedures—from harvest to bottling. The typical rum production process is discussed below.

Figure 7.2: Sugarcane Fields in Brazil

Base Material: As noted, all rum is produced from sugarcane or its by-products. Sugarcane itself is a tall tropical perennial plant of the grass family *Gramineae*; the species *Saccharum officinarum* is the most widely-used for the production of rum. There are different varieties of sugarcane grown in various parts of the world, most of which are actually hybrids developed from *Saccharum officinarum*. The varieties planted vary with soil and climatic conditions. For most rum producers, the choice of variety is not dictated, and the selection is based on what the producer thinks will grow best.

Harvesting: Sugarcane is harvested at maximum maturity, defined as the point at which the sugar concentration reaches its highest level before starting to decline. Once maturity has been reached, harvesting can be done either manually, which is labor-intensive and slow, or mechanically, which requires expensive machinery but is much faster. In some places, to facilitate the manual cutting of the cane, the cane fields are set on fire to burn away the razor-sharp sugarcane leaves and eliminate snakes and vermin. However, this process reduces moisture in the cane and makes pressing more difficult. Regardless of harvesting method, when the harvested sugarcane leaves the fields, its weight is between 10% and 13% sugar.

Initial Cane Preparation: Once harvested, the cane is washed to remove all debris and then chopped into fine pieces. The cane is then milled and crushed with added water to extract the sugar from the cane. Finally, the sugary juice obtained from the milling step is filtered to remove any cane residue. At this point, the raw sugarcane juice has a sugar concentration of about 16%.

Figure 7.3: Sugarcane after Harvesting and Cleaning

Sugarcane Juice: Many styles of rum, particularly those produced in the French Caribbean, are made from raw sugarcane juice. As their base ferment is made from a fresh agricultural product, these rums are known as *agricultural rum* or *rhum agricole*. They are differentiated from molasses-based rums, which are sometimes known as *industrial rum* or *rhum industriel*. About 10% of all rum produced is made with sugarcane juice.

Evaporation and Sugar Crystal Removal: The sugar production process continues through evaporation, which continues until the sugar concentration approaches 60%. At this point, the thick liquid is often referred to as *virgin sugarcane honey*, but, in essence, it is a very high-grade form of molasses. Following the evaporation stage, the molasses is boiled and concentrated further until sugar crystals begin to form.

A centrifuge is used to separate the sugar crystals from the saturated molasses. After all the sugar crystals are removed, the remaining molasses is stored in tanks until it is either used to make rum or processed for animal feed. The sugar crystals are sold as brown or raw sugar, or further refined to produce white sugar.

Molasses: Molasses is the very viscous, concentrated sugarcane juice left after the sugar crystals have been removed. Depending on the length of time that the juice is boiled and allowed to evaporate, along with how much sugar is removed in crystal form, the residue is graded. Grade A molasses contains the highest percentage of remaining fermentable sugar, followed in decreasing order by grades B, C, and D molasses and finally blackstrap molasses, which is the lowest in both quality and sugar content. Higher-quality molasses contains more fermentable sugar and fewer chemicals left over from the sugar extraction process and, therefore, produces higher-quality rum. Approximately 90% of all rum produced is made with molasses.

Mash Creation: To create a mash for fermentation, the sugarcane juice or molasses is diluted with water to reduce the sugar concentration to a level that will allow the yeast to ferment the sugary liquid.

Fermentation: Specific yeasts are then added to this liquid in order to create an alcoholic wash and to impart specific aromas and flavors to the finished product. Most distilleries use proprietary cultured yeasts to conduct their fermentations. When cultured yeasts are used, all of the sugar is typically converted to alcohol in two or three days. Fermentation times vary based on the type of yeast used, the fermentation temperature, the initial sugar concentration, and the type of nutrients available to the yeast. Faster-working yeasts are selected to create lighter-style rums.

Figure 7.4: Fermentation Tanks at Domaine de Séverin, Cadet, Guadeloupe

Some styles of rum are produced using *natural fermentation*, which relies on wild, naturally occurring yeast present in the air and in the cane juice. However, due to the high sugar content of the mash, it is often necessary to use cultured yeast at some point in the process in order to finish the fermentation. This type of fermentation can take from one to several weeks, and the results vary from batch to batch. Slower fermentations promote the creation of more esters, resulting in rums with more aromatic character and fuller flavor.

Distillation: As with most other aspects of rum production, there is no standard method used for distillation. Some distillers work in batches using pot stills, which are much less efficient than column stills but are ideal for producing the richer, aged styles of rum that generally command a higher price.

A unique style of pot still distillation uses a series of copper vessels—known as *retorts*—that are placed between the pot still and the condenser. The use of retorts allows the distiller to create a new make spirit using a single distillation. The retorts contain liquid—typically a mixture of alcohol (left over from the previous distillation) and water. Upon firing, the original vapors from the still will pass through the liquid in the first retort—this will cause the liquid in the retort to boil and release a batch of vapors that are concentrated to a higher proof than the original vapors. These concentrated vapors then pass onto the next retort where the process is repeated, and the resulting vapors are passed onto the condenser. Typically, the heads and tails of the run are used to fill the retorts for the next round of distillation. Retorts are associated with the Jamaican rum tradition and may be used—along with pot still distillation—in the production of rich, flavorful rum.

The lighter styles of rum, typically created via the use of continuous distillation in sets of column stills, are widely produced and very popular worldwide. Continuous distillation is the most cost-effective way to produce large quantities of rum with lower levels of congeners and consistent alcohol levels.

Distillers also have the option of blending rums from different types of stills together in order to combine different elements for their house style. For instance, Appleton White Rum from Jamaica blends pot still rums with column still rums, and Bacardi from Puerto Rico uses two parallel multi-column systems running at different temperature levels, the results of which are then blended together.

Maturation: In general, as rum is not required to be aged, the spirit that comes off the still may be reduced in strength and bottled immediately. These unaged "white" rums are often the lighter-style product of column still distillation. Although there are exceptions, heavier-style pot still rums are more likely to be aged than lighter styles.

As with other spirits, the maturation process influences the aroma and flavor of rum by creating congeners in the aging distillate through a series of natural chemical reactions. Unique to rum production, the tropical climate of most rum-producing countries matures the spirit at a much faster rate than brandies, whiskeys, and other aged spirits made in cooler regions. As a result, there is significant evaporative loss of product through the pores of the wooden barrels in which the rum is aged. While cognac and whiskeys typically lose between 1% and 3% of their volume annually, rum aged in wooden barrels may lose as much as 10% of their volume per year to evaporation.

Blending: After aging, rum is typically blended across types and ages to produce a product of a relatively consistent style. In some cases, a single-barrel rum may be produced. Each bottle of this finished product is clearly identified with a designation of the aging barrel from which it was filled. Single-barrel rums will have aromas and flavors unique to the batch.

RHUM AGRICOLE

Rum produced from fresh sugarcane juice, as opposed to molasses, is known as agricultural rum, or rhum agricole. This style of rum retains much of the flavor of the original sugarcane and tends to be smooth and light, with floral and herbal aromas. Rhum agricole is primarily produced in the West Indies, particularly the French islands of Guadeloupe and Martinique. A small amount is also produced on La Réunion Island and the island of Madeira. Rum made with cane juice is also produced in Haiti, Grenada, Brazil, and the Virgin Islands.

LEADING RUMS FROM AROUND THE WORLD

Jamaica

Jamaica is well-known for its high-ester, pot still rums; however, the country produces many different styles of rum using a range of fermentation techniques, distillation styles, and aging processes as well as blending. Most distilleries in Jamaica produce a range of new-make spirits, each according to a specific formula as to the base ingredients, length of fermentation, method of distillation, and resultant ester level. The formulas are known as marques (marks), and are registered with the Jamaica Spirits Pool Association.

A marque or finished rum is often classified by ester content, with each category equating to a certain flavor style. While many distilleries have their own naming system, the following traditional categories are still in use:

- **Common Cleans:** Products with the lowest level of esters are known as *common cleans*. These rums have light, floral aromas and may be produced using column still distillation. Common cleans typically contain an ester content between 80 and 150 parts per million (ppm).
- **Plummers:** Products with a medium ester level are known as *plummers*. This style of rum shows tropical fruit aromas and has a bit more structure. Plummers typically contain an ester content between 150 and 200 parts ppm.

Figure 7.5: Raw Sugarcane Juice

- **Wedderburns:** Medium-high ester rums are known as *wedderburns* and are more aromatic—with a degree of pungency—as well as more flavorful, and more structured. Wedderburns typically contain an ester content of at least 200 ppm.
- **Continental Flavoreds:** This style of rum was once designated as such for export to the European markets, where they would be added to lighter spirits as a flavoring agent. These very high-ester products are the most aromatic and flavorful, often showing pungent "medicinal" aromas or (when diluted) aromas of tropical fruit. These products may contain an ester content between 500 and 1,600 ppm, and are sometimes added to rum blends in small amounts in order to add flavor and body. Despite their intense flavors they are often consumed "as is" in Jamaica, and some very-high-ester products, such as Rum Fire produced by Hampden Estate, have made their way into the export market. These rums are likely to be produced via a long, slow fermentation—which may last from 5 to 10 days.

Rum production in Jamaica is unique in that a substance called *dunder* is sometimes used in the production process. Dunder is comprised of the highly acidic, yeast-rich foam "leftovers" that remain in the still after distillation is complete (similar terms used for these leftovers in other types of distillation include *stillage* and *backset*). Dunder is often stored in wooden tanks for use in subsequent distillation runs, or it may be aged and concentrated in tubs or pits dug into the ground. These are known as *muck pits*, with the resultant bacteria- and ester-rich concentrate known as *muck*.

Dunder or muck is typically added to the vat at some point during the fermentation process. *Skimmings*—the sugar- and mineral-rich froth residue created during the boiling and concentration of sugarcane juice—may also be re-used. Dunder, muck, and skimmings encourage the creation of highly aromatic esters, and are most likely to be used in the production of continental flavoreds and other high-ester rums.

In 2016, Jamaica passed a set of regulations establishing the Jamaica Rum Geographical Indication. Under these laws, Jamaica Rum GI must be fermented and distilled in a defined area limited to those portions of the island located within the limestone aquifer water basins (which limits the allowed area to about 50% of the island). The laws allow for Jamaica Rum GI to be produced using sugarcane juice, sugarcane syrup, molasses, or cane sugar from any source; Jamaica-grown sugar is not required. There are no limits to the type of yeast used, nor are there specifications as to methods of fermentation or distillation. Jamaica Rum GI may be unaged, or it may be aged in small wooden barrels. However, the use of caramel coloring is not allowed, and—according to the country's excise duty tax laws—other additives and sweeteners are also disallowed without prior approval from a commissioner. Finally, all rum bearing the label term "Certified Geographical Indication" and "Jamaica Rum" must be tested and approved by the technical committee of the Jamaica Rum and Spirits Traders Association (JRASTA).

Jamaica prides itself on its traditional, high-ester-content pot still rums while producing a wide range of rum and rum products. Leading producers and brands of Jamaican rum include Appleton Estate (which can trace its documented rum production back to 1749), Myer's Rum, Coruba Rum, Hampden Estate, Long Pond Distillery, and Wray & Nephew.

Martinique

Martinique, an overseas department of France, has appellation d'origine contrôlée (AOC) status for its rhum agricole—the only AOC for rum in existence.

The two main species of sugarcane approved for use are *Saccharum officinarum* and *Saccharum spontaneum*—hybrids of these two species are also allowed. There are limits on sugarcane yield and strict standards for harvesting and processing.

Fermentation must take place in open tanks. Once begun, fermentation must remain beneath the maximum allowed temperature of 38.5°C (101°F) and be completed within 120 hours. Distillation must occur in a specific style of continuous still that contains three elements—the heating chamber, a stripping column, and a condensation column. Rectification (repeated or continuous distillation to produce a high-ethanol spirit) is not allowed. The result is a new-make spirit of between 65% and 75% abv that retains a good deal of the sugarcane's original flavor.

For all versions of Rhum Martinique AOC, the words *Rhum Agricole* must be indicated on the label alongside the word *Martinique*. There are several styles of rhum agricole produced within the Rhum Martinique AOC. These include the following:

- **Rhum Blanc Martinique (White):** colorless rum that has aged for a minimum of eight weeks with no oak aging requirement; if aged in oak, the rhum must have been aged for no more than three months
- **Rhum Martinique Élevé Sous Bois (Cask-Aged):** rum that has been oak-aged for at least twelve months
- **Rhum Martinique Ambré (Rhum Paille):** amber or straw-colored rum that has been oak-aged for a minimum of 18 months
- **Rhum Martinique Vieux (Extra-Aged):** rum that has been oak-aged for at least three years with a capacity of less than 650 liters

The following aging designations are allowed to be used on the labels of Rhum Martinique:
- VO: a minimum of three years of oak aging
- VSOP: a minimum of four years of oak aging
- XO: a minimum of six years of oak aging

Any style of rum designated as *vieux* (three years) or older must have been aged in oak barrels with a capacity of less than 650 liters.

Leading producers of Rhum Martinique include Depaz, Rhum JM, La Favorite, Saint James, and Habitation Clément.

Figure 7.6: The Trois-Rivières Plantation, Martinique

Guadeloupe

Guadeloupe—a French overseas department and a producer of rhum agricole as well as molasses-based rum—has protected geographical indication (PGI) status for its agricultural rum. (It does not, however, have the higher-level PDO [AOC] status that is enjoyed in Martinique.) The area referred to as Guadeloupe Island—known as the "butterfly island" for its butterfly shape—is actually two islands separated by a saltwater river. Most of the sugarcane is grown on Basse Terre—the larger, western island—as well as on the northern side of the mountainous Grand Terre Island (to the east). Leading rum producers on Guadeloupe Island include Rhum Bologne, Diltillerie Mon Repos, Distillerie Damoiseau, and Domaine de Séverin.

The neighboring island of Marie-Galante produces a good deal of high-quality (and often, high-proof) rum. The small island has three rum producers: Rhum Bielle, Distillerie Poisson (producer of Rhum du Pére Labat), and Domaine de Bellevue (producer of Rhum Magalda).

Trinidad and Tobago

The twin-island nation of Trinidad and Tobago is situated just 6.8 miles (11 km) off the northern coast of South America. The islands were colonized by a series of countries—including Spain, Britain, and France—and began to cultivate sugarcane and make rum from molasses in the 1700s. This small country once had close to 50 distilleries with a good deal of its rum used in blends destined for the British Navy and other navy-style rums. However, as government subsidies for the sugarcane industry waned, so did the production of the distilleries. By 1950, only a handful of distilleries remained.

The Caroni Distillery, established in 1918, operated at a near-full capacity producing an artisan style of rum until 2002. Since its demise, the Caroni Distillery has become the stuff of legends and many rum aficionados mourn the loss of Caroni rum. However, some well-aged barrels have recently been uncovered and it is still possible (albeit rare) to find Caroni rum in the marketplace.

These days, on the island of Trinidad, Angostura Limited (better known for its world-famous bitters) produces a range of spirits—including Fernandes Black Label Rum and Angostura Single Barrel Reserve Rum. A portion of the base rum for Kraken Black Spiced Rum is also produced in Trinidad and Tobago. Some versions of Trinidad rum are produced in a traditional style known as puncheon rum—an overproof rum that may be as high as 75% abv.

St. Croix

The Caribbean island of St. Croix is a territory of the United States and the largest of the United States Virgin Islands. St. Croix is home to the Cruzan Rum Distillery, makers of Cruzan Rum. The Cruzan Rum Distillery was founded in 1769 (as Estate Diamond) by the Nelthropp Family, who owned the company for many generations and are still involved in the rum's production. The distillery uses both locally-grown sugarcane and imported molasses to make a range of rum products in a variety of styles, including their highly-regarded Cruzan Single Barrel—produced from variously aged rums blended together and then re-barreled in new oak for additional aging.

Captain Morgan, a brand of flavored (spiced) rum named after the Welsh privateer Sir Henry Morgan, is also produced on St. Croix.

Haiti

French colonists brought sugarcane to St. Dominique (as Haiti was known at the time) in the 1600s. Not long after that, rum was being made in the area. Today, one of Haiti's most famous exports is the array of rum produced by the Société du Rhum Barbancourt. This family business, which began on March 18, 1862, was founded by Dupré Barbancourt, a Frenchman from the cognac-producing region of Charente. Rhum Barbancourt is produced from sugarcane juice via double distillation. Some versions are aged for many years in a method similar to the aging of cognac.

Haiti also produces a unique style of naturally-fermented, sugarcane juice- or sugarcane syrup-based rum known as *clairin* (based on the Haitian Creole word for "clear"). Clairin is a traditional product made by hundreds of tiny distilleries based all over the island and typically consumed locally. However, it has recently been made available in limited amounts in the United States and other markets. The term clairin is not legally defined; however, bottlers have created some standards for the use of the term. These include the use of sugarcane varieties native to Haiti (excluding hybrids), hand-harvesting, the use of natural yeast, and small-batch distillation. Clairin is typically bottled in Haiti at distillation proof—which averages around 50% abv—with no water or other additives added after distillation is complete.

Demerara Rum
Demerara rum, named after the local river, has been produced in Guyana—a country on the northern coast of South America—for over three hundred years. English-speaking Guyana has been a sugar-producing country since the seventeenth century. It produced some of the original rums supplied to the British navy for use in "navy blends."

By the eighteenth century, over three hundred estates were growing sugarcane and producing their own rums in Guyana. Over the centuries, many of these estates have closed down or consolidated. Today, Demerara Distillers Limited operates Diamond Distillery, one of the few remaining distilleries in the area. Located on the east bank of the Demerara River, their main brand—produced in a range of styles and ages—is El Dorado Rum.

Demerara Distillery has preserved and is still using many of the stills original to the region. Among their unique stills are two wooden pot stills—each over 250 years old and known as the Demerara vat stills—and a four-column metal French Savalle still made by Armand Savalle (a leading still manufacturer in the nineteenth century). The distillery also has possession (and use) of the EHP wooden still—the last fully working wooden continuous Coffey still in existence. Built in 1880 using plans originally published by Coffey & Company, the EHP wooden still is the last remaining still from the Enmore Sugar Estate of Edward Henry Porter (EHP).

Barbados
Barbados was colonized by the British in 1627 and began to grow sugar after much of its tobacco trade was usurped by the Americans. Rum production was a natural by-product, and Barbados rum quickly became a favorite of the British. It was also appreciated by early Americans— including George Washington—who reportedly ordered a barrel for his inauguration in 1789.

Barbados produces a wide variety of rum, mainly from molasses. Several local distilleries capitalize on the long history of rum production in the area by using traditional pot stills and oak aging, while others produce a range of products, including blended rum using a combination of pot and column still distillation. Barbados white rum is sometimes referred to as "Bajan see-through" (to use an old-fashioned term). Barbados is often called the "birthplace of rum" and while this may be difficult to prove conclusively, the island is home to Mount Gay, the world's oldest documented rum brand—founded here in 1703.

Barbados is also home to the Foursquare Rum Distillery, opened in 1996 on the grounds of a former molasses and sugar plantation dating back some 350 years. Under its own label, the distillery produces a range of high-quality rum products including vintage releases, cask strength rums, ultra-aged versions, and "exceptional cask" selections that feature rum finished in a variety of specialty barrels—such as those that once held cognac, bourbon, Zinfandel wine, or port. In addition to the Foursquare brand, Foursquare Rum Distillery produces Doorly's Rum, Old Brigand Rum, and R. L. Seale Rum—in addition to "The Real McCoy" Rum named in honor of Bill McCoy, a famous rum runner of the Prohibition era.

Mauritius
Mauritius is an island nation located in the Indian Ocean about 1,200 miles (2,000 km) off the southeast coast of the African continent. Sugarcane was brought to the area along with Dutch colonization in the 1600s. The production of rum began in the 1850s, when Mr. Pierre Charles François Harel founded the first distillery in the area. Until recently, Mauritius only produced molasses-based rum; this changed in 2006 when the prohibition on the distillation of sugarcane juice was lifted. Today the country produces both molasses- and sugarcane juice-based rum as well

as "island rum"—a flavored rum infused with pineapple, coconut, passion fruit, vanilla, and other local products. Well-known brands of Mauritian rum include St. Aubin, Rhumerie de Chamarel, New Grove Rum, and Penny Blue.

Brazil

Cachaça is a Brazilian rum produced from sugarcane juice. It is by far the most popular distilled spirit among the 180 million citizens of Brazil, making it one of the most widely consumed spirits on the planet. Outside Brazil, cachaça is mainly known as the key ingredient in certain popular tropical drinks, namely the Caipirinha. Cachaça is made in many styles, from fiery, unaged spirits to smooth, aged sippers produced using temperature-controlled fermentation, alembic stills, and extended cask aging.

As of April 11, 2013, the United States Alcohol and Tobacco Tax and Trade Bureau (TTB) recognized cachaça as a type of rum and a distinctive product of Brazil. While the Brazilian standard allows cachaça to have as low as 38% alcohol by volume, any product imported into the United States will conform to the US minimum bottling standard of 40% by volume.

Brazilian standards also allow for a percentage of corn or corn syrup in the fermentation process; however, as the US definition of rum does not allow for the use of corn products, only those products made from 100% sugarcane-based ferment may be labeled as "rum" or "cachaça" in the United States. (Note: According to the TTB, in the United States the term may be spelled either with or without the diacritic mark, as in *cachaça* or *cachaca*.)

Venezuela

Venezuela has the perfect conditions to grow sugarcane and has produced rum for over 300 years. In 2003, the Autonomous Service of Intellectual Property of Venezuela (SAPI) approved a set of standards that created a designation of origin known as the *Denominación de Origen Ron de Venezuela*.

Under these standards, Ron de Venezuela must be produced using 100% Venezuelan-grown sugar cane. The specific style of distillation is not regulated; however, the alcohol must be diluted to 120 proof before it enters the barrel, and it must be aged in white oak barrels (of a maximum size of 150 liters)

Figure 7.7: Bottles of Cachaça (Brazilian Rum)

for a minimum of two years. Ron de Venezuela must be bottled between 40% abv (minimum) and 50% abv (maximum).

Sugarcane and rum production can be divided into three main regions in Venezuela:

- Central West Region: This region produces 80% of all Venezuelan rum. Rums produced in this region have a nose with fruity character and a sweetness expression in the palate. The main brands include Diplomático and Cacique.
- Central Region: This region produces about 15% of all Venezuelan rum. Main brands include Santa Teresa, Pampero, Roble Viejo, and Ocumare.
- East Coast: Only about 5% of all Venezuelan rum is produced in this region; however these rums have a very unique minerality, which can often be perceived in terms of "saltiness" and even iodized notes on the nose and the palate. The main brand is Carúpano.

Nicaragua

Sugar cane was introduced into Central America, including Nicaragua, in the 1880s—with the first Nicaraguan distilleries founded soon thereafter. Within a few decades, rum and other sugarcane products represented a significant part of the Nicaraguan economy. Many styles of rum are produced in

Nicaragua, with the majority being molasses-based and column-distilled. Nicaragua has a somewhat milder climate than the Caribbean, so the processes of wood aging are slower and as a result, many Nicaraguan rums are lightly wooded and quite aromatic. Today, the leading brands of rum produced in Nicaragua include Flor de Caña (produced by Compaña Licorera), Ron Fortuna, and Mombacho.

The Nicaraguan Revolution of the 1980s caused an interruption in international distribution as well as a period of hyper-inflation in Nicaragua. As a result, Compaña Licorera made a strategic decision to store large quantities of their product; today this reserve represents one of the largest collections of slow-barrel-aged rum in the world.

Puerto Rico
The rum produced in Puerto Rico tends to be a light style of rum with delicate, clean, floral notes. Most Puerto Rican rums are based on the traditional Cuban style developed in the 1860s. While most Puerto Rican rum is produced in continuous column stills from highly purified distillates, some specialty products are produced using pot stills. All Puerto Rican rum is required to be aged for at least a year. A good deal is subsequently carbon-filtered to remove any traces of color gained while aging. Today, more than 80% of the rum consumed in the United States is produced in Puerto Rico.

Today, the majority of the rum consumed in the United States is produced in Puerto Rico. Located in Cataño, Puerto Rico, Bacardi Limited runs one of the largest distilleries in the world, producing the very popular Bacardi Select and Bacardi Carta Blanca as well as a wide range of aged and flavored rums. Other brands of Puerto Rican rum include Ron Llave, Ron Palo Viejo, Don Q, and Ron del Barrilito.

Cuba
The Caribbean island of Cuba has grown sugarcane since the 1500s, when the plant was first introduced to the area. Cuba's fertile soil and tropical climate are ideal for the growth of sugarcane (as well as its other revered crops, such as tobacco). Due to current restrictions on commercial imports and distribution, Cuban rum is not available in the United States. It is, however, readily available in many other parts of the world—and many Americans get a taste of Cuban rum while on vacation in Europe, Canada, or elsewhere. Cuba was a pioneer of the light, clean, column-distilled style of rum now produced in many parts of the world. Cuban rum is produced from molasses—and the country has a large enough sugar industry that all of the molasses used is created from Cuban-grown sugarcane. The resulting molasses-based ferment, known as *vino de caña*, is typically distilled in copper-lined column stills. The new-make spirit is then placed into neutral oak barrels for aging. It must spend two years aging, and is subsequently filtered through charcoal. The resulting rum may then be blended, bottled, and sold as blanco (white) rum, or it may be aged longer. Cuban rum masters, known as *maestros roneros*, are responsible for the final blends and aging.

Havana Club is the most widely distributed Cuban rum in the world. The brand was created in Cuba in 1934 by the family of José Arechabala who, along with the Bacardi family, are considered among the "founding families" of Cuban rum culture. The Cuban rum industry—including the distilleries, sugarcane plantations, and the Havana Club brand—was nationalized after the Cuban Revolution of 1959. Soon thereafter, the Arechabala family and the Bacardi family were forced to flee the island.

Havana Club of Cuba rum is produced in a range of styles—including *Blanco, Reserva, 7 años, 15 años Gran Reserva, Selección de Maestros* (barrel proof), and *Máximo Extra Añejo* (a luxury ultra-aged rum with limited production). Other brands of Cuban rum include Ron Santero and Santiago de Cuba.

Havana Club of Cuba—produced by Havana Club International (a joint venture between Pernod Ricard and the Cuban government [Corporación Cuba Ron]) since 1994—should not be confused with the "Havana Club" brand of Puerto Rican rum. Puerto Rico's Havana Club rum is produced by Bacardi Limited (which holds a US trademark on the name), bottled in Florida, and distributed only in the United States. There is, needless to say, extensive, ongoing international litigation regarding the use of the name "Havana Club."

"New England Style" Rum
Early Americans were producing rum from imported Caribbean molasses as early as 1657. Because of the influence of settlers with brandy-making experience,

the rum produced in colonial times was created via pot still, was aged in oak barrels for short periods of time, and contained a high level of congeners. Interest in this historic "New England" style of rum has been revived, and several American craft distillers are using historic recipes and formulas to re-create an early American style of rum. Examples include Thomas Tew Rum produced by the Newport Distillery in Newport, Rhode Island; Privateer True American Rum produced in Ipswich, Massachusetts; and Prichard's Fine Aged Rum produced in Kelso, Tennessee.

Private Labels and Independent Rum Bottlers
Many of the rum products available for sale are either estate-bottled (produced and bottled by a specific distillery) or various "private label" (branded) products such as Gosling's or Pusser's. In addition, a range of rum products—many of them rare and some of them ultra-aged—are available via independent bottlers who purchase and bottle rum sourced from all over the world.

Independent rum bottlers can obtain their rum in a variety of ways, such as a purchase of rum directly from a distillery, the use of a rum broker, the purchase of private rum collections, or the acquisition of specific (often rare) casks or barrels. In some cases, an independent bottler will specialize in the *élevage* (aging, finishing, and blending) of rum.

Many warehouse facilities associated with independent bottlers are located in Europe, allowing for the rum to be finished in a continental climate as opposed to—or in addition to—the tropical climate of many rum-producing countries.

Examples of independent rum bottlers include Habitation Velier (Genoa, Italy), Bristol Classic Rum (Bristol, England), Smith & Cross (London), and Plantation Rum (located in France and associated with Maison Ferrand Cognac). Many independent rum bottlers also deal in private label rum and other sprits—such as Scotch whisky, gin, brandy, and liqueurs.

Figure 7.8: Thomas Tew Rum

CATEGORIES OF RUM

Rum is a difficult spirit to categorize, as there are few classification-wide legal requirements beyond the sugarcane base. In addition, it is not uncommon for a given region or even an individual distillery to produce many different styles of rum. As such, there has yet to be a singular, widely-accepted method of classifying rum into neat categories. Instead, there are quite a few (sometimes overlapping, and sometime contradictory) ways to approach the taxonomy of rum—including geographical indications, historical associations, production methodology, or color. Each of these systems has its benefits and its limitations, as discussed below.

Geographical Indications for Rum
Many of the leading spirits of the world are clearly classified based on specific geographical indications and country- or region-specific rules. This is certainly the case for whiskey, which has a set of government-backed regulations for individual products such as Scotch whisky, Irish whiskey, Bourbon, Tennessee whiskey, and Canadian whisky (among others). Rum has until quite recently been fairly devoid of such geographically-based rules and regulations, but there are exceptions. Martinique was awarded the first (and so far, only) appellation d'origine controlee designation (AOC) for rum in 1996. Other rum-producing localities have followed suit, including the following:
- Jamaica: Geographical Indication for Jamaica Rum (2016)

- Venezuela: Denominación de Origen Ron de Venezuela (2003)
- Cuba: Denominación de Origen Protegida Cuba Ron (2013)

Several other rum-producing areas have plans to legislate guidelines and regulations for their rums. This is a subject that will be interesting to watch in the future.

Classification Based on Color
Rum is generally produced in three different colors, which are somewhat aligned with a particular style.
- **White:** White rums are colorless and may be labeled as clear, crystal, blanco, silver, or plata. In terms of total volume of rum consumed worldwide, this color category is the most popular. White rum is usually a light style of rum that is unaged or lightly aged, made using column stills, and sometimes filtered to remove any color after a period of aging. Due to their clear color and lighter flavor profile, these rums are especially good for use in mixed drinks and cocktails. Puerto Rico is a leading producer of white rum.
- **Amber/Gold:** Also known as *oro*, the gold color category denotes some aging, as the color presumably comes from the time spent in a wooden barrel during the maturation process. As such, this style of rum is expected to have some richness and complexity. However, some distillers add caramel or molasses to white rum in order to produce an amber-hued rum that gives the impression of aging.
- **Dark:** Dark rums are presumably aged in charred oak barrels, some for as long as five to seven years or even longer. A smooth, rich mouthfeel and aromas of sweet spices and dried fruits—such as raisin, fig, clove, and cinnamon—are common in aged rums. However, as with gold rums, additives can mimic the effect of aging and artificially darken the color of rum. Deeply-hued versions of dark rum (which may be aged in heavily charred barrels) are sometimes referred to as "black rum."

Categories Based on Historical Associations
One system of rum classification is based on the historical European colonization—by France, Britain, and Spain—of portions of the Caribbean Basin and Central and South America. As such, certain rums may be described as British style, French style, or Spanish style, as described below:

- **French style:** French-style rums were originally modeled on traditional French brandies and produced using fermented sugarcane juice instead of molasses. These rums are characterized by fruity and floral notes. Guadeloupe, Haiti, Martinique, and Grenada are known for producing French-style rums.
- **British style:** British-style rum tends to be characteristically dark, rich, and heavy in style, with full body and pungent aroma. Jamaica, Guyana, Barbados, Trinidad and Tobago, and St. Lucia are considered to produce British-style rum.
- **Spanish style:** Based upon the traditional Cuban style of rum developed in the 1860s, the Spanish style tends to be lightest style of rum. Many are made in continuous column stills from highly purified distillates and are known for clean, floral, and delicate aromas. Producers of Spanish-style rum include Cuba, Puerto Rico, St. Croix, Guatemala, Dominican Republic, Nicaragua, Panama, Colombia, and Venezuela.

Categories Based on Production Methods
Like many spirits, rum is made using a wide range of production techniques; these include methods of fermentation, distillation, aging, and blending. As such, rum is produced in a range of styles that often seem to transcend regions of origin and local traditions. For these reasons, many rum experts believe that a meaningful classification system for rum would be based on these factors, and might include the following categories:
- Molasses-based, pot still distillation
- Molasses-based, column still distillation
- Molasses-based, blended
- Cane juice-based, pot still distillation
- Cane juice-based, column still distillation
- Cane juice-based, blended
- "Modern Rum," produced using multiple column still distillation

Each of these classifications could be further segmented based on one or more of the following:
- Length of aging
- Location of aging
- Barrel source and type
- Estate-bottled, private label, or independent bottler
- Type of fermentation (including such factors as commercial yeast versus wild yeast, temperature, length of time, use of dunder or other factors)

- Alcohol by volume
- Geographical indication or region of origin

The conversation regarding such classification systems for rum is complex and ongoing. Some of the leading contributors include Martin Cate of Smuggler's Cove, Luca Gargano of Habitation Velier, David Broom (author of "Rum: the Manual"), and Richard Seale of Foursquare Distillery.

DISCUSSING RUM STYLE

Aged Rum: The label of a bottle of rum may carry an age statement. In the United States, the age statement must represent the youngest spirit in a blend.

The term *añejo* seems to indicate a rum that has been significantly aged and is often used for premium products. However, as there are no universal standards or regulations governing the use of the term in reference to rum, actual years of age indicated by the term will vary by region or producer.

Flavored Rums: In the United States, flavored rums must be made with natural flavorings and must be bottled at a minimum of 30% alcohol by volume (60 proof). If there is a predominant flavor, then the name of the flavor must appear on the label, such as "orange-flavored rum" or "spiced rum." Most flavored rums are made using unaged white rums. Flavored rums may be sweetened or unsweetened. Fruit-flavored rums—including orange, coconut, lime, mango, and pineapple—are very popular, as are spiced rums flavored with vanilla, cinnamon, nutmeg, clove, and anise.

According to European Union guidelines, EU rum may not be flavored (although caramel coloring is allowed). However, flavored spirits based on rum are produced throughout Europe. These products may be classified as "other spirit drinks" such as Inländerrum (a spice-flavored spirit produced in Austria), or—if sweetened—as "liqueurs" such as Ronmiel de Canarias (produced in Spain).

Navy Rum: The British Navy has had a long and interesting association with rum, beginning with a failed invasion of the island of Santo Domingo (now known as Hispaniola) in 1655. Refusing to return to England in defeat, the fleet's commanders invaded

Figure 7.9: Rum Aging in Barrels at the Brugal and Company Distillery in Puerto Plata, Dominican Republic

the island of Jamaica, successfully seizing it from Spain for the English crown. In advance of the trip home, the captain and crew fortified their provisions with a large supply of the island's sugarcane spirit, and the sailors' daily ration of beer and brandy was thus replaced by West Indies rum. Over the years, with a ready supply of rum from the Caribbean, the practice of giving navy sailors a "tot" (a daily ration of "navy rum") became formalized.

Navy rum was typically high proof, and there are several versions as to the reasons why. One legend states that barrels of rum were often stored alongside barrels of gunpowder in the cramped space on navy ships. As such, the rum needed to be high enough in proof so that if the rum spilled onto the gunpowder, the gunpowder would still ignite. Thus, navy proof rum was typically 54% to 57% abv or higher. Another version of the same tale states that sailors liked to "prove" the rum had not been watered down by pouring it on gunpowder; only a high proof rum would allow the gunpowder to ignite and therefore "pass the test."

Over the years, the tradition of the daily tot evolved. In the beginning, it was a mid-day serving of full-strength rum; later versions involved serving the tot (a half measure at a time) twice a day in an attempt to reduce binge drinking. Age restrictions were eventually instituted, and finally, the navy began to add water and lime juice to the rum in an attempt to combat drunkenness and to prevent scurvy. Alas, as high-tech military maneuvers and alcohol are an ill-advised combination, the Royal Navy put an end to the daily rum rations for good on July 31, 1970—a day now known as Black Tot Day.

Table 7.1: Top-Selling Rum Brands

TOP-SELLING RUM BRANDS (GLOBAL SALES)	
	Brand
1.	Tanduay
2.	Bacardi
3.	Cachaça 51
4.	McDowell's No. 1 Celebration
5.	Havana Club (Pernod Ricard)
6.	Pitú Cachaça
7.	Velho Barreiro Cachaça
8.	Ypióca Cachaça
9.	Barceló
10.	Contessa
11.	Old Port Rum
12.	Appleton Jamaica
13.	Bozkov
14.	Cacique
15.	Negrita

Source: Drinks International (2018)

Despite Black Tot Day, the legend and spirit of navy rum refused to fade away, and in 1979 a distiller named Charles Tobias created a "navy-style" rum by replicating the mix of five West Indian rums that was once the basis for the Royal Navy rations. Sold under the brand name Pusser's—after the slang term for a ship's purser (supply officer)—this was the first of many navy-style rums on the market.

The terms "navy rum" and "navy-style rum" are not legally-defined, nor are they official categories of rum. However, the terms are often used to describe a particular style of amber-colored, high-proof, flavorful rum. Purists will add that true navy-style rum is crafted from a blend of Caribbean rum, including products from Guyana, Jamaica, Barbados, and Trinidad. Likewise, the term "navy-strength" is unregulated but typically taken to mean a strong rum in the 54 proof to 57 proof range.

Overproof Rum: While most styles of rum sold in the United States are bottled at 80 to 100 proof, or 40 to 50% alcohol by volume, *overproof* rum has a higher alcohol strength. Most overproof rums are bottled at 62.5%-75% alcohol by volume (125-150 proof) or even higher. US regulations prevent rums that are over 155 proof from entering the United States under most circumstances, so many manufacturers produce rums in the 150 proof range, such as Bacardi 151, Cruzan 151, and Gosling's 151. Classic rum punches are often made with high-proof rum. High-proof rums are also often used in cooking, given their ease in flambé. The same high alcohol content that allows the rum to catch on fire during cooking calls for extreme caution in the use of overproof rums.

OTHER SUGAR- AND SUGARCANE-BASED PRODUCTS

Many countries around the world use different forms of sugar to make their spirits, resulting in a diverse array of products that are related to rum.

Ronmiel de Canarias: Sugarcane was first brought to the New World from the Canary Islands, so it makes sense that this part of the world has a long history of making distilled spirits from sugarcane. While the Canary Islands—an autonomous community of Spain located in the Atlantic Ocean about 62 miles (100 km) off the western coast of Morocco—produce several types of rum, the region is particularly renowned for a rum-based liqueur known as *Ronmiel de Canarias*. Ronmiel de Canarias was awarded a Protected Geographical Indication by the European Union in 2008. Under these regulations, the product must be produced in the Canary Islands from a sugarcane-based distillate, flavored with a minimum of 2% honey, and diluted with water to create a finished product between 20% and 30% alcohol by volume.

Table 7.2: Tasting Rum – Typical Flavors and Aromas

TASTING RUM – TYPICAL FLAVORS AND AROMAS	
Sugarcane	Sugar, Molasses, Treacle
Sweet Aromatics	Vanilla, Butterscotch, Honey, Caramel, Maple, Brown Sugar
Wood	Fresh Oak, Smoke, Cedar, Pine
Nutty	Almond
Fruit	Apricot, Pear, Dried Fruit, Banana, Pineapple, Apple, Spiced Apple, Orange Peel
Floral	Dried Flowers
Spirit	Medicinal, Solvent, Ethanol
Spice	Cinnamon, Anise, Clove, Allspice
Earthy	Leather
Herbal	Mint, Tobacco

Table 7.3: Tasting Rum – Typical Descriptors for Palate and Style

TASTING RUM – TYPICAL DESCRIPTORS FOR PALATE AND STYLE	
Style	Clean, Clear, Focused, Heavy, Rustic
Palate	Light, Delicate, Pungent, Full-Bodied, Rich
Other	Mellow, Complex, Layered, Warm

Batavia Arrack: *Batavia arrack* is a spirit produced in Indonesia from sugarcane and red rice, fermented with local yeast. The name dates back to the 1600s when the Indonesian island of Java, then known as Batavia, was part of the Dutch East Indies. Batavia arrack is generally pot-distilled and consumed unaged. It has a reputation for being highly aromatic.

Seco Herrerano: *Seco Herrerano* is considered the national alcoholic beverage of Panama. Triple-distilled from sugarcane, it is a clear spirit that is quite neutral in flavor and is often compared to vodka. Seco Herrerano is traditionally served straight or mixed with milk in a drink known as *Seco con Vaca*. Because it has a neutral flavor, it is often mixed with coconut water—or with just about any mixer as a replacement for rum or vodka.

While Seco Herrerano is a sugarcane-based product, it is differentiated from rum in that it is often sold at 35% alcohol by volume. Also, it is allowed to be distilled at above 190 proof. There are actually multiple brands of seco, but Herrerano is the most widely available. In addition to seco, Panama produces several styles of "true" rum.

Tuzemák: *Tuzemák* is a traditional Czech spirit produced from potatoes or sugar beets. In the nineteenth century, many similar spirits were produced throughout the Austro-Hungarian Empire by populations with no access to the sugarcane produced by the tropical colonies. Tuzemák is typically sweetened and flavored with essences such as cinnamon, anise, and caramel.

Charanda: Charanda is a sugarcane distillate produced in Mexico and defined via the *Norma Oficial Mexicana* as a product derived from a base of sugarcane juice, molasses, or piloncillo (unrefined cane sugar). Charnada was awarded *denominación de origen* (DO) status by the Mexican government in 2002 and may only be produced in and around the city of Uruapan, located in the state of Michoacán. Charanda is produced in several defined styles, including *blanco, reposado, oro,* and *añejo*. Charanda is allowed to be bottled at 35% to 55% abv and as such, it does not always meet the US or EU definition of rum.

TASTING AND SERVING RUM

As unaged rums can be a bit fiery when sipped straight, white rums are generally served long, mixed with soda or juice, or in cocktails. The Cuba Libre, Daiquiri, and Mojito are among the world's favorite rum-based drinks, as are many punches and tropical drinks. The Caipirinha, Brazil's national cocktail made with rum, sugar, and lime, helped to introduce cachaça to the rest of the world. Aged rums mix nicely in drinks and cocktails, as well, but are often enjoyed as an after-dinner drink, to be sipped and savored on their own or over ice.

Silver or white rums should be crystal clear, while amber, dark, or aged rums may show a range of colors from golden to amber to brown. Demerara rums and Jamaican rums can be dark brown to almost black. Remember that color is not always an accurate indicator of age, as some styles of rum may contain caramel coloring.

Silver and white rums should smell fresh, clean, and slightly sweet, having subtle aromas of sugar, banana, flowers, and vanilla. They can also be a bit fiery on the nose, so caution is advised when taking that first sniff. You should remember to keep your nose above the rim of the glass. Amber, dark, or aged rums are more intense in aroma, particularly showing molasses, maple, toffee, spice, vanilla, caramel, and wood.

White rum may have a subtle sweet taste or flavors that mimic sweetness, such as marshmallow, vanilla, or fruit. White rum may also have some warmth, or a "bite," from the alcohol, but a high-quality rum should not "burn" or have a solvent-like character. Aged rums will have a complex range of flavors such as caramel, brown sugar, butterscotch, and tobacco, as well as an overall smooth, rich taste.

White rum should have a clean, sweet finish, while dark rums should have a lingering finish with a flavor or aroma of wood. It is worthwhile to go through the tasting process with a bit of water added to the rum, particularly for white rums and overproof versions.

CHAPTER EIGHT TEQUILA AND OTHER AGAVE-BASED BEVERAGES

TEQUILA AND OTHER AGAVE-BASED BEVERAGES

CHAPTER EIGHT

LEARNING OBJECTIVES

After studying this chapter, the candidate should be able to do the following:
- Define tequila in terms of base materials, distillation processes, aging, and other post-distillation procedures.
- Compare and contrast tequila and 100% agave tequila.
- Describe the plant known as the *Agave tequilana Weber*.
- Identify and discuss the various styles of tequila in terms of flavor profile, color, and aging regimen.
- Discuss the various other types of agave-based spirits available, including mezcal, raicilla, and sotol.
- Discuss the sensory evaluation of tequila and the typical procedures for the serving of tequila and tequila-based drinks.

Tequila—a type of spirit produced from the blue agave plant—has denominacion de origen (DO) status as a protected product of Mexico. Most tequila is made in the state of Jalisco, but it is also approved for production within portions of four nearby states.

This chapter begins with an overview of tequila, including the internationally accepted definition as outlined by the Official Standards of Mexico. It then proceeds to provide a short history of tequila and other agave-based beverages, including a discussion of the agave plant itself. The chapter continues with a discussion of the basic steps in the production of tequila in addition to typical blending, aging, and bottling regimens. The chapter concludes with a discussion of some other agave-based spirits and a short discussion on the tasting and service of tequila.

DEFINITION OF TEQUILA

The United States Standards of Identity define tequila as:
- An alcoholic distillate from a fermented mash derived principally from the *Agave tequilana Weber* ("blue" variety)
- Produced with or without additional fermentable substances
- Distilled in such a manner so that it possesses the taste, aroma, and characteristics generally attributed to tequila
- Bottled at no less than 40% alcohol by volume (80 proof)

The US standards recognize that "tequila is a distinctive product of Mexico, manufactured in Mexico, in compliance with the laws of Mexico." Thus, the Mexican standards for tequila, as described in the *Norma Oficial Mexicana* ("Official Standard of Mexico," often abbreviated as *NOM*), are considered to be the international standards for tequila.

The NOM for tequila recognizes two distinct types of tequila; one is known simply by the term *tequila,* and the other, which has higher standards of production and bottling, is known as 100% agave tequila. Tequila that is 100% agave must be labeled with one of the following statements: "100% de agave," "100% puro de agave," "100% agave," or "100% puro agave," to which the word *blue* may be added.

According to the NOM, both types of tequila are required to be:
- A regional beverage obtained by distilling the fermented must of material derived from the cooked or hydrolyzed hearts of the *Agave tequilana Weber* plant, which must be grown and harvested within the designated tequila-producing area
- Produced at an authorized manufacturer located within the designated tequila-producing area

- Bottled at 35-55% alcohol by volume (70 to 110 proof)
- Not "cold mixed," which is defined as the adding or mixing of any alcoholic beverage different from tequila at any point during the manufacturing process, including the finished product

In addition, the NOM for 100% agave tequila requires the following:

- It must be produced from a fermented must consisting of 100% blue agave.
- It must be bottled in a bottling plant controlled by the authorized manufacturer and located within the designated tequila-producing area.

The NOM for tequila allows for the following:

- It must be produced using a fermented product that is created with a minimum of 51% blue agave. The remaining 49% of the total volume must be other sugars of a non-agave source. These are typically molasses, cane sugar, or corn syrup. The sugars and liquids must be blended together prior to fermentation.
- With a Certificate of Approval from the Ministry of the Economy, it may be transported in bulk and bottled outside of the designated tequila-producing area.

With the notable exception of *blanco* tequilas, tequila is allowed to be treated with "mellowing agents." These are defined as caramel coloring, natural oak or Encino oak extract, glycerin, and sugar syrup—and are permitted up to an allowed maximum of 76 g/L for sugar, or a total of all such materials of 1% by volume. Tequila that is treated with mellowing agents may be referred to as "mellowed" or *abocado*.

Figure 8.1: *The Mezcal Drinkers,* Pre-Hispanic Sculpture on Display at the National Museum of Tequila

HISTORY OF TEQUILA

The agave (pronounced *ah-GAH-vay*) plant was used for many practical purposes before the native Mexicans discovered that it could be fermented into a palatable beverage. Of the many species of agave found throughout Mexico, about a dozen or so were recognized by the native inhabitants for use as food and medicine. Agave fiber was used as rope and binding cords. Its broad and durable leaves were perfect for roof thatching, and its thin, sharp thorns provided needles for sewing. Historians believe that around 200 CE, it was discovered that the juice of the agave plant could be fermented into an intoxicating beverage.

The Aztec civilization gave names to the products they created with agave. The fermented juice became known as *octili poliqhui,* named after Ometochtli, the Aztec god of drink. Tepoztecatl, the god of alcoholic merriment, was invoked during the use of octili poliqhui as a tension-releasing intoxicant after the day's rigorous activity. In an extreme, octili poliqhui was used as a narcotic during the human sacrifice rites of the era.

In the 1520s, upon their invasion of Mexico, Spanish conquistadors introduced the art of alcoholic distillation to the native population. The earliest experiments of making a distilled beverage using *pulque* (as octili poliqhui had come to be known) produced a spirit known as *mezcal wine* (alternately spelled "mescal"). The process was primitive, but the essential steps are still in use today. First, the agave was cooked. Then, it was pounded and crushed with mallets to squeeze the sweet juice from the agave fibers. This juice was fermented into the low-alcohol pulque. Finally, the fermented juice was distilled in clay pots. The resulting spirit was usually consumed unaged.

Mezcal wine was produced all over central Mexico from the many varieties of agave native to the region. Although production around the town of Tequila in the state of Jalisco was limited in the sixteenth and seventeenth centuries, distillation became the main enterprise of the area by the eighteenth century.

Near the end of the eighteenth century, from 1785 to 1789, under the Spanish ruler King Charles III, the production of mezcal wine was temporarily forbidden in hopes that the locals would then need to import Spanish wine and spirits, which would increase much-needed tax revenues for Spain. Much to the Spaniards' dismay, this attempt failed. In 1792, the new king, Ferdinand IV, allowed the legal resumption of fermentation and spirit distillation in Mexico. The first license to produce mezcal wine in the Tequila region was granted to Jose María Guadalupe Cuervo in 1795.

Many small distilleries proliferated during the nineteenth century by making and selling mezcal wine. They were set up as taverns and served the local populace and surrounding neighborhoods. At this time, mezcal wine was being distilled from the fermented juice of many different agave species. Eventually, producers narrowed down the agave source that produced the best-tasting mezcal wine to the blue agave grown around the village of Tequila. This agave plant was classified by a botanist named Frédéric Albert Constantin Weber in 1902 and was given the botanical name *Agave tequilana Weber azul*.

The mezcal wine industry was transformed after the blue agave was discovered to be the finest source of juice for distillation. In 1873, the blue agave-based "mezcal wine" from the region of Jalisco was officially renamed *tequila* in order to distinguish it from mezcal spirits produced in other parts of Mexico, such as those produced in Oaxaca.

By the first decade of the twentieth century, there were almost ninety tequila distilleries operating in the state of Jalisco. Organizations designed to advance the tequila industry began to form. In 1949, the first official Norma Oficial Mexicana for tequila was established. Similar to the regulations that protect the agricultural products of other countries, the NOM for tequila protects the appellation of origin, regulates production, and establishes standards to ensure quality and authenticity. Those companies that comply with the regulations of the tequila NOM are certified by the Consejo Regulador del Tequila (CRT) as authentic producers. Every approved tequila producer (distillery) is assigned a four-digit NOM number that appears on either the front or back label of the tequila bottle. Every brand produced by a given distillery will carry the same number.

THE AGAVE PLANT

Over 200 different varieties of agave are known to exist. While many of them are used for industrial or agricultural purposes, only a few are suitable or desirable as a source for alcoholic beverages.

Figure 8.2: The Blue Agave Plant

Most people mistake the agave plant for a cactus. While the plants look similar and grow in the same type of climate, the agave is not a cactus. Rather, the agave belongs to the *Asparagaceae* family and is classified as a succulent. *Asparagaceae* is a large family of flowering plants that includes asparagus, the spider plant, yucca, and lily of the valley as well as the large sub-family of agave *(Agavoideae)* plants. There are several agave subspecies that are used to produce distillates. Several others are used to make fermented beverages.

All varieties of the agave plant have long leaves (known as *pencas*) with thorns on their tips and along their edges. The pencas grow in the form of a rosette. Agave plants can grow to be very large. Specifically, the blue agave may reach from five to eight feet (1.5 to 2.4 m) in height and eight to twelve feet (2.4 to 3.7 m) in diameter. The maturation rate is very slow; the blue agave variety requires six to eight years of maturation before it is ready to be harvested.

For use in tequila, the flower stalk is removed before it has a chance to blossom, preventing the plants from reaching sexual maturity. This injurious process causes the central rosette stem to swell with juice, or *aguamiel* (literally, "honey water"). This swollen portion of the agave has two names: *piña,* as it resembles a pineapple, and *cabeza* ("head"), as it somewhat resembles the shape of a human head.

Commercially grown agave plants are generally created via asexual reproduction. This occurs when the plant sends out horizontal underground stems called *rhizomes,* which develop their own roots and eventually become new agave plants. When the parent plant is approximately four to six years old, it is severed from the offspring. The small offspring is allowed to grow for another year before being transported to a nursery area, where it is kept for another year. At age two, it is moved to its final growing site, where it becomes a new parent plant.

Figure 8.3: Blue Agave *Cabezas* at Harvest

THE TEQUILA-PRODUCTION REGION

The Mexican state of Jalisco is by far the largest grower of the agave plant as well as the largest producer of tequila; more than 80% of all blue agave cultivated for use in tequila is grown in Jalisco. Jalisco—located in the midsection of the country on the west coast—covers approximately 31,210 square miles (80,830 square km) and comprises 4.1% of the total area of Mexico.

The center of tequila production is the small town of Tequila, located about forty miles (sixty-five kilometers) west of Guadalajara, the capital city of the state of Jalisco. Blue agave may be grown, and tequila may be produced, throughout the entire state of Jalisco. Tequila is also produced in portions of the nearby states of Tamaulipas, Guanajuato, Nayarit, and Michoacán.

Figure 8.4: Map of the Tequila-Producing Regions

In Jalisco, there are two main regions for the cultivation of blue agave, both located near the town of Tequila—the Amatitán/Lowlands region and Los Altos/The Highlands. These two regions, which vary somewhat in their climate and soil, are detailed below.

The Amatitán/Lowlands Region
- Located in the east-central section of Jalisco
- Overall, the warmer of the two regions
- Altitude: 1,300 m (4,200 ft) above sea level

Los Altos/The Highlands Region
- Located in the north-central section of Jalisco
- Overall, the cooler of the two regions
- Altitude: 2,000 m (6,500 ft) above sea level

These two primary areas, because of significant differences in terroir, produce agaves that show distinctive expressions. Los Altos/The Highlands region tequilas are softer, fruitier, and highly floral in nature; the Amatitán/Lowlands tequilas tend to be crisper, more vegetal, and earthy, with clear black pepper spice flavors.

THE PRODUCTION OF TEQUILA

Every tequila distillery uses a combination of factors to craft its product. By varying any of these factors, a distillery can change the character of its specific brand.

- **Agave:** The quality of the agave plant determines the final product developed. The finest tequilas are produced from 100% blue agave. The plants themselves vary according to the soil, climate, and rainfall of the growing regions, as well as the maturity of the plant.
- **Other Base Material:** Some types of tequila are produced using a minimum of 51% blue agave aguamiel. In these products, the choice of the secondary sugar source, such as cane sugar or corn, has an influence on the final product.
- **Water:** Water used in production may be potable water from natural sources or processed water.
- **Fermentation:** As there are few regulations concerning the fermentation process used in the production of tequila, each distillery uses its discretion in the choice of natural yeast or cultured yeast and, if a cultured yeast, a proprietary strain vs. a generic strain.
- **Distillation:** The distillation proof, type of still, still material, and choice of double or triple distillation all influence the final character of the spirit.
- **Maturation:** Tequila is produced in a wide range of ages, from "silver" tequila, which is aged for less than two months, to "extra-añejo," which is aged for a minimum of three years.

The production of tequila can be divided into the following steps: the harvest, cooking, extraction, fermentation, distillation, dilution, maturation, and bottling. Each of the processes is discussed below.

The Harvest: A few months prior to harvest, a fieldworker known as a *jimador* uses a sharp cutting tool known as a *coa* to prepare the matured plant for harvest. This preparation includes the removal of the central flower spike, which forces the plant to send its growth and sap into its heart, causing a swollen piña to form. At harvest, the plant is cut from its roots and rolled onto its side. From this position, the plant's leaves, known as *pencas,* are sliced off, leaving a relatively smooth piña to be hauled to the distillery.

Amatitán piñas are 35 to 75 kilos (75 to 165 pounds) in weight, while piñas grown in the Highlands can range from 50 to 90 kilos (110 to 200 pounds). The piñas are trucked to the distillery, where workers with axes cut them into halves and quarters.

Figure 8.5: *Jimador* Using a *Coa* to Remove the *Pencas* of a Blue Agave Plant

Cooking: Upon harvest, the aguamiel sap located inside the cabeza is partially composed of *inulin*, a polysaccharide (complex carbohydrate) which must be converted into fermentable sugars. This conversion involves a process known as *hydrolysis*—the chemical breakdown of a compound due to a reaction with water—combined with prolonged exposure to moderate heat. During this process the inulin will be converted into fructose and glucose—highly fermentable simple sugars—along with a number of other compounds. The use of heat also assists with softening the piña, which permits it to be more easily milled later on.

The cut-up piñas are placed in steam ovens called *hornos* and cooked for thirty-six to forty-eight hours at an average temperature range of 140-185°F (60-85°C). Alternatively, some producers may cook their piñas for a longer time at a lower temperature, or for a shorter time at temperatures up to 200°F (93°C). After the cooking period, the steam is turned off, and the cooked piñas are left in the oven for another two days. During this time, additional cooking takes place, followed by cooling.

Some distilleries use modern high-pressure steel autoclaves instead of traditional brick ovens. These modern ovens use higher temperatures and shorter cooking times, generally requiring six hours of direct heating followed by six hours with the steam turned off. While the obvious advantage of an autoclave is the speed, it must be carefully controlled to avoid overcooking or burning the piñas.

During cooking, a small amount of sweet liquid which may contain as much as 20% fermentable sugars oozes from the plant material. This liquid is collected, reduced in strength with water, and stored for later addition to the must. After cooling, the cooked agave is removed from the ovens and moved to the crushing–juicing equipment for the extraction of additional sugars.

Extraction: In addition to the juice that readily seeps out, there is much more to be extracted from the pulp of the cooked agave. Historically, the juice was separated from the fibrous pulp by crushing it beneath a *tahona,* a huge stone wheel drawn by oxen or horses. As the agave was crushed, it would create a raft of juice resting atop a mat of fibers. The juice would then be scooped up in buckets and placed in the fermentation tanks. The leftover fibers, known as *bagazo,* are sometimes used later in the production process.

The old-fashioned crushing method has now been almost exclusively replaced by the use of modern grinder–juicer machines similar to those used in the sugarcane industry. A third option called the *diffuser process* (diffusion) bypasses the initial cooking process altogether and mechanically shreds the piñas, permitting the raw extraction of the sap, which then goes through a heating and cooking process.

Figure 8.6: Traditional Agave Grinder and Brick Ovens

Fermentation: After the extraction process, the juice is ready to be fermented. Some traditional producers still use wooden vats as their fermentation vessels, but most producers now use temperature-controlled stainless steel fermenters. As the juice is placed in the fermenters, it is typically diluted with water to a sugar level of between 8% and 16% by weight. If a distillery is making a basic tequila (meaning a non-100% agave tequila), the non-agave sugar portion is added to the fermentable must of agave juice just before the yeast is added.

The decision of whether to use natural or cultured yeast is left up to each distillery. In practice, nearly all distilleries use cultured yeast, either a proprietary strain or a commercially available one. As the role of the yeast is critical to the final outcome of the product, specific information about the type of yeast used is a tightly held secret.

During the fermentation process, several of the more artisanal producers will add some of the bagazo (leftover agave fibers) to their fermentation vessels to impart complexity. Fermentation typically takes from three to ten days. Once the alcohol is created, the fermented liquid is known as *mosto.*

Table 8.1: Top-Selling Tequila Brands

TOP-SELLING TEQUILA BRANDS (GLOBAL SALES)	
Brand	
1.	Jose Cuervo
2.	Sauza
3.	Patrón
4.	Don Julio
5.	El Jimador
6.	Hornitos

Source: Drinks International (2018), *Wall Street Journal*

Distillation: When fermentation is complete, the alcohol content of the mosto can range from 4% to 8%. The variation in alcohol content is the result of several factors, such as the type and ripeness of the harvested agave, thermal conditions in the ovens, efficiency in the extraction phase, dilution in the fermentation vats, efficacy of the yeast and strain(s) used, and, if a non-100% agave tequila is being produced, the amount and type of sugars added to the must.

As there are no regulatory limitations on the type of still used for the distillation of tequila, copper or stainless steel pot stills, single column stills, and even continuous distillation towers may be used. The vast majority of tequila producers use the pot still for two separate distillations.

The desired distillate (the heart of the run, or *el corazón*) from the first distillation has an alcohol content of around 25% and is called *ordinario* or, sometimes, *tequila primero*. The heads and tails of the first distillation are either discarded or redistilled with the mosto in the next batch. Since one objective of making tequila is to maintain the agave's vegetal flavors and not distill the must to high alcohol levels, the tequila coming off the second distillation is usually no higher than 55-60% alcohol by volume (110-120 proof).

In a typical second distillation, either in a new pot still or with the must returned to the cleaned-out first pot still, the middle portion of the run is taken off at about 55% alcohol by volume and is called *tequila refino* or *vino refino*. Those distillers who will mature the tequila in barrels may distill their tequila at higher levels to allow for some evaporation during aging. Distillers who wish to produce unaged tequila with a full-bodied, silky texture and distinct flavor will take the distillate off the second distillation at a lower alcoholic strength (40% alcohol by volume) and bottle it without dilution.

Dilution: Although some unaged tequilas are distilled to 40% and bottled undiluted, most tequila is distilled at a higher alcohol by volume and is thereafter diluted with water. Distilled or demineralized water is preferable for purity.

Maturation: All tequila is clear (water-white) as it comes off the still. This first stage of tequila is called either *blanco* or *plata,* meaning *white* and *silver,* respectively. It is from blanco that all other styles of tequila are made.

Figure 8.7: Tequila Maturing in Barrels

While some styles of tequila are "mellowed" with caramel coloring or other additives, the natural coloring of tequila is gained via barrel maturation. As with other aged spirits, this transformation from a clear spirit to one with an amber hue is caused by the interaction between the spirit and the wooden barrel over a period of time. The longer the aging period, the darker the tequila becomes.

However, if the barrels have been used continuously for many years, their coloring and congener extractives become slowly depleted. Accordingly, the distillery may choose between using newer barrels and a mixed regimen of new and used barrels, or allotting the extra time necessary for producing the desired character. Without regulations on barrel age or the preparation of the inside surface of the barrels, the producer has a great deal of latitude in the maturation regimen.

A new trend, borrowed from certain Scotch whisky methods used to impart exotic flavors, is to age the tequila in used barrels for the requisite time and then to rack it into "finishing barrels" (which were used for port or sherry, for example) for a brief period before bottling.

Bottling: Once maturation is completed, the tequila is prepared for bottling. Some styles of tequila, particularly those that are aged for a year or less, are often blended in order to achieve a certain style consistency with regard to both color and flavor. At this stage, some tequilas may be conditioned with "mellowing agents," as detailed in the NOM.

Older tequilas are not typically blended, as the tequila NOM regulations stipulate that the age statement on a label be determined by the age of the youngest component in the bottle. Thus, older tequilas are bottled directly from the barrel, with the sole addition of water, if necessary, to bring them to the desired bottling proof.

STYLES OF TEQUILA

Tequila is produced in several styles based on aging, blending, and other finishing procedures. In discussing these styles of tequila, it is important to remember the distinction between 100% agave tequila and a product labeled simply with the term *tequila,* which may be produced using up to 49% other base materials. Before the 1930s, all tequilas were 100% agave. Production of the product using a mixture of sugars began because of the increased demand for the product coupled with a limited supply of the blue agave.

A few important distinctions between the two main types of tequila are discussed below; aging classifications are discussed in the next section.

100% Blue Agave Tequila
- All 100% agave tequila must be distilled entirely from the fermented juice of the blue agave plant.
- All 100% agave tequilas must be bottled in Mexico.
- These tequilas may be aged and labeled in the following styles: blanco, oro, reposado, añejo, and extra-añejo.

Tequila
- Tequila may be fermented and distilled from a minimum of 51% agave juice and up to 49% non-agave sugars.
- It may be bulk exported and bottled outside of Mexico.
- This style of tequila, originally called mixto, makes up the great majority of tequila consumed outside of Mexico. Although the term does not appear on the label, if a product label does not read "100% agave" in some way, then it is, in fact, mixto tequila.
- It may be aged and labeled in the following styles: blanco, joven abocado (known in the United States as gold tequila), reposado, añejo, and extra-añejo.

FLAVORED TEQUILA

As of 2004, flavored tequila has been on the market. Chili pepper, rose, orange, coconut, mango, strawberry, and almond are among the many styles of flavored tequila available today.

AGING CLASSIFICATIONS FOR TEQUILA

Tequila is produced in several strictly regulated aging categories that are described below.

Blanco: Also known as "plata," "white," or "silver," this style of tequila is water-white in the bottle. It can be bottled immediately after distillation, with a possible addition of water to adjust bottling strength. It may be allowed to rest in stainless steel tanks prior to bottling. Blanco tequila may be either 100% agave tequila or tequila.

Figure 8.8: Various Types of Tequila

Oro: The term *oro* or *gold,* somewhat confusingly, means something entirely different when applied to 100% agave tequila versus non-100% (mixto) tequila. When applied to 100% agave tequilas, the term indicates tequila produced via the blending of young tequilas with aged tequilas. Such products are rare, but they do allow for tequila to be labeled as oro or gold and still maintain the 100% agave status.

In the United States, it is far more common for gold tequila to be mixto tequila. In such cases, the tequila is considered to be joven abocado. The term *joven abocado*, which may only be used on non-100% agave (mixto) tequilas, translates to "young and smooth" or "young and mellowed." It should be noted that the only difference between white and "gold" mixto tequilas is the addition of coloring and mellowing agents.

Reposado: *Reposado* tequila is "rested" for a minimum of two months in oak vats or barrels. The vats may range from 10,000 to 30,000 liters (264 to 790 gallons) in size. Barrels for this purpose are typically used barrels, such as those previously used by whiskey producers in the United States. Reposado may be 100% agave tequila or tequila.

Añejo: This aged tequila must be matured in oak barrels no larger than 600 liters (160 gallons) for a period of no less than one year. Like blanco and reposado, añejo may be 100% agave tequila or tequila.

Extra-Añejo: Introduced in 2006, this is the newest classification in the tequila registry. This style of tequila must be aged in oak barrels no larger than 600 liters (160 gallons) in size for a minimum period of three years. Like the previous classifications, it may be 100% agave tequila or tequila.

Table 8.2: Styles of 100% Agave Tequila

Classification	Definition	Equivalent Labeling Terms
Blanco	Unaged	White, Silver, Plata
Oro	While rarely used, this term may be used for a blend of blanco tequila with an older tequila	Gold
Reposado	Aged for a minimum of 2 months in oak vats or barrels	Aged, Rested
Añejo	Aged for at least 1 year in oak barrels	Extra-aged
Extra-Añejo	Aged for at least 3 years in oak barrels	Ultra-aged

Table 8.3: Styles of Mixto Tequila

Classification	Definition	Equivalent Labeling Terms
Blanco	Unaged	White, Silver, Plata
Joven Abocado	Unaged; typically has caramel coloring added	Gold Tequila
Reposado	Aged for a minimum of 2 months in oak vats or barrels	Aged, Rested
Añejo	Aged for at least 1 year in oak barrels	Extra-aged
Extra-Añejo	Aged for at least 3 years in oak barrels	Ultra-aged

BOTTLING TEQUILA

Some styles of tequila are allowed to be shipped in bulk from Mexico and bottled in the United States. This practice was made official when the two countries signed an agreement in January 2006. However, in an effort to control quality, the Mexican government imposes various restrictions on these bulk shipments.

More specifically, the restrictions are as follows:
- All 100% agave tequilas must be bottled in Mexico.
- An importer is not permitted to resell bulk tequila to other bottlers.
- The label must identify both the producer and the importer.
- The 2006 agreement created a Tequila Bottlers Registry to identify approved bottlers, as well as an agency that monitors this registry.
- The agreement encourages bottlers to include the NOM number or tequila distillery registration number on the label. While this is not mandatory for imported bottling, tequila bottled in Mexico is required to have this NOM number on either the front or back label.

OTHER AGAVE-BASED BEVERAGES

While the vast majority of agave-based spirits on the global market are tequilas, there are several other agave-based beverages that are less common. Some of these are currently strictly local products, while others, such as mezcal, have more international fame.

Pulque: Pulque is a fermented beverage, as opposed to a distillate. Just as grain can be used to make beer as well as whiskey, agave makes both a simple fermented beverage and a more complex distillate. The fermented product made from agave is commonly called *pulque*. Pulque may be produced from several different agave subspecies and is typically consumed as a local beverage soon after fermentation is complete.

The sap (as opposed to the cooked hearts) of the *Agave americana*, commonly referred to as maguey, is the typical base material for pulque. When the plant reaches maturity—which typically takes 10 to 12 years—the floral bud and central leaves of the plant are removed, and a small cavity is carved into the center of the base. After a few days, the sap starts to flow into the cavity, and it is harvested once or twice per day. The cavity is scraped at regular intervals, which allows the plant to continue to produce sap for three to six months.

After the sap is harvested, it is brought to the production facility—known as a *tinacal*—and placed in a large vat. Fermentation, via ethanol-producing *Zymomonas mobilis* bacteria, is induced by the addition of some freshly-made (and still-fermenting) pulque to the vat of fresh sap. Fermentation typically takes 7 to 14 days.

Because pulque spoils rapidly within a few days, this milky-looking product is essentially a locally produced product, and most pulque is consumed in neighborhood bars called *pulquerías*. In recent years, brewers have found a way to store pulque in cans, like beer, but purists claim that this significantly changes the flavor.

Figure 8.9: *Agave americana* field in Oaxaca

Mezcal: Mezcal was, until quite recently, a traditional term referring to all agave spirits. However, in 1994, mezcal was awarded its own set of standards, and as of 2016 these standards (as described in the Norma Oficial Mexicana and the standards of the spirit's denominacion de origen) were updated such that the term *mezcal* may only be used to refer to certain specific agave-based beverages produced within certain defined geographic areas. Mezcal derives its name from a Nahuatl Indian word, *mexcalmetl*, which loosely translates as "agave plant."

While the Mexican state of Oaxaca is the traditional center and leading producer of mezcal, the NOM allows for the production of mezcal in a total of nine Mexican states. In addition to Oaxaca, approved production areas include the Mexican states of Guerrero, Durango, San Luis Potosí, Puebla, and Zacatecas as well as portions of the states of Tamaulipas and Michoacán—plus the town of San Luis de la Paz (located in the state of Guanajuato).

A range of agave plant species and varieties are approved for use in the production of mezcal, however, close to 90% is made using *Agave espadín (Agave angustifolia)*. Other approved species include *Agave esperrima, Agave weberi, Agave patatorum,* and *Agave salmiano*. The rules also allow for the use of "other agave species" as long as they are not specified in the use of other NOM-regulated beverages within the same state. This means that many different agave plants may be used to produce mezcal, resulting in a wide selection of unique and artisanal beverages.

Mezcal often has a "smokier" or "earthier" aroma than tequila, in part because of the varieties of agave used but also because of the tradition of cooking the piñas in earth-covered pits. Grinding methods vary, and some versions of mezcal use agave fibers (bagazo) in the fermentation and distillation stages of production in order to add character.

Mezcal made using only agave may be labeled as 100% Agave Mezcal. Products without this label designation must be produced using a minimum of 80% agave (the remaining 20% being non-agave sugars).

Mezcal is typically bottled in an unaged expression, but it may be oak-aged prior to bottling. Regulations allow for the following aging designations on the label of a bottle of mezcal:
- Joven: No aging requirements
- Reposado: Must be aged in oak barrels for a minimum of two months
- Añejo: Must be aged in oak barrels for a minimum of one year

With the update of the official standards in 2016, three categories of mezcal were created. Products with labels using just the term *Mezcal* have few production requirements regarding the specific procedures for cooking the piñas, milling the cooked product, fermentation, and/or distillation. Such products are likely to use industrial-style equipment including stainless steel ovens, stainless steel fermentation tanks, and column stills.

The following two label categories may be used for those products made using specific artisanal or traditional production methods:
- **Mezcal Artesanal:** In the production of Mezcal Artesanal, the agave must be cooked in pits or cement ovens (no stainless steel allowed), fermentation must be completed in a vessel made of stone, cement, wood, clay, earthenware or animal skins, and distillation must be fueled using direct fire.
- **Mezcal Ancestral:** Mezcal Ancestral must be produced using traditional methods, such as cooking the agave in pit ovens and milling the agave with wooden bats or a stone wheel. Fermentation must be accomplished in a vessel of stone, cement, wood, clay, earthenware or animal skins; and agave fibers (bagazo) must be included. Distillation, which must also include agave fibers, must be accomplished via cement vessels fueled using a direct fire.

As of the passage of NOM 199 in July 2016, agave-based distillates produced outside of the geographical limits (or other standards) of the Mezcal NOM may not use the term *mezcal* but instead must be named according to another designation or labeled as "Aguardiente de Agave."

Bacanora: This agave distillate is made in the state of Sonora in the north of Mexico. Bacanora is produced using the agave subspecies *angustofolia* (also known as *Agave yaquiana*). Here, the piñas are roasted in underground pits of volcanic rock and heated with mesquite charcoal. Bacanora is named for the town in Sonora where it was first produced. The methods used in the production of Bacanora have been passed down over the generations for at least three hundred years. However, it wasn't until 2006 that the Mexican government officially declared its denomination of origin, specifying that Bacanora can only be produced in certain municipalities within the state of Sonora. Bacanora is 100% agave, so the quality tends to be quite high. The finished product has pleasant hints of both smoke and earth.

Raicilla: *Raicilla* is a locally distilled product made in central Jalisco. Raicilla does not qualify as tequila, as it uses the *lechuguilla* or *angustifolia* subspecies of agave, not blue agave. This spirit has traditionally been overshadowed and overlooked, even by the Mexican government, because of its more popular cousin. It is, in effect, a type of moonshine that is often bottled at more than 100 proof, and consumed primarily by the locals. Now, given tequila's rising popularity and the search for artisanal spirits, legally produced raicilla is starting to be commercially bottled.

Figure 8.10: The Sotol Plant

Sotol: *Sotol* is distilled in the states of Chihuahua, Durango, and Coahuila and is produced using the *Dasylirion wheeleri* plant, also known as the desert spoon or simply the sotol plant. The sotol plant was formerly considered a variety of agave but was recently reclassified. The harvesting and production methods used for sotol are, however, still largely the same as those used for mezcal. Sotol received a denomination of origin from the Mexican government in 2004. Before commercial production was popular, it would have been common to use only wild desert spoon plants to produce sotol. However, since the wild plants can take up to fifteen years to mature, they are now cultivated. Sotol is typically less smoky and earthy than mezcal.

TASTING AND SERVING TEQUILA

Tequila has a reputation for being downed in a single shot—sometimes accompanied by a bite of lime and a lick of salt. While some traditions die hard, high-quality tequila deserves to be savored. Riedel even has a long-stemmed tequila glass designed with input from the master distillers at Cuervo. A stemmed white wineglass will do for a formal tasting, as well.

There are over 350 brands of tequila in Mexico. That diversity, combined with the various aging categories and the differences in base ingredients between tequila and 100% agave tequila, makes for a wide possibility of tastes, flavors, and colors. Tequila flights can be arranged to compare several brands of tequila with 100% agave, the same product from different distillers, or a "horizontal" tasting of one distiller's range from plata to extra-añejo.

Figure 8.11: Classic Margarita

Silver/white tequilas are generally crystal clear in color; a high-quality example should show excellent clarity and brightness. Some plata tequila may develop a silver "sheen." Non-100% agave tequilas with a golden or amber hue most likely contain caramel coloring, while older 100% agave tequilas will show a range of colors reflecting their time in barrel, from gold to amber to almost brown.

Young tequilas tend to be spicy, with aromas of citrus and herbs and a distinctly earthy scent. The aroma of agave, which is delicate, earthy, and almost floral, should be detectable in young tequila. The term *agave intensity* is often used to describe the level of this particular scent. The typical aromas to be found in aged tequilas include wood, smoke, and sweet aromatics such as caramel and vanilla. Tequila that is 100% agave will show the highest level of fruit, floral, and earthy characteristics, as compared to those versions made from a lower percentage of aguamiel.

On the palate, young tequila tends to have a fiery, spicy character due to the influence of the agave. Older versions will feel richer and smoother and will show vanilla and wood-influenced flavors. It is interesting to note if the aromas are mirrored on the palate as flavors; oftentimes with tequila, this is the case.

Young tequila should have a long finish. A bit of "heat" is to be expected. High-quality aged tequila will have a lingering, warm, smooth aftertaste. The aroma or flavor of blue agave should be noticeable in the finish of tequila; it may be delicate and subtle or else show more "agave intensity." In any case, a short, harsh, musty, or medicinal finish is likely to be a sign of an inferior product.

Tequila, particularly the silver and plata versions, is the star of many of the world's most popular cocktails, led by the Margarita (basically, a Tequila Sour), the Tequila Sunrise, the Paloma, the Brave Bull, and the Bloody María.

Table 8.4: Tasting Tequila – Typical Flavors and Aromas

\multicolumn{2}{c}{TASTING TEQUILA – TYPICAL FLAVORS AND AROMAS}	
Fruity	Apple, Banana, Lemon, Grapefruit, Orange Peel, Citrus
Agave, Vegetal	Baked Yam, Celery, Jicama, Asparagus, Bell Pepper
Floral	Violet, Lilac, Rose, Jasmine
Earthy	Cardboard, Wet Cement, Mushroom, Wet Earth
Sweet Aromatics	Vanilla, Chocolate, Caramel, Honey, Nutty
Spicy	White Pepper, Black Pepper, Anise, Cinnamon
Herbal	Dried Herb, Dill, Herbaceous, Juniper
Mineral	Salt, Flint
Wood	Oak, Dust, Smoke, Pine, Balsam

Table 8.5: Tasting Tequila – Typical Descriptors for Palate and Style

TASTING TEQUILA – TYPICAL DESCRIPTORS FOR PALATE AND STYLE	
Style	Young, Clean, Rich, Sharp, Harsh
Palate	Fiery, Spicy, Warm, Smooth, Sweet, Bitter
Other	"Agave Intensity," Lingering, Smoky, Complex, Warm

CHAPTER NINE
LIQUEURS

LIQUEURS

CHAPTER NINE

LEARNING OBJECTIVES

After studying this chapter, the candidate should be able to do the following:
- Define the distilled spirit category known as liqueurs in terms of base materials, sweeteners, and flavorings.
- Identify the elements of liqueur flavor and describe the various flavoring procedures used in the production of liqueurs.
- Identify and describe the leading members of the following liqueur categories: fruit liqueurs; botanical liqueurs; bean, nut, and seed liqueurs; cream liqueurs; and whiskey liqueurs.

Simply put, a liqueur is a spirit that has been sweetened and flavored. The large and diverse spirits category of liqueurs is international in nature, as liqueurs are produced in many different parts of the world. Certain products, such as the rum-based, coffee-flavored liqueur known as Kahlúa, which is made in Mexico, have been produced for so long in a particular area or country that their product is globally recognized as the standard of excellence for that particular type of liqueur. For many others, however, the original product types have lost their designation of origin.

This chapter begins with a discussion of the definition of the terms *liqueurs* and *cordials*. Defining these terms accurately requires quite a bit of detail, given the diverse character of the category as well as the difference in usage between the United States and the European Union. The chapter then continues on with a discussion of the history of liqueurs, followed by an overview of the various ways in which liqueurs are produced and flavored. The chapter concludes with a discussion of many of the leading types of liqueurs available on the market today. They are categorized into groupings that include fruit liqueurs; botanical liqueurs; bean, nut, and seed liqueurs; cream liqueurs; and whiskey liqueurs.

THE DEFINITION OF LIQUEURS

According to the United States Standards of Identity, the terms *cordials* and *liqueurs* are used interchangeably. Both are defined as:
- Products obtained by the mixing or redistilling of distilled spirits with fruits, flowers, plants, juices, extracts, or other natural flavorings.
- Products containing no less than 2.5% sugar (by weight of the finished product). Note that this is about one-quarter of the level of sugar required by the European Union. In addition, in the United States, the word "dry" may be used on the label of a liqueur that contains less than 10% sugar by weight.

The following US products are further regulated, as stated below:
- Rye liqueur, rye cordial, bourbon liqueur, and bourbon cordial must be bottled at no less than 30% alcohol by volume (60 proof), must be at least 51% rye or bourbon whiskey, and must have a predominant flavor derived from such whiskey.
- Rock and rye, or rock and bourbon, must be bottled at no less than 24% alcohol by volume (48 proof), must be at least 51% rye or bourbon whiskey, must have a predominant flavor derived from such whiskey, and must contain rock candy or sugar syrup.
- Rum liqueur, gin liqueur, and brandy liqueur must be bottled at no less than 30% alcohol by volume (60 proof), and the distilled spirit base must be entirely rum, gin, or brandy, respectively.

The European Union defines a liqueur (but not a cordial) as:
- A drink produced with a spirit base that is sweetened and flavored with agricultural products such as cream, milk, fruit, wine, or aromatized wine.

- A drink that has a minimum sugar content of 70 g/L (7%) for cherry liqueurs, 80 g/L (8%) for gentian liqueurs, and 100 g/L (10%) in all other cases, except for those products that are further defined by name.
- A drink bottled at no less than 15% alcohol by volume (30 proof).

The European Union has slightly different regulations, particularly for sugar and alcohol content for a few specific products, the most well-known of which are listed in table 9.1.

Note: In the European Union, the term *cordial* is not considered synonymous with the term *liqueur*. A cordial is instead defined as a nonalcoholic, flavor-enhancing ingredient used for mixed drinks, cocktails, and nonalcoholic beverages.

Table 9.1: Selected Liqueurs, as Defined by the European Union

SELECTED LIQUEURS, AS DEFINED BY THE EUROPEAN UNION		
Product	Flavor	Specifications
"Crème" Products, as in Crème de Cacao	Varies	Minimum sugar content of 250 g/L (25%)
Crème de Cassis	Black Currant	Minimum sugar content of 400 g/L (40%)
Sambuca	Anise or Star Anise	Minimum alcohol strength of 38% alcohol by volume, minimum sugar content of 350 g/L (35%), natural anethole content between 1 and 2 g/L
Maraschino	Marasca Cherries	Must be colorless, with a minimum sugar content of 250 g/L (25%) and a minimum alcohol strength of 24% alcohol by volume
Nocino	Walnuts	Must be flavored via maceration and/or distillation with whole green walnuts; must have a minimum sugar content of 100 g/L (10%) and a minimum alcohol content of 30% alcohol by volume
Advocaat (Advokaat)	Egg, Sugar, and Honey	Minimum sugar or honey content of 150 g/L (15%), minimum pure egg yolk content of 140 g/L, and minimum alcohol content of 14% alcohol by volume

THE HISTORY OF LIQUEURS

Balms, crèmes, elixirs, oils—all of these terms have been used throughout history to refer to liqueurs. Originally, liqueurs were created for use as medicinal remedies, love potions, and general cure-alls. In the early Middle Ages, the monks and healers, with their limited chemical knowledge, used spirits and botanicals familiar to them to create medicines they deemed beneficial for various maladies.

During the fifteenth century, the physician and philosopher Paracelsus suggested that the goals of those working in the field of medicine should focus less on bloodletting and purging and more on the preparation of imbibable cures and tonics. By then, the therapeutic value of certain seeds, herbs, and roots was well-known. Through trial and error, those plant parts that had little or no value as a medicine were set aside, while others were retained and are still in use today. A modern pharmacopoeia still lists caraway seed, angelica root, oils of orange and lemon, and various herbs as being beneficial to a person's digestion or general constitution.

Figure 9.1: Advertisement for the "Tonic" Liqueur Produced by the Abbey of Saint-Martin-du-Canigou (1911)

In this manner, up to the end of the eighteenth century, liqueurs were primarily flavored with plants, herbs, and spices that were chosen not for their flavor but for their ability to aid a person's health. But by the beginning of the nineteenth century, when chemistry became the dominant science and the preoccupation with the better things in life was in full swing, the evolution of liqueurs appreciated for their flavors and sophistication expanded and became a thriving business in many parts of Europe. France and Italy became the primary producers of liqueurs during the 1800s and remained so until the early twentieth century.

Concurrently, other countries were becoming famous for their liqueurs. Holland became known for orange-flavored liqueurs. Germany gained fame for its herbal products, notably caraway seed preparations. Denmark and Spain found fruit and spice combinations to be very profitable. Scotland and Ireland produced liqueurs using their whiskeys as a base for fruit and herbal concoctions.

The twentieth century brought a large and diverse assortment of liqueurs to the worldwide market. This trend continues today. What started with the production of brandy-based herbal medicines during the Middle Ages has evolved into a broad spirits-based industry. Producers use whiskey, rum, tequila, vodka, neutral spirits, and gin, as well as tried-and-true brandy, as the base spirit. Increasingly complex flavors, new sweeteners, and additives such as dairy products have expanded—and will continue to expand—the range and versatility of the liqueur category.

THE PRODUCTION OF LIQUEURS

The production of liqueurs basically requires the following four steps:
- Selection of the base spirit and flavor source
- Flavor extraction
- Sweetening
- Finishing, which may or may not include coloring or aging

Base Spirit and Flavor Source Selection: A base spirit and a flavor source are selected along with the method that will be used to infuse the flavor into the spirit. A producer may decide to use a base spirit from any spirit category or may simply use a neutral spirit.

These selections are very often dependent on the availability of and proximity to the ingredients. For example, the Scots and the Irish chose to use their whiskeys as the spirit base. The flavorings they chose for their liqueurs came from the available plantings in those countries. More specifically, Drambuie, produced in Scotland, is a product of Scotch, cloves, nutmeg, herbs, and honey.

Alternately, large companies, especially those in countries with no historical tradition of liqueur production, likely take a broader approach in their selection of base spirit and flavorings to produce a product that conforms to marketing trends and meets consumer demand.

Flavor Extraction: Once the flavor profile of the liqueur has been determined, there are two basic ways to extract the flavors: the cold method and the hot method. The choice of method depends on both the desired flavor and the source of the flavor. Generally, fruit flavors are extracted by the cold method, while plant products such as seeds, leaves, roots, and flowers have their flavors extracted by the hot method. For these two basic methods, there are several different processes, again dependent on the ingredients used.

The Cold Method of Flavor Extraction: Generally used for fruit-flavored liqueurs, cold methods are most effective when the flavoring material is sensitive to heat and would, therefore, be damaged by a hot method. The cold method is very time-consuming, sometimes taking up to a year to complete. The cold method has four different processes, the choice of which depends on the nature of the flavoring material.

- **Infusion:** This cold method entails steeping the fruit in a liquid in order to extract the flavor. In the case of infusion, the liquid is usually water. This is the gentlest process. It is used with flavor sources that are very delicate and ethereal. When working with less delicate fruits, the infusion liquid may contain alcohol as well.
- **Maceration:** Similar to the infusion method, maceration is used with hardier fruits and berries. Maceration is more destructive in that the flavor source is cut, crushed, and pressed to expose as much surface area as possible. The flavoring material is then steeped in an alcoholic solution, usually in the 120 proof range, and the mixture is left to extract the desired flavors. A water extraction is rarely used in the maceration procedure.
- **Percolation:** Another method of cold extraction is percolation, or brewing. Leaves, herbs, or other delicate plant materials are placed in an apparatus resembling a large coffee percolator, and the spirit is then continuously pumped over and passed through the flavoring material. The extracting spirit is allowed to flow through the mass of flavorings and extract the aroma and flavor components in a slow, time-consuming manner.
- **Compounding:** Essences and/or concentrates of the flavoring agents are simply blended into the base spirit.

In all four cold methods, the water or alcohol eventually absorbs almost all of the aroma, flavor, and color of the fruit, seed, or other flavoring agent. When the desired flavor is finally obtained, the liquid is drawn off, allowed to settle, filtered, and sweetened to the desired richness. If it is a water-extracted flavor, it will be added to a spirit base.

Figure 9.2: Colorful Array of Liqueurs

The Hot Method of Flavor Extraction: The hot extraction method, sometimes called distillation, is typically used for products flavored by seeds and flowers. These items contain flavors that are more difficult to extract and so require more than a simple soak in a cold liquid to effectively produce the flavor. The flavor components of beans, nuts, seeds, and flowers can generally withstand moderate heat and may also benefit from a quicker extraction of flavor than is possible by using the slower cold methods.

Specifically, the hot method utilizes distillation to extract the essential oils from the flavoring agent. This distillation is normally carried out in small- to medium-sized copper pot stills that resemble those used to make gin.

The normal procedure is to steep the flavoring agent in alcohol for several hours, after which time it is placed in the still with additional spirits and then distilled. The heads and tails are either discarded or redistilled with the next batch.

A variation of this process is used on delicate flowers and herbs, such as mint, roses, and violets, whose aromatics dissipate soon after they are picked. These are distilled quickly and gently in an aqueous solution rather than a spirit. In order to preserve more of the aromas, vacuum distillation is used, which permits the water to boil at a lower temperature.

In practice, a liqueur might use a combination of cold and hot methods, depending on the individual ingredients used. For instance, if both orange and coffee flavors are desired, one might macerate the orange peels to get an orange essence while, perhaps, using a distillation (hot) method with the coffee beans.

Sweetening: Once the flavor has been integrated into the base spirit, regardless of the method used, the liqueur is reduced in strength and sweetened. Sweetening agents include sucrose, high fructose corn syrup, rectified grape must, and honey.

Finishing: Some liqueurs are left to reveal their natural coloration, while others are intentionally colored with either naturally derived coloring or approved food dyes. The addition of color is generally done for marketing purposes, enabling the producer to make its product more attractive or distinctive. For example, crème de menthe is marketed in various hues of green, as well as gold, red, blue, and white (colorless) versions.

While most liqueurs are unaged or perhaps left to age for only a short period of time in order to allow the flavors to meld or mellow, some liqueurs may be barrel-aged before bottling. The proof at bottling is left to the discretion of the producer, within the guidelines of the various legal definitions of the particular product; however, the usual range is from 15% to 40% alcohol by volume (30 to 80 proof).

THE CATEGORIZATION OF LIQUEURS

As there is no distinct formula or set of requirements to produce a liqueur other than the use of a base spirit, flavor, and sugar, the number of combinations is limitless. Consequently, a vast set of liqueurs currently exists, and new products are continually being developed and marketed.

Generic and Proprietary: Within the diverse universe of liqueurs, there are two main classes: generic and proprietary. Generic liqueurs include general flavor categories and may be branded but not trademarked. Thus, there are many similar products on the market. Proprietary liqueurs are the exclusive property of their creators and are made according to a unique recipe, even if the liqueur may fit into an existing flavor category. For example, there are many generic products called coffee liqueur; however, both Kahlúa and Tia Maria are unique, proprietary versions of coffee liqueur. Crème de cacao is generic chocolate liqueur; Godiva Chocolate Liqueur is proprietary. Many proprietary liqueurs are believed to be made according to "secret formulas," and several are based on ancient texts. Producers go to great lengths to guard their recipes.

Irrespective of their class, liqueurs can be categorized into broad types according to the source of their key flavor. These categories include the following:

Fruit Liqueurs: These liqueurs get their dominant flavor from the pulp, skin, peel, or pit of a fruit. While citrus fruits are the most commonly used, there are products flavored with melons, soft fruits, stone fruits, berries, and many others.

Figure 9.3: Proprietary Liqueurs

Botanical Liqueurs: This category includes products flavored with flowers, herbs, roots, or spices. This category is quite varied, as many botanical liqueurs include multiple herbs and spices in their recipes. Some even claim to have hundreds of ingredients in the "secret formula."

Bean, Nut, and Seed Liqueurs: Liqueurs in this category are flavored with various types of nuts, beans (such as cacao and coffee), and seeds. Coffee, chocolate, almond, and hazelnut are among the favorite flavors worldwide.

Cream Liqueurs: This style is relatively new, as the shelf life of cream liqueurs posed problems in the past. In order to avoid spoilage, these products typically use a homogenized mixture of cream, sugar, alcohol, and sodium caseinate. Through this process, the fat globules in the cream are significantly reduced in size in order to stabilize the product. Cream liqueurs that use acidic flavoring agents such as lemon are made with nondairy creamers to avoid spoilage. The cream in such products is not meant to be the key flavor. Rather, it is added to provide a mellowing, textural component to the liqueur. The recent popularity of cream-based liqueurs has led many producers to extend their existing brands with cream versions.

Note: It is important to know that crèmes and creams are quite different. Creams are essentially dairy products (or products made with liquids that resemble dairy products), as described above. Alternately, a crème is a generic liqueur that is more concentrated in flavor and much sweeter than the original liqueur. Regulations stipulate that crèmes are also quite sweet (minimum sugar requirements do, however, vary) and low-alcohol. A crème liqueur has a minimum alcohol content of 15% by volume.

Whiskey Liqueurs: These liqueurs use whiskey as their base spirit, which provides the dominant sensory impression. Examples are Drambuie made with Scotch whisky, and rock and rye made with American rye whiskey. Although this style of liqueur has added flavorings, the aroma and flavor of the base spirit override those of the flavoring element.

Table 9.2 provides examples of both the generic and proprietary liqueurs within the various categories described above.

Table 9.2: Examples of Generic and Proprietary Liqueurs by Category

Category	Flavor	Generic Examples	Proprietary or Branded Examples
Fruit			
	Orange	Triple Sec	Cointreau
	Apple	Sour Apple Schnapps	DeKuyper Sour Apple Pucker
	Melon	Melon Liqueur	Midori Melon
	Cherry	Maraschino Liqueur	Luxardo Maraschino
	Black Raspberry	Black Raspberry Liqueur	Chambord
Botanical			
	Mint	Crème de Menthe	Bols Peppermint Liqueur
	Violet	Crème de Violette	Crème Yvette
	Cinnamon	Cinnamon Schnapps	Goldschläger
	Herbs	(usually proprietary)	Chartreuse
	Elderflower	Elderflower Liqueur	St. Germain
	Ginger	Ginger Liqueur	Canton
Bean, Nut, Seed			
	Hazelnut	Crème de Noisette	Frangelico
	Cacao	Crème de Cacao	Godiva Chocolate Liqueur
	Coffee	Coffee Liqueur	Kahlúa
Cream			
	Egg	Advocaat Liqueur	Baitz Advokaat
	Whiskey	Irish Cream	Bailey's Irish Cream
Whiskey			
	Scotch Whisky	Whisky Liqueur	Drambuie
	Bourbon	Bourbon Liqueur	Jeremiah Weed

THE ESSENTIAL LIQUEURS

While this list is not intended to be exhaustive, it covers what are generally considered to be the most important liqueurs to have in a well-stocked bar. This list also contains some items with historical or traditional significance, and some trendy products as well.

FRUIT LIQUEURS

Triple Sec: The name *triple sec* is a generic term for orange-flavored liqueurs. The origins of the product (and term) remain somewhat debated; however, it is generally accepted that triple sec was first made in France, perhaps as a result of the sudden popularity of Dutch orange liqueurs in the 1800s.

In 1834, one of the earliest versions—known at the time as *Curaçao Triple Sec*—was produced at the Combier Distillery located in Saumur (France). As the story is told, the word *triple* referred to the three-stage, copper pot distillation process that was used. The word *sec* (French for "dry") may refer to either the fact that the orange peels used to flavor the liqueur were dried before distillation, or to the fact that triple sec was intended to be less sweet than other versions of orange liqueur. The Combier Distillery is still in operation and currently produces several versions of triple sec, including *L'Original Combier Liqueur d'Orange*—a proprietary product based on their original 1834 formula. These days, numerous distilleries produce their own versions of orange liqueur using the generic name triple sec. (Generic)

Curaçao: The term *curaçao* is also used as a generic term to refer to orange-flavored liqueur. Oranges were originally brought to the Caribbean island of Curaçao—along with Spanish occupation—in the 1500s. The Spaniards planted Valencia Orange orchards on the island, despite the fact that the climate was not ideal for citrus. The trees managed to survive, however, and eventually adapted to their new environment while producing a small, bitter fruit with inedible flesh but highly fragrant peels. When the Dutch arrived on the island of Curaçao, they used their knowledge of distillation to turn this ungainly fruit into a delectable, sweet style of orange-flavored liqueur. The oranges of Curaçao are now known as *Lahana Oranges*, or by the botanical name of *Citrus aurantium currassuviensis* (meaning "Golden Orange of Curaçao").

The term "curaçao" is not a geographical indication and versions of curaçao liqueur are produced all over the world. One firm, known as Senior & Company, founded on the island of Curaçao in 1896, was among the first local businesses to produce a liqueur from Lahana Oranges. They remain based on the island of Curaçao, and their products may be labeled as "the Genuine Curaçao Liqueur" or "Curaçao of Curaçao."

While typically clear, curaçao is available in a range of colors. Blue curaçao is particularly well-known for its role in brightly-hued cocktails such as the Blue Margarita and the Blue Hawaii. (Generic)

Cointreau: Cointreau is a French orange-flavored liqueur. It was developed by Édouard Cointreau in 1875, at a time when orange liqueurs were all the rage in France. Cointreau was developed as a much drier (less sweet) alternative to popular products such as curaçao. Both bitter and sweet orange peels are used in the initial infusion, which has a neutral spirit as its base. This infusion is then distilled, preserving the orange flavors and aromas but leaving behind the bitter elements of the orange peels. Technically, Cointreau is a type of triple sec, and there are those that claim that Cointreau was the first company to use the term to refer to an orange liqueur. The word triple—in this version of the story—may refer to the third (and final) formula used in the recipe trials for Cointreau, or to the three different types of oranges used for flavoring. (Proprietary)

Grand Marnier Cordon Rouge: Grand Marnier's signature liqueur, made from a distillate of bitter tropical bigaradia orange peels and cognac, was created in 1880 by Alexandre Marnier-Lapostolle of Neauphle-le-Château, France. It is still owned by the Marnier-Lapostolle family today. Originally known as Curaçao Marnier, the product was reportedly christened with the name Grand Marnier by César Ritz (of the Ritz Hotel), who felt that Marnier-Lapostolle should have "a grand name for a grand liqueur." A less sweet and more cognac-forward version known as Cuvée 1880, and the super-premium Quintessence are also available. In certain European markets, you may also see Grand Marnier Cordon Jaune, which uses neutral spirits instead of cognac and is intended to be used more for cooking than drinking, as Grand Marnier is featured in many recipes, including soufflés, crêpes suzette, and duck à l'orange. (Proprietary)

Mandarine Napoléon: Mandarine Napoléon is an orange and tangerine-flavored liqueur originally produced in Belgium. According to legend, the liqueur was created in the 1700s for Napoléon Bonaparte by Dr. Antoine-François de Fourcroy, the emperor's personal physician. Commercial production of the product dates back to 1892, when a Belgian chemist by the name of Louis Schmidt reportedly discovered the recipe for Napoléon's favorite drink in Dr. Fourcroy's diary.

Mandarine Napoléon is made with Sicilian and Corsican mandarins (tangerines) plus a proprietary blend of botanicals—believed to include clove, nutmeg, cinnamon, and cardamom as well as green and black tea. In the first step of production, these flavorings are macerated in a combination of spirits and water which is later distilled in copper pot stills. This flavored distillate is then aged, blended with cognac, sweetened, and finished to a typical bottling proof of 38% abv.

Chambord Liqueur Royal de France: Chambord is a French black raspberry-flavored liqueur. According to a local legend, a wild raspberry liqueur was introduced to King Louis XIV when he visited the Château de Chambord in the Loire Valley. This inspired the modern incarnation, which is still produced in the Commune de Cour-Cheverny in the Loire Valley. It is produced using a time-honored technique of infusing neutral spirits with fresh raspberries and blackberries. A second infusion extracts even more flavor from the fruit. After six weeks total, the berries are pressed, and the infused alcohol, along with the fruit juices and sugars, is then blended with extracts of black raspberries, black currants, vanilla, herbs, and cognac. (Proprietary)

Ginjinha: Ginjinha is a traditional morello cherry liqueur of Portugal. It is particularly popular in Lisbon, where many shops will serve a drink of Ginjinha to customers, and storefront Ginjinha bars abound. Ginjinha is made by infusing ginja berries (as sour Morello cherries are locally known) in brandy. Sugar is also added, along with cinnamon and (perhaps) other ingredients. Ginjinha is traditionally served in a shot form with a piece of the fruit in the bottom of the cup. Homemade Ginjinha is common, although there are many commercially produced varieties as well. (Generic)

Heering Cherry Liqueur: Often referred to as Cherry Heering, this liqueur is produced by Peter Heering, a Danish producer of spirits and liqueurs. Heering Cherry Liqueur has been produced since 1818 and is used in such cocktails as the Singapore Sling and the Blood and Sand. (Proprietary)

Licor 43: Licor 43 *(Cuarenta y Tres)* is a golden-hued liqueur produced in Cartagena, Spain. The name is derived from its unique blend of 43 different flavorings. The exact formula remains a secret of the founders (the Zamora family), but is known to contain Mediterranean citrus, vanilla, and spices. Licor 43 is one of the top-selling liqueurs in Spain, where it is served in a range of styles, including neat, over ice, or as an ingredient in coffee drinks. (Proprietary)

Limoncello: Limoncello is a traditional Italian lemon liqueur produced mainly in southern Italy, especially in the regions around the city of Naples, the Almafi Coast, and the island of Capri. Limoncello is traditionally made from the zest of Sorrento lemons (also known as Femminello Santa Teresa lemons). Two versions of limoncello produced in Italy— Liquore di limone di Sorrento and Liquore di limone della Costa d'Amalfi—have PGI status in the European Union. While many commercial versions exist, there is a significant tradition of homemade limoncello in many parts of Italy. American versions, made primarily with California lemons, are also produced. (Generic)

Figure 9.4: Various Brands of Limoncello for Sale in Capri

Luxardo Maraschino: The city of Zadar on the Dalmatian Coast of Croatia has been known for centuries for the quality of its sour marasca cherries. As far back as the 1700s, when the city was part of the Venetian Republic, high-quality liqueurs produced from marasca cherries were well-known and appreciated throughout the region. Girolamo Luxardo, using his wife's recipe for homemade cherry liqueur, began producing a commercial version of maraschino liqueur in the area in 1821. After the city of Zadar suffered bombings and other tragedies in World War II, the company moved to Italy's Veneto region. The company's iconic green-tinted, squared-off glass bottles with a straw cover are reminiscent of the method used to transport bottles on long ocean journeys during the days of the Venetian Republic. Luxardo Maraschino's use in pre-Prohibition era cocktails such as the Mary Pickford, and in modern classics such as the Hemingway Daiquiri, has fueled a renewed interest in maraschino liqueurs. (Proprietary)

Malibu: A rum and coconut liqueur made in Barbados, Malibu is a traditional concoction that took off in the cocktail culture of the 1980s. Its primary use is to simplify the recipe for a piña colada, as it provides both the rum and the coconut flavors when added to pineapple juice. (Proprietary)

Midori Melon: This muskmelon-flavored liqueur from Japan was first introduced by Suntory in 1978. Although it is made from orange-fleshed melons, the signature bright green color of this liqueur makes it a standout on back bar shelves. In fact, *midori* is the Japanese word for *green*. It is now made in Japan, Mexico, and France. Midori Melon is used in popular cocktails such as the Midori Sour, Sex on the Beach, and the Japanese Slipper. (Proprietary)

Pimm's No. 1 Cup: Pimm's No. 1 Cup is an English specialty drink known as a fruit cup—that is, a beverage intended to be made into a tall drink through the addition of ice, a mixer (typically sparkling wine, sparkling water, ginger ale, or citrus-flavored soda), and a variety of fruit, vegetable, and/or herb garnishes. While generally used in the production of tall drinks, Pimm's No. 1 Cup can technically be classified as a citrus- and herbal-flavored liqueur.

Pimm's was originally produced in 1823 by James Pimm. Pimm owned an oyster bar in the city of London and invented the drink—based on gin and a secret blend of fruit and botanicals—as a digestif. By 1851 the liqueur was in wide-scale production and distribution, and a series of other "cups" had been created to include No. 2 (based on Scotch), No. 3 (based on brandy), No. 4 (based on rum), No. 5 (based on rye whiskey) and No. 6 (based on vodka). All of these new iterations were eventually phased out, but seasonal variations such as Pimm's Vodka Cup and Pimm's Winter Cup (based on brandy) are sometimes available.

Tall drinks made from Pimm's are very popular across England and are a standard cocktail offering at polo matches, garden parties, the Chelsea Flower Show, and Wimbledon. (Proprietary)

BOTANICAL LIQUEURS

Domaine de Canton French Ginger Liqueur: A revival of a Chinese ginger liqueur produced until 1997, Domaine de Canton was first released in 2007. It is a cognac-based French liqueur with ginger as the primary flavor, complemented by orange blossom, honey, and vanilla. (Proprietary)

Figure 9.5: Wild Violets in Provence

Crème Yvette: Crème Yvette is a liqueur flavored with violet petals as well as blackberries, raspberries, wild strawberries, orange peel, and vanilla. It was originally produced in 1890 by the Sheffield Company of Connecticut. Later, it was purchased by Charles Jacquin et Cie and made in Philadelphia until 1969, after which it became unavailable for a while. However, the company revived the production of Crème Yvette in 2009. The new version of the product is made in France and flavored with dried violet petals from Provence. It stars in the classic Blue Moon cocktail as well as in a modern drink known as the Stratosphere, which is a mixture of Champagne and Crème Yvette. (Proprietary)

Liquore Galliano L'Autentico: This sweet herbal liqueur from Italy derives most of its flavor from anise and vanilla, although it also contains extracts of star anise, citrus, ginger, lavender, musk yarrow, cinnamon, peppermint, and juniper. It was first created in Tuscany in 1896 by Arturo Vaccari, who named it for the Italian war hero Giuseppe Galliano. (Proprietary)

Liquore Strega: This Italian liqueur, made from over seventy different ingredients, has been produced since 1860. *Strega* means *witch* in Italian, which may be a reference to the liqueur's city of origin, Benevento, which is purported to have been an historic gathering place for witches. Its recipe is said to be based on a witches' brew believed (by some) to be a love potion. Strega has a vibrant yellow color from the addition of saffron, and a flavor of mint, juniper, and anise. (Proprietary)

Italicus Rosolio di Bergamotto: Italicus Rosolio di Bergamotto is a fairly new product, launched by Italian spirits specialist Giuseppe Gallo in 2016. The concept, however, is based on a very old product known as *rosolio*. Rosolio is a traditional Italian aperitivo flavored with rose petals that dates back to the 15th century. Rosolio was very popular with the Royal House of Savoy and was once produced all over Italy. However, with the passing of the generations (along with the rise and fall of nations), rosolio fell out of favor. Italicus Rosolio di Bergamotto, a modern re-interpretation of this historic product, incorporates a range of botanicals including bergamot orange, chamomile, lavender, cedro lemon (citron), and yellow roses. The result is a bittersweet liqueur with clean, floral-and-citrus flavors and a lingering finish. (Proprietary)

Goldschläger: The word *goldschläger* literally means "gold beater" in German, referring to a metalworker who would pound gold bars into thin sheets of gold leaf. Some of the gold beater's work might make its way into this version of the traditional Swiss cinnamon schnapps with tiny flakes of gold leaf floating in it. (Proprietary)

St. Germain: St. Germain, launched in 2007, is based on an old European tradition of making elderflower syrup and cordials from Alpine elderflowers. Elderflowers are notoriously difficult to use in a distillate, as they tend to lose their aromas unless processed very quickly after picking. St. Germain is produced using modern techniques that overcome these limitations, and the resulting floral flavor of the liqueur tends to shine through in a variety of cocktails. (Proprietary)

Figure 9.6: Elderflowers

Sambuca Romana: Sambuca Romana is one of the most popular brands of traditional Italian anise- or licorice-flavored liqueur. It is a neutral spirit base flavored with anise, elderberries, and a secret recipe of other essences. It is usually served neat with three coffee beans that are said to either represent the Holy Trinity or the wish for health, happiness, and prosperity. Like other anise-flavored spirits and liqueurs, Sambuca tends to "louche," or turn cloudy, with the addition of ice or cold water. (Proprietary)

Note: Many botanical liqueurs, including Chartreuse, Bénédictine, and Jägermeister, contain bittering agents. These products are discussed in chapter 10 under the heading "Spirit Amari." In addition, some products flavored with anise or caraway, such as absinthe, Pernod, pastis, and ouzo, are discussed in chapter 4 under the headings "Anise-Flavored Spirits" and "Other Flavored Spirits."

BEAN, NUT, AND SEED LIQUEURS

Amaretto: *Amaretto* is a generic term for almond-flavored liqueurs. The earliest versions were produced in Saronno, Italy and flavored with bitter almonds. Modern versions are quite sweet and only slightly bitter, and are typically flavored with apricot pits, peach pits, almonds, or extracts. In many such cases, the chemical *benzaldehyde* provides the product's almond-like flavor. Amaretto is popular served as a digestif, in coffee drinks such as the Café Amore, or in a range of cocktails such as the Amaretto Sour, the Godfather, and the Toasted Almond. (Generic)

Disaronno Originale: According to legend, in 1525 a pupil of Leonardo da Vinci by the name of Bernardo Luini was painting a fresco of the Virgin Mary in Saronno, Italy, and used a local innkeeper's daughter as the model. As a gesture of thanks, the model gave the artist a flask of a traditional local liqueur. Years later, Giovanni Reina discovered the recipe for this liqueur and passed it down from father to son within the Reina family. In the early 1900s, the Reina family started to produce it commercially under the name Disaronno Originale. During the twentieth century, it was bottled under the name Amaretto di Saronno Originale and then Amaretto Disaronno, but the decision was made in 2001 to return to the traditional moniker of Disaronno Originale. It is still produced in Saronno, Italy. (Proprietary)

Although the flavor of Disaronno Originale is one of bittersweet almonds, the product is actually an infusion of apricot kernel oil along with a secret recipe of other herbs and fruits.

Frangelico: Frangelico is a relatively modern liqueur, first released in the 1980s, whose bottle and label evoke a historical reference to a monk by the name of Fra Angelico. The bottle is shaped like a monk in his robe and even includes a rope belt tied around the bottle's "waist." Frangelico is made in the Piedmont region of Italy with the primary flavor of local Tonda Gentile della Langhe hazelnuts. The hazelnuts are toasted and crushed and then placed in a solution of alcohol and water. After the infusion of flavor is complete, the solution is distilled to concentrate the hazelnut aromas and flavors. As a final step, the distillate is sweetened and blended with extracts of cocoa, vanilla, and other flavorings. (Proprietary)

Kahlúa: Kahlúa is a rum-based coffee liqueur from Mexico. Kahlúa, which also contains hints of vanilla and caramel, was first produced in 1936 by Pedro Domecq. It is indispensable for making several famous cocktails and mixed drinks such as the B-52, the White Russian, the Black Russian, the Mudslide, and the Espresso Martini. (Proprietary)

Figure 9.7: Espresso Martini

Nocino: Nocino is a walnut liqueur originally from Italy's Emilia-Romagna region. It is produced by steeping green walnuts in spirits. Other ingredients may include cinnamon, clove, or other spices. Nocino has intense aromas and a distinctive bittersweet taste. It is traditionally homemade, although several commercial brands are available. (Generic)

Tia Maria: Tia Maria is a dark liqueur flavored with coffee beans, Madagascar vanilla, and Jamaican rum. Originally produced in Jamaica, Tia Maria is often served on its own, in desserts such as the Tia Maria Torte (made with sponge cake or cookies layered with whipped cream) or in cocktails. Coffee-based cocktails such as the Tia Maria Espresso Martini are especially popular. (Proprietary)

Tuaca: Tuaca is a vanilla-flavored liqueur originally produced by the Tuoni and Canepa families of Livorno, Italy, and now produced by the Tuaca Liqueur Company of Louisville, Kentucky. According to the company website, Tuaca is based on a five-hundred-year-old Tuscan recipe dating back to Lorenzo di Medici. Tuaca is golden brown in color, made with a brandy base, and flavored with citrus (primarily orange) and vanilla. (Proprietary)

CREAM LIQUEURS

Amarula: Amarula is a cream liqueur from South Africa. It is made with sugar, cream, and the fruit of the African marula tree (*Sclerocarya birrea*). The beautiful, leafy, and drought-resistant marula tree grows abundantly in the wild in many parts of South Africa. The fruit of the marula tree is the size of a small plum and has light golden-yellow skin. The white-fleshed fruit has been described as lychee-like, creamy, citrusy, and nutty. The marula tree is also called the elephant tree, as its fruit is a favorite treat of elephants. As such, the elephant is the "symbol" of Amarula and features prominently on the label. (Proprietary)

Bailey's Irish Cream: Shelf-stable cream liqueurs were not a commercial product until the 1970s, when it was discovered that emulsifying the cream and alcohol with refined vegetable oil ensured that the product would not separate at room temperature. Introduced by Gilbeys of Ireland in 1974, Bailey's Irish Cream was one of the first liqueurs on the market that took advantage of this new technique.

The original Bailey's Irish Cream is a blend of aged Irish whiskey, cream, and chocolate; in addition, there are now several variations on the original recipe available, including hazelnut, caramel, and vanilla-cinnamon. (Proprietary)

RumChata: RumChata—the label also reads *Horchata con Ron*—is a cream liqueur made using a base of Caribbean rum. RumChata, produced in the United States, is flavored with cinnamon, vanilla, and other proprietary ingredients. RumChata is typically served on the rocks or in sweet cocktails (similar to those made using other cream liqueurs). The flavor of RumChata is derivative of horchata—a drink enjoyed in Spain and across Latin America made from grains (such as rice or barley) seeds (such as sesame seeds), and/or nuts and flavored with spices such as cinnamon, vanilla, and nutmeg. (Proprietary)

Figure 9.8: The Marula Tree

WHISKEY LIQUEURS

Drambuie: Drambuie is a Scottish liqueur made from Scotch malt whisky and heather honey, with a secret recipe of herbs and spices. The origins of the recipe are in some dispute, but the legend states that in 1746, when Bonnie Prince Charlie lost a battle with the English, the MacKinnon clan helped him escape to the island of Skye. As thanks, the prince granted the MacKinnons this recipe. The recipe ended up in the hands of John Ross, who owned a hotel on the island. He served the liqueur to his guests and coined the name from the Gaelic phrase *an dram buidheach*, "the drink that satisfies." Drambuie was commercially produced for the first time in 1914, coincidentally by another MacKinnon, Malcolm, who had acquired the recipe and the trademarked name from the Ross family. (Proprietary)

Irish Mist: Irish Mist is a blend of Irish whiskey, honey, and spices. The company website claims that the origins of this liqueur can be traced back over a thousand years to a traditional recipe for heather wine. Desmond E. Williams (the "D.E.W." in Tullamore D.E.W.) claimed to have found the recipe in an old Irish manuscript brought to him by a traveler. He began producing Irish Mist in 1947. (Proprietary)

Rock & Rye: Rock & Rye first became popular in America in the 1800s, when bartenders would mix rock candy, sugar, and citrus with young rye whiskey to make a refreshing drink intended to take the edge off of the widely-available—but rather rough-tasting—rye whiskey of the time. With time, the concoction began to blur the line between beverage and medicine as Rock & Rye became known as a useful home remedy. Some versions even managed to remain in distribution through American Prohibition, dispensed by pharmacies and described as an "alcoholic medicinal preparation."

American rye whiskey has improved quite a bit since the 1800s, but Rock & Rye has managed a comeback nonetheless. Today's bartenders may make their own back-bar versions using rye whiskey and rock candy (or—more likely—simple syrup) and flavorings that range from citrus and cloves to vanilla and maraschino cherries. Commercial Rock & Rye liqueurs are also being produced once again. Examples include Hochstadter's Slow & Low Rock and Rye (produced by the Cooper Spirits Co. of Philadelphia) and Mister Katz's Rock & Rye (flavored with cherries, cinnamon, and citrus) produced by New York Distilling Company. (Generic)

Southern Comfort: This American liqueur is an invention of a New Orleans bartender named Martin Wilkes Heron. In 1885, he mixed bourbon with vanilla bean, lemon, cinnamon, cloves, cherries, peaches, and oranges and then let the mixture infuse for a few days. To finish the beverage, he sweetened it with honey. Originally, he called the concoction Cuffs and Buttons, but when he patented his creation and began bottling it, he changed the name to Southern Comfort. The modern version may contain neutral spirits as its base.

# CHAPTER TEN VERMOUTH, AMARI, AND BITTERS

VERMOUTH, AMARI, AND BITTERS

CHAPTER TEN

LEARNING OBJECTIVES

After studying this chapter, the candidate should be able to do the following:
- Discuss the taste component of bitter and its importance to both the alcoholic beverage industry and mixology.
- Define and discuss the various styles of aromatized wines, including vermouth, vini amari, quinquina, and americano.
- Identify and describe the various types and styles of bittered spirits.
- Describe the leading brands of cocktail bitters and explain their use in cocktails, mixed drinks, and other beverages.

Within the family of beverages, there is a broad and fascinating category that varies widely in base source materials, flavor profiles, methods of production, and uses, and yet can be considered a singular category unified by the common use of bittering agents. Within this category, there is a large group of products known as aromatized wines, which include many varieties and types of *vermouth* as well as *vini amari, chinato, quinquina,* and *americano*. Other products in this category include a wide range of bittered spirits known as *amari* or *amer,* and a type of flavoring agent commonly referred to as cocktail bitters.

Technically, aromatized wines may be considered fortified wines instead of spirits; several types of amari may be classified as liqueurs; and cocktail bitters are considered a flavoring agent that is classified as a food, as opposed to a beverage. And yet, all of these products are included in this Study Guide, and specifically in this chapter, because of the unique role they play in the world of spirits and mixology. These products are used throughout the world as aperitifs and digestifs, and also represent some of the most important cocktail ingredients in the bartender's arsenal.

This chapter begins with a discussion of the "bitter" taste component and its importance, both historical and modern, to the world of adult beverages. It then continues on to a discussion of aromatized wines, including the various styles of vermouth, vini amari (bittered wines), quinquina, and americano. This is followed by an examination of bittered spirits categorized into groupings including Italian amari, French amer, and those spirits from other origins. The chapter then concludes with a discussion of cocktail bitters.

THE TASTE COMPONENT OF BITTER

As mentioned in chapter 2, bitterness is one of the five widely accepted basic taste components, the others being sweetness, acidity, saltiness, and umami (the taste component associated with protein). Bitterness is the single most sensitive taste component, meaning that it can be discerned at lower levels than the other tastes. This is possibly because, in many cases, bitterness is nature's way of warning humans and other animals of potential toxicity. Bitterness is, in a way, nature's way of saying, "Don't swallow this; it may kill you."

However, as with other taste components such as saltiness and acidity, bitterness is attractive in small amounts and can serve to sharpen flavors by contrasting with other tastes. While the taste of bitterness is not as widely appreciated in the cuisine of America as it is in many other cultures, some widely appreciated foodstuffs contain some level of bitterness, such as coffee, chocolate, beer flavored with hops, endive, radicchio, and, to a certain extent, vegetables like broccoli and asparagus.

The taste of bitterness stimulates saliva, which causes increased appetite and releases the first enzymes of the digestive process. Individuals may have a widely divergent sensitivity to the taste of bitterness as well as differing levels at which they appreciate the taste, given that bitterness in foods and beverages is most definitely an acquired taste. Concerning all foods and beverages, each of us has different likes and dislikes. Therefore, what may seem unpleasantly bitter to one individual may not even be noticed or detected by another, and what seems delicious to one person may be intolerable to the next.

As a very general rule, Europeans tend to appreciate a bitter taste in both foods and beverages because it has been a standard component in their cuisine for generations. In contrast, Americans, with their so-called sweet tooth for sugars and starches, are not as familiar with or appreciative of bitters.

AROMATIZED WINES

Since the time when wine and beer were first fermented, humans began to add flavorings to these beverages. This may have been done to disguise off-flavors or to enhance, intensify, or preserve the beverage through the addition of sweet, savory, and bitter aromatic compounds.

One of the oldest discovered remains of a fermented beverage in China included aromatized wines—this find dates back to roughly 1250 BCE. The beverage was cited by Dr. Patrick McGovern as being "obviously aromatized with herbs, flowers, and pungent tree resins." Another archaeological team documented the discovery of aromatized wines in Hajji Firuz Tepe, Iran, dating back to circa 5400 BCE.

In Greco-Roman cultures, the most highly sought and expensive wines were often aromatized. A beverage called hippocras, which was a wine infused with absinthium, or wormwood, was a highly sought-after drink in ancient times—one deemed to have healthy and invigorating tonic effects. It was consumed as both a stimulant and a restorative.

Figure 10.1: *Artemisia absinthium* (absinthe wormwood)

People eventually lessened the medicinal focus of these ancient aromatized wines, at which time they evolved into the modern beverages still appreciated today for their stimulative and tonic-like effects. These beverages retain the common element of bitter additives and are enjoyed before a meal as apéritifs (French) or aperitivi (Italian)—or as digestifs/digestivi, which are consumed after a meal in order to aid in digestion. The largest subcategory of aromatized wines is vermouth.

DEFINITION OF AROMATIZED WINES

Aromatized wines, referred to as *vini aromatizzati* in Italian, are wine-based beverages that are flavored with aromatic botanicals. They may have additional spirit alcohol added for purposes of stabilization. Thus, they may technically be classified as fortified wines. Sugar, natural flavorings, and caramel colorings are allowed. Since this is a diverse category of products, aromatized wines may be classified into the following groups: vermouth, vini amari/chinati, quinquina, and americano. These product groupings are detailed in table 10.1.

Table 10.1: Overview of Aromatized Wines

OVERVIEW OF AROMATIZED WINES	
Vermouth	Aromatized, fortified wines typically flavored with artemisia (wormwood) and other approved natural herbs, fruit, spices, or flavorings
Vini Amari/Chinati	Aromatized, unfortified wines produced using a variety of bitter and herbal flavorings
Quinquina	Aromatized, fortified wines flavored with cinchona bark (also known as quina, kina, or china (this last is pronounced *kina* in Italian))
Americano	Aromatized, fortified wines flavored with wormwood and gentian

Aromatized wines have clear definitions and parameters under the laws of the European Union. According to these EU statutes, aromatized wines (with the exception of retsina) must conform to the following:
- Obtained from a wine base of 75% before enhancement
- May have added grape must, fresh or fermenting, to which alcohol has been added (primarily for arresting fermentation and for stabilizing purposes)
- Flavored with the aid of natural flavoring preparations, aromatic herbs, spices, or flavoring foodstuffs
- Generally sweetened and possibly colored with caramel
- Have an alcoholic strength of 14.5% to 22% alcohol by volume, with the following exceptions: "extra-dry" products must have a minimum alcoholic strength of 15% abv; "dry" products must have a minimum alcoholic strength of 16% abv

The EU regulations, which were updated in 2014, also specify finished sugar levels for aromatized wines:
- Extra-dry: Sugar content of less than 30 g/L
- Dry: Sugar content of less than 50 g/L
- Semi-dry: Sugar content of between 50 and 90 g/L
- Semi-sweet: Sugar content between 90 and 130 g/L
- Sweet: Sugar content of more than 130 g/L

The terms *semisweet* and *sweet* may be replaced by an indication of the sugar content expressed in grams of invert sugar per liter.

The European Union also defines the following aromatized wine drinks and cocktails:
- **Sangria:** A red-wine-based beverage with citrus fruit and spices, sometimes including brandy, served over ice. As of 2014, the European Union requires that products labeled as sangria must be a product of either Spain or Portugal. Sangria produced outside the Iberian Peninsula must be labeled with the place of origin, as in "German sangria."
- **Clarea:** A white-wine-based beverage made with honey and spices. The original recipe, prepared for King Fernando I of Naples, dates to the 1500s.
- **Zurra or Zurracapote:** Similar to sangria, zurra is a Spanish red-wine-based beverage made with fruit such as peaches and lemons that, for several days before drinking, are macerated with sugar, cinnamon, fruit juice, and, sometimes, brandy.
- **Kalte Ente:** A sweetened drink made with white wine, sparkling wine, and lemon, traditionally made in Germany with Riesling and sparkling wine.
- **Glühwein or Gluehwein:** A red or white wine flavored with sugar, cinnamon, and clove. Traditionally served warm, especially at Christmastime, in Germany, Austria, and Alsace.
- **Maiwein:** An aromatized wine drink flavored with *Asperula odorata* (sweet woodruff). Other ingredients may include strawberries, brandy, sparkling wine, and sugar. Also known as May wine, maiwein is a traditional German beverage served on May Day and throughout the spring.

- **Cremovo:** An egg-based aromatized wine made with marsala. Produced exclusively in Sicily, where it may also be called *Marsala all'Uovo*.

Under the laws of the United States, aromatized wines—including vermouth—are included in the classification of *aperitif wines*. According to the regulations that define vermouth and other aperitif wines, they must be:
- A product based on grape wine,
- fortified with brandy or other alcohol to a minimum alcoholic content of 15% by volume,
- flavored with herbs and other natural aromatic flavoring materials,
- produced with or without the addition of juice, concentrated juices, sugar, and/or caramel coloring.

VERMOUTH

Vermouth is produced using a wine base that has been aromatized with some version of the *artemisia* herb, along with any other approved natural herbs, fruits, spices, or flavorings. The word *vermouth* itself is derived from the name of the herb artemisia, which is commonly known as *wormwood* in English and as *vermut* in German. In the EU, vermouth is defined as a fortified, aromatized wine that must be flavored with Artemisia (and may contain other flavorings and sweeteners).

The type of wine base varies, as do the botanical formulas used by each producer. Most vermouth is made with a white wine base, although the variety of wine varies widely. Many of the products known as red vermouth are colorized via the botanicals used in the production process, as well as with allowed caramel food coloring. One exception to this rule is P. Quiles Spanish vermouth, which uses a red wine base made using the Mourvèdre grape variety.

Vermouth is generally fortified with spirits to stabilize the product. Some styles are produced with enhanced complexity via oxidative barrel aging and exposure to the elements.

Vermouth was originally consumed either straight or diluted with other liquids to create a tonic beverage to stimulate the appetite and enhance digestion. Over the centuries, however, vermouths have been used as flavoring ingredients in mixed drinks and cocktails. They now constitute a major segment of the cocktail industry. Many classic cocktails, such as variations of the Martini, the Manhattan, and drinks in the Americano/Negroni family, include vermouth. Also, vermouth is used extensively in cooking, primarily to add aromatic and flavor complexity to dishes.

With its wine base, vermouth is subject to increased oxidation when left open and unrefrigerated. Consequently, many of the vermouths used in bars and restaurants seem flat, dull, and stale, bereft of the very aromatics that are supposed to define them. However, with tight seals, refrigerated storage, and the absence of direct sunlight, vermouth (as well as most other aromatized wines) can usually maintain sufficient vivacity for a few weeks. Unless high usage dictates larger bottles, it is advisable to use smaller (375 ml) packages of aromatized wines when available in order to promote freshness.

There are several dominant vermouth-producing regions as well as several types of vermouth recognized, primarily in Europe but increasingly in other parts of the world. Among the most highly prized and widely distributed are the following examples:

Chambéry: Located in the French Alps, the city of Chambéry has a long and storied history. At one time, Chambéry had numerous producers of fortified and aromatized wines and was considered one of the centers of vermouth production. Today, however, only a few houses remain.

The House of Dolin, one of the original producers of Chambéry vermouth, pioneered the light, dry style of vermouth in France in 1832. This original product, Dolin Dry White Vermouth, is described as a clean, fresh, floral style of vermouth. Other products produced by Dolin include Dolin Blanc, a traditional herbal-focused style vermouth, and a full-bodied rouge/red vermouth that—while being somewhat drier than most red vermouths—is still quite sweet and has noticeable characteristics of bitter wormwood. In addition to vermouth, Dolin produces a wide range of assorted aperitif and digestif wines and spirits as well as a local favorite, *Chamberyzette*, which blends Dolin dry vermouth with the juice of wild strawberries.

Chambéry is also home to the *Distillerie des Alpes*, a producer of vermouth and liqueurs—some of which are based on formulas passed down from Philibert Routin, an herbalist who lived in Chambéry in the late 1800s. Routin vermouth products are based on white wine from Savoie, and include Routin Blanc (infused with a range of flavorings including vanilla, thyme, and elderflowers), Routin Dry (produced using 17 botanicals including bitter almonds, rosemary, and rose petals), and Routin Original Rouge, produced using Philibert Routin's original formula from 1883.

Figure 10.2: Noilly Pratt, Carpano Antica Formula, and Lillet

Noilly Prat: The Noilly Prat brand is today's main producer of Marseilles-style vermouth. As a port city, Marseilles was once another large center for vermouth production. The Marseilles style of vermouth is noted for its oxidative, lightly wooded, almost marsala-like properties.

Founded in 1813, Noilly Prat is produced in Marseillan (which, despite the similarity in names, is a 130-mile drive from Marseilles). Historically, its vermouths were produced with proprietary secret recipes, all based on white wine, and with an emphasis on barrel-aging.

Styles produced by Noilly Prat today include dry white vermouth, sweet red vermouth, and *ambre*. Although the recipes remain secret, Noilly Prat has cited chamomile, gentian, nutmeg, and bitter orange peel in the recipe for its original dry white vermouth, and saffron, cloves, and cocoa beans for its sweet red vermouth. The amber version is rich and slightly sweet with mellow flavors of herbs and spices. The company has acknowledged the inclusion of cardamom, cinnamon, and lavender in its proprietary ambre blend.

Torino-Style Vermouth: The city of Torino (Turin) in the Piedmont region of northwestern Italy is the uncontested center of Italian vermouth production. Torino-style vermouth is, in turn, quite likely the dominant style of red/rouge vermouth worldwide. This style of vermouth tends to favor slightly more sweetness through the addition of sugar. Also, it emphasizes floral notes and spices over the herbal components.

One notable producer of Torino-style vermouth is *Carpano*, founded in Turin in 1786 by Antonio Benedetto Carpano. Antonio Carpano is often credited with being the "original inventor of vermouth." The company, which currently produces several styles of vermouth, is well-known for the *Carpano Antica Formula* and *Punt e Mes*. (As of 2001, the Carpano brand is owned by the Milanese firm Branca.)

Carpano Antica Formula Vermouth is high-end red vermouth created from the resurrected ancient recipe. It is designated as *vermouth alla vaniglia* for its heavy addition of natural vanilla.

Carpano Punt e Mes engendered an entirely new type of vermouth now known as *vermouth con bitter* or *vermouth amari*. As the story goes, the local stockbrokers who gathered each night at their favorite drinking establishments frequently refreshed themselves with vermouth cocktails. One style that became popular was the Punt e Mes, or "Point and a Half," curtly ordered in stockbroker sign language with an upthrust thumb—a point—and a sideways swipe and a half of the palm. Upon seeing this, the bartender would add a hefty dollop of bitters to a glass of vermouth. The Carpano family capitalized on the popularity of the local drink by blending bitters with vermouth and bottling it as Punt e Mes.

Giulio Cocchi was another of the earliest producers of Torino-style vermouth. He began making aromatized wines and sparkling wines in the town of Asti (about 30 miles/48 km southeast of Turin) in 1891. His distillery—and his and chain of Cocchi Tasting Bars located throughout Piedmont—were soon famous for their Barolo Chinato, Cocchi Aperitivo Americano, sparkling wines, and a range of vermouths. Today, known as Giulio Cocchi Spumanti Srl, the company creates a wide range of products, including grappa, sparkling wine, and amari. Their flagship products include Cocchi Storico Vermouth di Torino—a sweet, amber-hued vermouth produced from Giulio Cocchi's original, 120-year old recipe. The formula remains a closely-guarded secret, but it is reported to contain cocoa, rhubarb, citrus peel, and Moscato wine (in addition to artemisia).

Other vermouth producers abound in and around Torino, most of which produce Torino-style red vermouths as well as a range of other products. These firms include Martini & Rossi, Cinzano, Contratto, Gancia Rosso, and Casa Martelletti. Boissiere, which produces Boissiere Extra Dry and Sweet Red Vermouth, was for many years produced in Chambéry, but the company was purchased and moved to Torino in 1971. Their dry white vermouth is considered stylistically reminiscent of the original style of Chambéry vermouth, but it is now produced (along with their sweet red vermouth) in Torino.

Vermouth di Torino PGI: While many styles of vermouth are produced surrounding the city of Turin (Torino), a specific product referred to as Vermouth di Torino has protected geographical indication (PGI) status in the European Union. Under these standards, which were updated in early 2017, Vermouth di Torino PGI must be produced within the region of Piedmont using a base of Italian wine, and must be fortified with the addition of spirits. The main flavoring must be artemisia (with additional herbs

Figure 10.3: Cinzano Vermouth

and spices allowed), and the alcohol by volume must be between 16% and 22%. The standards also allow for a Vermouth di Torino Superiore PGI, with a minimum of 17% alcohol by volume. At least 50% of the base wine and the flavorings used for Vermouth di Torino Superiore PGI (aside from the artemisia) must be grown in Piedmont.

Trieste Vermouth: Trieste, an Italian city since the end of World War I and, prior to that, a largely Slovenian province of the Austro-Hungarian Empire, is home to Stock Spirits Group (Stock SpA), a large producer of a wide portfolio of spirits, wines, and vermouths. While the Stock rosso, bianco, and extra-dry vermouths are made in Trieste, they are considered to be of the Torino style.

Spanish Vermouth: Spanish vermouths (known as *vermut* in some parts of Spain) are abundant but are generally not familiar to Americans for the simple reason that until quite recently, Spanish vermouths were not widely exported to the United States. However, vermouth is very popular in Spain, so much so that a gathering of friends (what Americans might call "happy hour") is often referred to as *fer el vermut* ("doing vermouth"). Spanish vermouth is routinely consumed on the rocks with a splash of soda water, and garnished with—perhaps—a wedge of orange or some green olives.

Table 10.2: Common Brands and Styles of Vermouth

COMMON BRANDS AND STYLES OF VERMOUTH		
Brand/Type	Region of Origin	Notes
Dolin	Chambéry, France	Produces a range of styles, but known for creating the "light, clean" style of dry white vermouth
Routin	Chambéry, France	Range includes Routin Blanc, Routin Dry, and Routin Original Rouge; produced by Distillerie des Alpes
Noilly Prat	Marseillan, France	Originally produced in Marseilles; the "Marseilles Style" is oxidative and lightly wooded
Giulio Cocchi	Torino, Italy	Makes a range of products, including some versions produced according to the Vermouth di Torino PGI
Carpano Antica Formula Vermouth	Milan, Italy	High-end red vermouth with a heavy addition of vanilla; originally produced in Torino
Carpano Punt é Mes	Milan, Italy	Red Vermouth with bitters—Vermouth con amari—originally produced in Torino
Martini & Rossi Cinzano Contratto Gancia Rosso Casa Marteletti	Torino, Italy	Most produce "Torino style" red vermouth as well as a complete line of other styles
Boissiere	Torino, Italy	Produces "Extra Dry White" and sweet red, originally located in Chambéry
Stock S.p.A.	Trieste, Italy	Produces a complete line of vermouth; considered to be "Torino Style"
Perucchi	Badalona (Catalonia), Spain	Produces red, white, extra-dry, reservas, and special releases
Yzaguirre	Reus (Catalonia), Spain	Produces red, white, rosé, reservas, and special releases
Miró	Reus (Catalonia), Spain	Founded in 1957, produces a wide range of products including white, red, and "fusion"
Casa Mariol	Tarragona (Catalonia), Spain	Especially well-known for Casa Mariol Vermut Negre (black vermouth)
P. Quiles	Alicante, Spain	Made using a red (Mourvèdre) wine base
Lustau Vermut	Andalucía, Spain	Based on two types of Sherry, described as "Premium Red Sherry Vermouth"
Gallo Vermouth Triburno Vermouth Vya Vermouth Sutton Cellars Vermouth Imbue Bittersweet Vermouth Ransom American Vermouth Atsby Vermouth Uncouth Vermouth +Many more producers	New World	Varies, including non-traditional flavors

The Spanish are very supportive of their local vermouths, many of which are house-made in restaurants and bars. Catalonia—particularly the town of Reus—has been the epicenter of Spanish vermouth production for well over a century. Red vermouth is the main style produced; however, Spanish red vermouth tends to be somewhat lighter and less bitter than red (Torino-style) vermouth produced in Italy. A range of Spanish vermouths, featuring those that are best-known outside of the country, are discussed below.

- **Perucchi:** Perucchi vermouth has been produced in the Catalonian town of Badalona (just north of Barcelona) since 1876. Perucchi produces a range of products including red (rojo), white (blanco), extra-dry, reservas, and special editions—all based on Spanish wines from Empordà, Valencia, and La Mancha. Perucchi vermouths, produced using over 50 specific botanicals, are often noted for their characteristic aromas of chamomile, ginger, lemon verbena, cinnamon, mint, and orange blossom.
- **Yzaguirre:** Bodegas Yzaguirre is located in the province of Tarragona in Catalonia, Spain. Begun in 1884, it produces a range of vermouths, including red, white, rosado (rosé), and reserva versions as well as special releases. Yzaguirre is a classic "mistela" vermouth, with some products made using a base of unfermented grape must (juice) fortified with spirits to arrest fermentation. Some versions are oak-aged and cited for a unique balsamic character.
- **Miró:** Vermouth Miró was founded in 1957 in Reus, a Catalonian city long-known for the production of vermouth. A range of Miró products are produced, including classic red and white styles as well as extra dry and reserva styles. Unique products, such as Miró & Paco Perez Red Fusion (a red vermouth with a touch of salinity) and a canned vermut with cola—*vermucola*—are made as well.
- **Casa Mariol:** Casa Mariol Vermut is made by the Vaquer family, producers of artisan Spanish wine and vermouth for over 100 years. The company, located in Tarragona (Catalonia), produces a range of products, but is especially known for Casa Mariol Vermut Negre (black vermouth). Vermut Negre is produced using a base of local white wine made from Macabeo (also known as Viura) grapes and fortified with grape neutral spirits. Over 160 botanicals are used as flavorings, including green walnuts, thyme, rosemary, orange peel, and cardamom. After the blend is completed, the vermouth spends up to six months in a solera-style oak-aging system.
- **Primitivo Quiles:** Primitivo Quiles vermouth, better known by its label as P. Quiles, is produced in the Alicante area of Spain's Valencian Community. Primitivo Quiles produces traditional "alpine style" vermouths in a bodega dating back to 1780. While most vermouth is made with white wine (gaining its color from the botanical ingredients), P. Quiles vermouth uses red wine based on the Mourvèdre grape variety. Because of this, it has a deep, natural coloration. Primitivo Quiles cites cinnamon, clove, ginger, and nutmeg as part of its proprietary formula of botanicals.
- **Lustau:** Recently, the area of Jerez (in Andalucía) has begun to revive the tradition of making vermouth based on sherry—the fortified wines of Jerez. Bodegas Lustau has created their own version—Vermut Lustau—described as a "premium red sherry vermouth." Vermut Lustau uses two kinds of well-aged sherry as its base—one sweet (Pedro Ximénez), and one dry (Amontillado). The resulting vermouth is lightly sweet with a noticeable sherry influence as well as aromas and flavors of dried fruit, orange peel, cinnamon, and herbs.

NEW WORLD VERMOUTH

Many aromatized wines are now being produced throughout the New World, particularly in the United States. Many craft wineries and distilleries, taking advantage of the somewhat less restrictive regulations placed on these products, are beginning to explore the creative possibilities of aromatized wines. Some strive to produce classical but proprietary versions of Old World vermouths, while others are creating entirely new styles and flavor profiles.

This highly creative sector of the US beverage industry changes frequently; however, the following new brands have established themselves as vermouth producers to watch:
- Vya Vermouth from California
- Sutton Cellars Vermouth from California
- Imbue Bittersweet Vermouth from Oregon
- Ransom American Vermouth from Oregon
- Atsby Vermouth from New York City

Another producer, *Uncouth Vermouth* from Brooklyn, embodies the "new style" of American vermouth. Their product has very little relation to traditional vermouth styles and has a more fruit/herb/spice-focused character. Uncouth Vermouth flavors include apple and mint; pear, ginger, and butternut squash; beet and eucalyptus; and Serrano chili and lavender. More such brands and types are entering the market with increasing frequency.

Other American wine and spirits companies have been producing vermouth for quite some time. Among the best known, Gallo Wine Company has long produced a modestly priced, widely distributed line of red and white vermouths. Another line of vermouth, the low-priced Tribuno brand, has been produced for many years by the Wine Group.

VINI AMARI/BITTERED WINES

As with the category of aromatized wines, there is a wide variety of products that fall under the category of wine-based amari, or *bittered wines*. These wines differ from typical vermouth in that they are unfortified. Currently, there are only a few of these products available in the United States; however, with renewed interest in artisanal beverages of all kinds, this is likely to change in the future.

One of the most well-known examples is a traditional beverage of Piedmont, Italy, known as *Chinato d'Erbetti,* the last word of which translates as "bitter and herbal." A version known as *Barolo Chinato,* produced with Piedmont's renowned Barolo wine, is becoming both well-known and widely distributed. Barolo Chinato consists of Barolo wine (which, by definition, is a sturdy red wine produced from 100% Nebbiolo grapes) steeped in a proprietary selection of bitter herbs.

Craft winemakers and distillers in the United States are beginning to copy the style of Chinato d'Erbetti. For instance, winemaker Patrick Taylor of Cana's Feast in Oregon produces a highly lauded product based on wine made from the Nebbiolo grape variety and including extracts of (at last count) eighteen different botanicals, including mace, fennel, coriander, black pepper, rhubarb, elderflower, dried orange peel, rose, clove, cinnamon, and a few "undisclosed" secrets.

Figure 10.4: Purple Cardoon

Another interesting example of vin amaro, and one of the few available in the United States, is *Cardamaro*. Cardamaro is flavored with cardoon and blessed thistle, both relatives of the artichoke, which were used in the Middle Ages and the Renaissance to combat the plague. Cardamaro is produced in Piedmont, Italy, and based on Moscato wine. Being based on a sweet white wine, Cardamaro is milder, mellower, and less intensely bitter than other bittered products. It typically shows a decidedly nutty, oxidized, and aldehydic sherry-like character.

Table 10.3: Common Brands and Styles of Vini Amari

COMMON BRANDS AND STYLES OF VINI AMARI		
Brand/Type	Region of Origin	Notes
Barolo Chinato	Piedmont, Italy	Based on Barolo wine (made with the Nebbiolo grape variety); representative of Piedmont's traditional Chinato d'Erbetti, a bitter and herbal beverage
Cardamaro	Piedmont, Italy	Based on Moscato wine, flavored with cardoon and blessed thistle
Cana's Feast Winery Chinato d'Erbetti	New World	Produced in Oregon; representative of New World creations based on the vini amari tradition.

QUINQUINA

Quinquina wines, like vermouths, are flavored and fortified, but *cinchona bark* (the original quinine base used to treat malaria), rather than wormwood, is the primary botanical. The bark, which is generally from either Peru or India, is either chipped or powdered and then macerated in the wine. Sugar and other botanicals, as well as fortifying spirits, may be added. Europe has a long history of using cinchona bark, which is also known as *quina, kina,* or *china* (pronounced *kina* in Italian), for medicinal and beverage purposes.

Some of the more well-known versions of quinquina are discussed in the sections that follow.

Figure 10.5: Cinchona Bark

Lillet: *Lillet,* a mild quinquina, was created in Podensac, Bordeaux, in 1887 from locally sourced wine, fruits, and herbs. The original product, based on white Bordeaux wine, was dubbed *Kina Lillet.* This original Lillet was reformulated in 1986 to make it a bit less bitter and a bit less sweet. It is now known as *Lillet Blanc.* The change did not sit well with some people, so there are many consumers who still mourn the loss of the "original" Kina Lillet. Nevertheless, *Lillet Rouge* was introduced in 1962, followed by *Lillet Rosé* in 2010. As of 2013, reserve versions of Lillet—intended to be able to improve over 15 to 20 years of proper bottle aging—were created, based on the more prestigious wines of Bordeaux. Two styles of Lillet Réserve are currently available, albeit in very small quantities: Réserve Jean de Lillet Blanc (based on Sauternes) and Réserve Jean de Lillet Rouge.

Bonal Gentiane Quina: Produced in France, *Bonal Gentiane Quina* is based on mistelle (grape juice fortified before fermentation begins or very soon after the start of fermentation). The mistelle is infused with gentian root, cinchona, and a variety of herbs found in the local Chartreuse Mountains. Bonal is reddish brown in color and has a balanced flavor that is sweet, bitter, and noticeably woody in aroma and flavor.

Dubonnet: *Dubonnet* was originally created in Paris, France, in 1846 as Quinquina Dubonnet; the name was later simplified to Dubonnet. It is generally considered to be one of the lightest products in the quinquina category. Since World War II, American Dubonnet has been produced, via licensing agreement, by Heaven Hill Distilleries in Kentucky.

That said, there is some question as to how closely the American version follows the European version. In any case, the original Dubonnet was rouge. The blanc version of Dubonnet was a later addition, made only for the American market.

Figure 10.6: Dubonnet Poster by Jules Chéret (1895)

Byrrh: *Byrrh,* originally produced in the Roussillon region of France, combines a mistelle made using the grapes of the region, mainly Carignan and Grenache varieties, with selected dry red Roussillon wines. This mixture is then soaked with dried, crushed cinchona bark and other botanicals before being aged for three years in *foudres* (large wooden barrels).

Invented by brothers Pallade and Simon Violet in 1866 as a health tonic, Byrrh was imported to the United States until Prohibition. The brand was purchased by Pernod Ricard in 1976, which produces Byrrh at their location in Thuir (in the South of France). As of 2012, it is available in the United States once more.

In 1999, a high-end version known as *Byrrh Rare Assemblage* was introduced. Byrrh Rare Assemblage is aged for a minimum of ten years in small oak barrels. It has been described as having a mahogany hue, intense aromas of candied red fruit, and flavors of vanilla, coffee, and spice.

St. Raphael: *St. Raphael* is a quinquina created in 1830 with a mistelle base flavored with quinine extract, bitter oranges, cocoa, vanilla, and other ingredients. The original inventor, a French physician known to history simply as Doctor Juppet, reportedly became nearly blind while working on his quinquina-based elixir. However, he recalled the biblical story of Tobias, who was cured of blindness by the archangel Raphael. The good doctor claimed that he invoked the protection of the angel and then his sight was restored. In homage, he named his new product St. Raphael. St. Raphael has a balanced level of sweetness and bitterness characterized by red fruits with a hint of chocolate complexity. It is generally served on the rocks with a twist of lemon as an aperitif. Both an amber and a rouge version are produced.

In addition to wine-based quinquina, there are several popular nonalcoholic soda and tonic brands based on cinchona bitters.

Table 10.4: Common Brands and Styles of Quinquina

COMMON BRANDS AND STYLES OF QUINQUINA		
Brand/Type	Region of Origin	Notes
Bonal Gentiane Quina	Saint-Laurent-du-Pont, France	Based on mistelle, gentian root, cinchona, and local herbs. Balanced with a slightly woody flavor.
Dubonnet	Originally produced in Paris, France; versions for the US market are made in Kentucky	Considered to be one of the lightest versions of the category. Originally produced as a rouge. A blanc version was created for the American market.
Lillet	Bordeaux, France	Currently produces four versions: blanc, rouge, rosé, and the limited edition Cuvée Réserve Jean de Lillet.
Byrrh	Roussillon, France	Based on red grapes native to the Roussillon region of France. Two versions, including a high-end "Rare Assemblage," are produced.
St. Raphael	Lyon, France	Produced in both amber and rouge styles.

AMERICANO

Americano is a category of aromatized, fortified wines flavored with wormwood and gentian. Gentian is a flowering plant that grows throughout Europe's mountainous regions including the Alps, the Pyrenees, the Vosges, and the Massif Central. Several varieties of gentian—including *Gentiana lutea* (yellow), *Gentiana punctata* ("spotted"), and *Gentiana purpurea* (purple)—are used in the production of flavored wines, spirits, and other beverages.

These aromatized wines, despite the name americano, are not to be confused with the popular Americano cocktail, which is a concoction of Campari, sweet red vermouth, soda, and citrus peel. In this instance, the word does not reference America, but *amer,* the French word for *bitter.*

Some of the better-known examples of americano are described below.

Cocchi Americano: Produced in Piedmont, Italy, by the house of Giulio Cocchi, the classic white version of Cocchi Americano is based on Moscato d'Asti wine and is flavored with cinchona bark, citrus peel, spices, and other botanicals. A red version, based on a wine produced from a blend of Brachetto and Malvasia grapes, contains the same flavorings as the white version, with the extra addition of rose petals and ginger.

The white version of Cocchi Americano is considered to be the one contemporary product that comes closest to the flavor of the "original" Kina Lillet. It is often mentioned as a substitute in classic drink recipes that list Kina Lillet as an ingredient, such as the Vesper Martini (as ordered by James Bond in *Casino Royale*) and the Corpse Reviver #2.

Contratto Americano: Produced in Piedmont, Italy, by the house of Giulio Cocchi, the classic white version of Cocchi Americano is based on Moscato d'Asti wine and is flavored with cinchona bark, citrus peel, spices, and other botanicals. A former producer of Vermouth di Torino, Contratto currently produces red and white vermouth, fernet, and americano rosso, along with a portfolio of still and sparkling wines. *Contratto Americano Rosso* is based on white wine made from the Cortese grape (a specialty of the Piedmont region), botanicals steeped in brandy, caramelized sugar, and over thirty other ingredients including mint, ginger, hibiscus flower, nettle, wormwood, lemon peel, licorice, angelica, and bitter orange peel.

Table 10.5: Common Brands and Styles of Americano

Brand/Type	Region of Origin	Notes
Cocchi Americano	Torino, Italy	Produces both a Moscato-based blanco and a "rosa" version made with Brachetto and Malvasia grapes.
Contratto Americano	Torino, Italy	Produces a rosso based on Cortese grapes, colored with caramelized sugar and flavored with over thirty botanicals.

SPIRIT AMARI

The beverage world abounds with spirit amari (bittered spirits), which may be classified as aperitifs, which are generally served in diluted forms as cocktails to stimulate the appetite, or as digestifs, which are often served in more concentrated forms to enhance digestion after a meal. The digestif versions usually contain botanicals with carminative properties intended to lessen gastric discomfort after rich meals. Botanicals known for their carminative properties include angelica, aniseed, basil, caraway, cardamom, cinnamon, coriander, cumin, dill, fennel, ginger, hops, nutmeg, parsley, and sage.

Spirit amari are made in a variety of styles and flavors. The more highly sweetened versions may technically fall within the classification of liqueurs if they have sufficient amounts of sugar. Others may be categorized as proprietary or specialty beverages that do not easily fit within the typical spirit classifications. Spirit amari may be produced with a primary overriding botanical base or be composed of a complex botanical blend. Some purport to have more than a hundred savory ingredients as part of a secret formula.

ITALIAN SPIRIT AMARI

Amari (the plural of *amaro,* the Italian word for *bitter*) are very popular in Italy, where they are commonly consumed neat or on the rocks, either before or after a meal as an aperitivo or digestivo, respectively. Amari produced in Italy are also the most likely versions of spirits amari to be distributed in the United States and other locales outside of Europe. A few, but by no means all, of the most well-known examples of Italian spirit amari are discussed in the sections that follow.

Fernet Branca: *Fernet Branca* was invented in Milan in 1845 by Bernardino Branca. It soon became famous worldwide and led to the founding of the Fratelli Branca Distillery. A sweeter, mint-flavored version of fernet known as Branca Menta is also produced.

Fernet has recently become quite popular in the United States as both a beverage and a hangover cure, but its popularity long precedes the craft cocktail scene. So popular is it among industry professionals that a shot of Fernet Branca has been called the "bartender's handshake." In Prohibition-era San Francisco, fernet was legally consumed on the grounds of its being "medicinal." San Franciscans still drink it—over 30% of the fernet consumed throughout the entire United States is consumed in San Francisco. Argentina consumes more fernet than any other nation. The beverage's popularity is reflected in the fact that a leading *cuarteto* (a popular, upbeat dance-hall music genre) song is titled "Fernet con Cola."

The secret recipe for Fernet Branca is reportedly known by only one person, Niccolò Branca, the current president of the Fratelli Branca Distillery. It is said that Niccolò personally measures out the flavorings for each production run.

The Branca brand, while definitely one of the better-known, is not the only producer of fernet. Fernet is actually a type of herbal-based bitter that is made by other producers as well. Many Italian companies, including Luxardo, Cinzano, and Martini & Rossi, produce fernet. Fernet is produced internationally as well, such as in Mexico, where the popular Fernet-Vallet is made.

Each brand of fernet has its own secret combination of herbs and botanicals. However, a good fernet is likely to include myrrh and saffron, both known for their "digestivo" and antioxidant properties. Other ingredients rumored to be included are linden, galangal, peppermint oil, sage, bay leaves, gentian root, St. John's wort, rhubarb, chamomile, cardamom, aloe, and bitter orange.

Figure 10.7: Various Bottles of Fernet

Cynar: *Cynar*, currently produced by the Campari Corporation, was first produced in Italy in 1949. Cynar is a member of a unique class of amari that are made with artichokes, which are known as *carciofo*. The name Cynar references the Latin name (*Cynara scolymus*) of the artichoke. Cynar contains *cynarin*, a chemical compound found in the artichoke that, for many people, makes things taste sweeter. Wine professionals are well aware of the unique food-and-wine interactions that can occur when wine is paired with artichokes. Cynarin is the culprit.

Cynar is made from a secret recipe of thirteen botanicals in addition to artichokes. Despite its ingredients, Cynar does not necessarily taste like artichoke, although there is definitely a vegetal and herbal flavor. In Italy, it is generally consumed neat or with a single ice cube as an aperitivo, or mixed with soda. Cynar has been available in the United States for more than a decade. It is also popular in Italy, Brazil, and Switzerland.

Zucca: Ettore Zucca created his eponymous amaro in 1845 using rhubarb, gentian, cardamom, and vanilla, as well as spices and botanicals advised by Chinese herbal medicine. The spirit was much appreciated by King Vittorio Emmanuel. Consequently, Ettore Zucca was awarded a contract to supply the royal house of Italy with his amaro.

Zucca has a bittersweet, smoky flavor profile and is often served neat as an aperitivo or over ice with soda. Zucca is somewhat difficult to find outside of Europe, but in Italy, it is well-known as the featured drink at the Zucca bar in the galleria at the Piazza del Duomo in Milan.

Campari: *Campari* is an amaro with an intense bitter-orange flavor. Originally called *Bitter Uso Campari,* it was invented by Gaspare Campari in the Novara region of Italy (west of Milan) in 1860. By 1880, Campari was widely popular as an aperitivo rather than a digestivo, which gained it a unique place in the market. Just after 1900, Campari opened its first large-scale production plant in Sesto San Giovanni and began exporting Campari overseas.

Campari was one of the first Italian amari to become popular outside of Europe. This popularity can be at least partially attributed to a few well-known cocktails featuring Campari. The Americano (originally called the Milano Torino) features Campari, sweet vermouth, and soda over ice; the equally popular Negroni is made with Campari, sweet vermouth, and gin, served over ice. Today, Campari sells almost three million cases per year.

Figure 10.8: The Negroni, a Classic Cocktail Made with Campari

Averna: In the 1800s, Sicilian businessman Salvatore Averna was a generous benefactor of the local Santo Spirito Abbey. As a token of their appreciation, in 1859, the monks gifted Salvatore with the recipe for their famous bitter health elixir made with Sicilian herbs. He soon began to make the elixir for his friends and family. Sometime later, his son Francesco began to produce *Averna* in greater quantities, aggressively marketing the product at wine fairs in Italy and abroad. Today, the company is still owned by the Averna family and is managed by their fourth generation.

Averna is a smooth, rich, brown amari with flavors of licorice, cola, sassafras, chocolate, and citrus. Averna is generally used as a digestivo and in unique cocktails such as the Black Manhattan, which combines Averna with bourbon and bitters (shaken and strained into a chilled glass).

Amaro Nonino: The House of Nonino was founded in 1897 in Friuli. Since then, it has been producing unique, single-variety grappas and single-vineyard grape brandies, as well as fruit brandies, liqueurs, and other spirits. In 1933, Nonino produced its first amaro based on grape brandy and local herbs from the Carnia Mountains.

Their current amari offering, *Amaro Nonino Quintessentia,* has been produced since 1993. Based on Nonino single-variety grape brandy, the product is flavored with a wide variety of botanicals, including gentian, rhubarb, orange peel, quassia wood, tamarind, saffron, and licorice. Whenever possible, local products are used. Amaro Nonino Quintessentia has a smoothness not always seen in other amari, a result, no doubt, of five years of aging in oak barrels of Nevers, Limousin, and ex-sherry origin.

Ramazzotti: Amaro Ramazzotti, based on a proprietary blend of 33 herbs, roots, and other botanicals, was originally created by Ausano Ramazzotti in 1815 in Milan—making it one of the oldest commercially-produced amari in Italy. In 1848, the first Ramazzotti bar was opened near the La Scala Opera House in Milan, where the locals would often drink Ramazzotti in place of coffee. Ramazzotti is dark brown in color with a strong herbal and spicy aroma (often compared to root beer, licorice, or chocolate) and a bittersweet flavor redolent of citrus zest, herbs, coffee, and spices.

While the formula remains a closely-guarded secret, it is known to contain Sicilian orange peels, bitter oranges from Curaçao, star anise, clove, cardamom, galangal root, myrrh, cinchona, rhubarb, gentian root, and caramel. Ramazzotti is often enjoyed as a digestivo, served either neat or on the rocks with a slice of lemon or orange.

Amaro Montenegro: Amaro Montenegro was first created by Stanislao Cobianchi in Bologna in 1885. Stanislao was an adventurer who traveled the world seeking out unique flavorings, and his amaro is said to contain botanicals from "the four corners of the world." The amaro is named in honor of Princess Elena Petrović-Njegoš of Montenegro, who would become the second queen of Italy several years after her 1896 marriage to Victor Emmanuel III of Italy. The overall flavor of Amaro Montenegro is complex, often described as slightly sweeter and less bitter than most amari.

The formula remains undisclosed; however, the company does admit to its use of artemisia, nutmeg, cloves, cinnamon, marjoram, oregano, coriander seeds, and oranges. The production process includes macerating, boiling, and distilling 40 component botanicals into a series of extracts designed to provide the following six aromatic notes: bitter and herbaceous, spicy and floral, sweet and roasted, fresh and balsamic, fruity and vegetal, and warm and tropical. A final ingredient—known as the *premio*—is produced from a secret blend of five botanicals and added at the end of the production process.

Aperol: *Aperol* was invented in 1919 by Silvio and Luigi Barbieri in Padua, Italy. The two brothers wanted to produce a slightly less bitter, lower-alcohol amaro and so created Aperol, which has between 11% and 15% alcohol by volume and a bright orange color. The spirit is flavored using sweet and bitter oranges, tangerines, herbs, spices, and vanilla. After its introduction, Aperol quickly became successful and has remained so ever since. Aperol is often served as an aperitivo as well as in a cocktail known as the Aperol Spritz, which combines Aperol, Prosecco, and a splash of soda, served over ice with an orange twist.

Table 10.6: Selected Brands of Italian Spirit Amari

SELECTED BRANDS OF ITALIAN SPIRIT AMARI		
Brand/Type	Primary Flavors	Style
Fernet Branca	Herbal blend	Very bitter and complex; used as a digestivo. A mint-flavored Branca Menta is also produced.
Cynar	Carciofo (artichoke)	Herbal and astringent; used as an aperitivo and mixer.
Zucca	Rabarbaro (rhubarb)	Tart, bright, and bitter; used as an aperitivo.
Averna	Sicilian root herbs	Cola and sassafras flavors; used as a digestivo and mixer.
Amaro Nonino	Citrus, floral, tamarind, herbs	Bright, citrusy, and floral; used as an aperitivo, digestivo, and mixer.
Campari	Bitter oranges	Bright, fruity, and floral; used as an aperitivo and mixer.
Aperol	Orange, tangerine	Fruity and citrusy; used as an aperitivo and mixer
Ramazzotti	Citrus, roots (root beer), spices	Bitter, spicy, and complex; used as a digestivo served neat or on the rocks.
Amaro Montenegro	Citrus, floral, cinnamon	Bittersweet, used as a digestivo or mixer.

FRENCH AMER

Chartreuse: Chartreuse is a spirit with a long and fascinating history. The story begins in 1605, in a suburb of Paris, when François Annibal d'Estrées, a marshal of King Henry IV, gave the monks of the Carthusian Order a mysterious ancient document. The manuscript, a formula for an "Elixir of Long Life," was most likely the work of a sixteenth-century alchemist who had great knowledge of using herbs and plants to treat illness.

The formula, containing over 130 ingredients, was so complex that it was never fully deciphered by the monks at the monastery. Thus, in the early 1700s, they sent the manuscript to the Grande Chartreuse—the head monastery of the Carthusian Order. The apothecary for the Grande Chartreuse undertook an exhaustive study of the formula and, by 1737, had unraveled the mystery and designed a practical formula for the preparation of the elixir.

The monks began producing the formula, which was sold in the town of Grenoble and other villages located close to the Grande Chartreuse Monastery. The elixir had a natural, clear green color. From the fame of the liqueur, the color became known as chartreuse. Today, Chartreuse still bills itself as "the only liqueur to have a color named after it."

Figure 10.9: Promotional Poster for Chartreuse (1940)

The monks protected their secret recipe throughout the centuries, including the tumultuous time surrounding the French Revolution when all religious orders were expelled from France. The Chartreuse monks left France in 1793, but one monk remained behind with a copy of the manuscript. Another monk secretly retained the original. Shortly after leaving the Grande Chartreuse Monastery, he was arrested and sent to prison in Bordeaux. However, he was not searched and eventually passed the original document to a friend, Dom Basile Nantas. Dom Basile was convinced that the monks of the Grande Chartreuse would never return to France, so he sold the recipe to a pharmacist in Grenoble by the name of Monsieur Liotard. Monsieur Liotard, however, never attempted to produce the elixir. When he died, his heirs returned the manuscript to the monks of Chartreuse.

The monks of Chartreuse were allowed to return to their monastery in 1816. They resumed the production of their Chartreuse elixir and, in 1838, introduced Yellow Chartreuse, a sweeter version flavored with saffron.

In 1903, the French government expelled the monks once again, and the Chartreuse distillery was nationalized. The monks fled to Spain and built a new distillery in Tarragona, where they produced a liqueur they called Une Tarragone.

In the years following the nationalization of the distillery and monastery, the French government sold the Chartreuse brand and trademark to a company that set up an operation known as the Compagnie Fermière de la Grande Chartreuse. The company went bankrupt in 1929. Upon the announcement of the bankruptcy, friends of the monks purchased the remaining shares and gifted them back to the monastery.

After regaining ownership of their brand and trademark, the monks returned to their distillery located in Fourvoirie, not far from their original monastery, and resumed production of authentic Chartreuse liqueurs. When, in 1935, the Fourvoirie distillery was severely damaged by a landslide, the monks moved to Voiron, where the production facility still exists today.

The selection and preparation of the secret blend of over 130 herbs is still done today in the monastery. Once prepared, the ingredients are taken to the production facility in Voiron, where they are macerated, distilled, and aged in oak casks for several years. In addition to Green Chartreuse and Yellow Chartreuse, a special bottling known as VEP (the acronym for "Vieillissement Exceptionnellement Prolongé") Chartreuse is produced. VEP is aged longer than the other two products and is packaged in a reproduction of the bottles used in 1840. Each bottle of VEP is individually numbered, sealed with wax, and presented in a wooden box.

Since 1970, a company known as Chartreuse Diffusion handles the packaging, marketing, and distribution of Chartreuse products. However, the Carthusian brothers still prepare and produce the liqueur. To this day, they remain the only people who know the secret formula for their "Elixir of Long Life."

Figure 10.10: The Grande Chartreuse Monastery, Located in a Remote Mountain Valley North of Grenoble, France

Suze: Suze was created in Paris in 1889 by a distiller named Fernand Moureaux. The original recipe called for wild gentian root harvested from the mountains of the Jura and Auvergne regions of France. Other ingredients in this highly aromatic, bright yellow liqueur include vanilla, dried wildflowers, fennel, bitter oranges, and honey.

Now produced by Pernod Ricard, Suze has long been popular in Europe and is among the top-selling aperitifs in France. The fame and reputation of Suze received quite a boost in 1912 when it was featured in the painting *Verre et bouteille de Suze* (*Glass and Bottle of Suze*) by Pablo Picasso (currently on display at the Kemper Art Museum in St. Louis). Suze has recently become available in the US market.

Bénédictine: The legend surrounding the origin of Bénédictine tells us that it all began in 1510, when Dom Bernardo Vincelli, a monk at Fécamp Abbey in Normandy, created a recipe for a secret elixir. The legend continues 350 years later, in 1863, when Alexandre Le Grand, a merchant and collector of religious art, discovered the lost recipe among his collection of religious artifacts.

There is some debate as to whether or not the part of the legend involving Bénédictine monks is true. Some people claim that the formula was, in fact, developed by Alexandre Le Grande in the nineteenth century and that the tale concerning the monks was created for marketing purposes.

Nevertheless, the cognac-based liqueur is today produced in a flamboyant palace in Fécamp, built in homage to the original Abbey of the Bénédictine Order. Every distinctively shaped bottle of Bénédictine bears the initials "D.O.M.," which stand for "Deo Optimo Maximo" ("To God most good, most great"). This abbreviation, used as a dedication, appears at the top of all official documents of the Bénédictine Order.

The liqueur is based on a closely guarded secret blend of twenty-seven herbs, spices, and other botanicals. It is believed that the main ingredients include angelica, hyssop, lemon balm, wormwood, and herbs from the French Alps. The company also produces B&B (Bénédictine and Brandy), which is not as sweet and is less intensely herbal in flavor than the original recipe. A high-end version packaged in a unique black bottle, Bénédictine Single Cask, is available only at the company's retail store in Fécamp.

The Vieux Carré, a classic cocktail invented at New Orleans' famed Carousel Bar, combines Bénédictine with rye whiskey, cognac, and sweet vermouth.

Figure 10.11: Alembic Still on the Grounds of the Bénédictine Museum in Fécamp, France

Picon: The original version of Picon was developed by a gentleman named Gaétan Picon in 1837. Distinctly bitter orange in flavor, it enjoys quite a following as an aperitif and mixer in France.

Picon is locally renowned in the Basque regions as a main ingredient in Picon Punch, a cocktail featuring Picon, grenadine, and soda water served over ice with a twist of lemon. The cocktail is described as "the Basque national drink." Other cocktails featuring Picon include the Brooklyn—a variation on the Manhattan that features Picon, rye, dry vermouth, and maraschino liqueur—and the Liberal Cocktail, which is made with Picon, sweet vermouth, and orange bitters.

The legendary "original" formula for Picon has been revised several times; currently, it is produced in two styles, Picon Club and Picon Bière, the latter being a lighter version intended for mixing with pilsner or wheat beer. Picon is still difficult to find outside of Europe, so recipes for the classic cocktails featuring Picon sometimes must be made with a different version of bittered spirits. What makes for the best substitution is the topic of many a great bar-based debate.

Table 10.7: Selected Brands of French Spirit Amers

SELECTED BRANDS OF FRENCH SPIRIT AMERS		
Brand/Type	Primary Flavors	Style
Chartreuse	Alpine herbs	Bright, sharp, and floral, made in both green and yellow; used as an aperitif and mixer.
Suze	Gentian, honey	Bitter and lightly sweet; used as an aperitif and mixer.
Picon	Bitter oranges	Fruity, floral, and spicy; orange aroma and flavor; used as an aperitif and mixer.
Bénédictine	Alpine herbs	Bittersweet and herbal; used as a digestif and mixer.

BITTERED SPIRITS OF OTHER ORIGINS

Jägermeister: Jägermeister is the top-selling bittered spirit in the world and one of the leading spirit exports of Germany. The spirit is produced using a closely guarded formula of fifty-six different botanicals; the company's website does, however, admit that the top five are ginger root, cinnamon, star anise, green cardamom, and orange peel. The botanicals are macerated with the base spirits for five months and are then aged in large oak casks for at least a year. This style of herbal liqueur is widely produced and appreciated in Central Europe, where as a category it is known as *kräuterlikör* (herbal liqueur).

The name Jägermeister means "master of hunters" in German and references Curt Mast, the original distiller of the product. Mast was an enthusiastic hunter, and upon perfecting his formula of purely natural ingredients in 1934, he dedicated his product to all hunters and their honorable traditions.

This respect for hunting is reflected in Jägermeister's iconic label, which depicts a glowing cross between the antlers of a stag. This trademark reflects the story of Saint Hubertus, the patron saint of hunters, who is said to have converted to Christianity after experiencing a vision of a Christian cross between the antlers of a stag.

Zwack Unicum: Unicum, produced in Budapest, Hungary, is a bold, bitter liqueur created using over forty different botanicals. It is aged for six months in oak barrels. Unicum was invented in 1790 by Dr. József Zwack, royal physician to the Hungarian court, in order to settle the stomach of Emperor Joseph II, then the Holy Roman Emperor and King of Hungary. The beverage is said to have received its name when Emperor Joseph proclaimed, "Dr. Zwack, das ist ein Unicum!"—meaning the drink was "rather unique!"

In 1840, the doctor's son, József Junior, founded J. Zwack and Partners, the first Hungarian liqueur manufacturer. Soon, J. Zwack and Partners was one of the leading distilleries in eastern Europe, producing over two hundred varieties of spirits and liqueurs and exporting them all over the world. The distillery was handed down through the generations and successfully operated until the facility was completely destroyed during World War II.

After the war, in 1948, the distillery was seized from the Zwack family and nationalized by the communist regime. János and Péter Zwack, the respective grandson and great-grandson of the founder, escaped the country with the original Zwack recipe. Another grandson, Béla, remained behind with a "fake" Zwack recipe and became a regular factory worker.

Figure 10.12: Zwack Unicum

Meanwhile, János and Péter migrated to the United States and settled in the Bronx. Péter worked diligently in the liquor trade until 1988, when, one year before the fall of the communist regime, he returned to Hungary and repurchased the Zwack production facility from the state. By 1990, production of the original Zwack formula and many other products resumed. The Zwack Company has since recovered its position as the leading distillery of eastern Europe and is now run by the sixth generation of the Zwack family.

Becherovka: Becherovka, produced in the city of Karlovy Vary in the Czech Republic, was invented by British-born Josef Vitus Becher in 1807. Becher ran a general store and pharmacy featuring herbal remedies and tonics in addition to his homemade alcoholic beverages. For many generations, Becherovka was produced by a succession of Becher family members. Today, it is produced by Pernod Ricard and is distributed to many parts of the world, including the United States.

Becherovka is made from a closely guarded recipe of over twenty botanicals, many of them sourced from the area around Karlovy Vary. Today, only two people know the secret formula and are permitted to enter the production plant's "Drogikamr room" where, several times a year, they meet to measure and weigh the precise amounts of dried flowers, leaves, barks, and roots that will flavor the next batch of Becherovka.

Becherovka is bittersweet with spicy flavors of ginger, cinnamon, and clove. As with many bittered spirits, it is meant to be consumed neat, chilled, or over ice as a digestif. A cocktail known as the Beton (a conflation of the words *Becherovka* and *tonic*) was invented to be served in the Czech Pavilion at the 1967 World Expo in Montreal and has been popular ever since. The Beton consists of Becherovka and tonic with a squeeze of lemon, served tall over ice.

Gammel Dansk Bitter Dram: Gammel Dansk was created in 1964 at De Danske Spritfabrikker (Danish Distillers) in Aalborg, Denmark. J. K. Asmund, the production manager of the facility, and his staff wanted to create a commercially produced bitter liqueur using the rowanberry, in homage to the long tradition of locally produced rowanberry bitters. While the complete recipe of twenty-nine botanicals is a company secret, Gammel Dansk is purported to include, in addition to rowanberry, star anise, nutmeg, ginger, laurel, gentian, Seville orange, and cinnamon. The spirit is copper-colored, moderately bitter, and quite spicy.

Gammel Dansk translates as "Old Danish." The beverage is enjoyed as a traditional drink at festivals, weddings, and gatherings of all kinds. As birthday celebrations in Denmark traditionally begin in the morning, the spirit is a favorite at birthday breakfasts as well.

Margerum Amaro: Produced in Santa Barbara, California by winemaker Doug Margerum, Margerum Amaro is a product of the producer's lifelong love of Italian Amari. Margerum Amaro is based on late-harvest, red grape-based wine fortified with grape neutral spirits. The product is then infused with various botanical roots and barks along with dried orange peel and a range of herbs including sage, thyme, and lemon verbena. Finally, it is aged in neutral, 225-liter French oak barrels that are kept outdoors in order to give the amaro a unique level of complexity via maderization.

Table 10.8: Bittered Spirits of Other Origins

Brand/Type	Source	Primary Flavors	Uses
Jägermeister	Germany	Ginger, green cardamom, cinnamon, herbs, and spices	As an aperitif, digestif, and mixer
Becherovka	Czech Republic	Ginger, cinnamon, root herbs	As a digestif and mixer
Gammel Dansk Bitter Dram	Denmark	Rowanberry, anise, gentian, ginger, cinnamon	As an aperitif, digestif, and mixer
Zwack Unicum	Hungary	Complex; roots, spices, herbs	As a digestif
Margerum Amaro	United States	Botanical roots and bark, dried citrus peel, herbs, and caramelized sugar	As a digestif and mixer

Bittered spirits were fairly unknown in the United States until the recent revival of cocktail culture, but the category is becoming more accessible and popular, albeit from a relatively small base. Significant growth has occurred in on-premise venues that singularly serve bitters as aperitifs or digestifs. The increasing practice of including amari in cocktails has also contributed to this growth.

Table 10.9: Top-Selling Bittered Spirits Brands Worldwide

Rank	Brand
1.	Jägermeister
2.	Fernet Branca
3.	Aperol
4.	Campari
5	Ramazzotti

Source: Drinks International (2018)

COCKTAIL BITTERS

Cocktail bitters reside in a class by themselves. Essentially, cocktail bitters are aromatics and flavoring extracts that have been macerated in neutral spirits. Cocktail bitters are so intensely concentrated as not to be considered potable on their own—or, as the official phrasing has it, "Not for singular consumption." Most cocktail bitters are botanicals in a neutral spirit base, although, while uncommon, it is possible to produce bitters with a glycerin base.

In the United States, cocktail bitters are considered "food extracts" and are therefore regulated by the Food and Drug Administration (FDA) rather than by the Alcohol and Tobacco Trade and Tax Bureau (TTB) or other alcohol-regulating agencies. Thus, they have wider distribution than wines and spirits, including in most food and grocery stores.

Cocktail bitters began, much like many other spirit groups, as medicinal and restorative tonics created by infusing botanicals in alcohol in order to extract their (presumed or actual) health benefits. One of the most prevalent forms of bittering agents used was Peruvian cinchona bark, also called quinine, which became popular as part of the potions used to treat malaria and tropical fevers. Other common bittering botanicals were used as well, and many are still in use today, such as caffeine, hops, gentian, and burdock root, as well as many other forms of herbs, roots, leaves, barks, and spices.

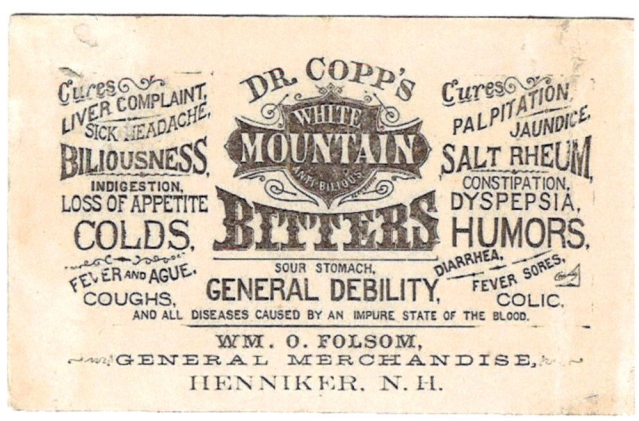

Figure 10.13: Advertisement for Dr. Copp's White Mountain Bitters (1849)

Some of these medicinal elixirs were favored as refreshing beverages, while others remained in highly concentrated form as tonics. In many cases, the tonics came to be used to flavor other beverages, as in the Gin and Tonic, the Pink Gins, and other such drinks, where a dash of bittering agents is called for to liven the drink. Bitters were so much a part of beverage culture that the earliest definition of a cocktail included a bittering agent. To be exact, the definition, formulated in 1806, listed "spirits of any kind, sugar, water, and bitter."

Outside of FDA regulations regarding use of certain approved foodstuffs, there is no limit or regulation on what may constitute a recipe for cocktail bitters; thus, much is left up to the discretion and whim of the creator. Cocktail bitters have found a new popularity, and there are many unique, creative products on the market today. However, there are four "classic" brands of cocktail bitters that have stood the test of time; at least one of these is generally found in any good bar, whether commercial or at home. These are discussed below.

Angostura Bitters: The most well-known of the cocktail bitters began with the House of Angostura. Angostura Bitters were created as a medical concoction in 1824 by Dr. Johann Siegert, a doctor in Simón Bolivar's Venezuelan army. It was named after the town of Angostura (later, Ciudad Bolivar), although, oddly enough, the recipe did not contain the local angostura bark as an ingredient, even though other bitters did. The House of Angostura later relocated to Port of Spain in Trinidad, where it resides today. The company also owns and operates rum distilleries on the island, both for the Angostura brand and by general contract for several others. Readily recognizable with its bright yellow cap and oversize paper label, Angostura is easily the world's dominant brand of bitters.

Peychaud's Bitters: Peychaud's Bitters were invented by the Haitian Creole Antoine Amédée Peychaud in his apothecary shop in New Orleans, circa 1830. The concoction was originally designed to go in his powerful spirit libations said to be served in dainty eggcups known by the French term *coquetiers* (a possible explanation for the origin of our term "cocktail"). This is a savory, exotic style of bitters with highly lifted aromatics. Peychaud's Bitters are an integral part of the original recipe for the Sazerac cocktail.

Figure 10.14: Flowering Gentian Plant. The root of the gentian plant is a common ingredient in bitters.

Fee Brothers Bitters: The Fee brothers and their extended family began their company with a saloon, eventually becoming a supplier to other saloons and grocers by providing bar products. Their most notable product was Fee Foam, a foaming agent used to enhance or replace egg whites in cocktails. The company soon branched out, very successfully, to provide a full range of bar products such as botanical waters, cocktail brine, cordial syrups, Margarita salt, and mixers. The Fee brothers created and expanded their repertoire of flavored bitters until they became the third most prevalent cocktail bitters brand in the United States. Fee Brothers Bitters come in over a dozen flavors, including Aztec chocolate, black walnut, cherry, celery, West Indian orange, peach, and gin-barrel-aged orange.

Regan's #6 Orange Bitters: Orange bitters were once very common; however, with time, they dwindled down to such obscurity that only a few examples remained—and even these were seldom seen in bars. In 1990, Gary and Mardee Regan, writers and cocktail ambassadors of the first order, were so frustrated by the lack of the good orange bitters they needed to make their classic pre–Prohibition era cocktails that they decided to create their own. They progressed through several renditions until they arrived at the perfect formula, which they named Regan's #6 Orange Bitters. The success of Regan's #6 Orange Bitters has been emulated to the extent that other companies are now making their own versions of orange bitters.

As a pleasant side effect of the current cocktail renaissance, the bitters market is exploding with artisanal and local versions of cocktail bitters, with more entering the market each day. Bittermen's, the Bitter Truth, Bittercube, Basement Bitters, and Bar Keep Bitters are among the many artisan-produced bitters available today. A plethora of flavors are also being produced; one can find bitters based on fennel, lavender, grapefruit, rhubarb, dandelion, molé, pineapple, apple, curry, and Jamaican jerk seasoning. The creativity for bitters, it seems, knows no bounds.

CHAPTER ELEVEN MIXOLOGY

MIXOLOGY

CHAPTER ELEVEN

LEARNING OBJECTIVES

After studying this chapter, the candidate should be able to do the following:
- Identify the key ingredients, glassware, and equipment needed to properly stock a full-service bar.
- Compare and contrast cocktails and mixed drinks, citing several examples of each.
- Discuss the various mixing methods used in the preparation of drinks, and identify the style of drinks best prepared by each.
- Identify and describe the twelve basic drink families.
- Describe the importance of responsible beverage alcohol service.

Mixology is a modern term referring to the study of beverages, particularly spirits, and the art of preparing mixed drinks and cocktails. Those who practice the craft are often called mixologists. While some people still prefer the term *bartender* to *mixologist*, many like to think that the renewed interest in classic recipes, craft cocktails, and unique, fresh ingredients combined with the high level of skill required by today's practitioners of the craft calls for a new term.

This chapter begins with a very brief history of mixology, followed by a definition and clarification of "cocktails" and "mixed drinks." It then proceeds to the basics of bar setup, such as the necessary fixtures, equipment, and tools to operate efficiently. The chapter concludes with a discussion of the most common mixing methods, a taxonomy of drink families, and some notes on responsible beverage alcohol service.

A selection of recipes for making cocktails and mixed drinks is provided later in this guide, in appendix C.

A (VERY BRIEF) HISTORY OF MIXOLOGY

Some of the earliest alcoholic beverages may be considered mixed drinks. The earliest-known wine-beer concoction dates back to the Neolithic period, around 7000 BCE. This beverage is believed to have been produced in the region around Jiahu, China, using a base of fermented rice combined with grape wine, honey, and herbs. According to Dr. Patrick McGovern, the concoction was typical of alcoholic beverages in early times. According to his book *Origins and Ancient History of Wine,* alcoholic beverages in ancient Greece and the Middle East were similar blends, created both to preserve the beverage as long as possible and improve the palatability of those early alcoholic drinks. The addition of botanicals and resins, such as pine resin and juniper, continue as a tradition to this day.

The evolution of mixed drinks took another broad leap forward during the seventeenth century, when the widespread availability of rum in Great Britain and the American colonies led to the development of many early recipes to create punches, shrubs, sangarees, flips, caliboguses, crustas, bounces, and syllabubs, to name but a few of the beverages enjoyed at the time. There is no doubt that the rough, unrefined flavor of these early alcoholic beverages was a driving force behind these early "mixed drinks."

The American Revolution proved to be another turning point in the evolution of popular drinks. At the beginning of the conflict, when the importation of rum and other spirits from Great Britain was banned, Americans found themselves without alcoholic refreshment. So, Americans began distilling their own whiskeys in earnest, although most were of dubious quality. By mixing whiskey with sugar and bitters, the taste was improved; by serving it on ice, it became even better still.

American whiskeys, thanks in good part to immigrants from Scotland and Ireland, improved and became more distinct. As these American whiskeys made their way down the Ohio and Mississippi Rivers to New Orleans, the Sazerac—one of the original American cocktails—was born. Served (or, perhaps, as some versions of the story tell, measured) in a two-sided eggcup called a coquetier (pronounced *cock-tee-ay*), the Sazerac also lays claim to the origin of the word *cocktail*.

Figure 11.1: Jerry Thomas Demonstrating His Famous Blue Blazer (1862)

In 1787, American whiskeys were used to create another of America's favorite cocktails, the Mint Julep. While the landed gentry used expensive imported brandies to create their versions, the general public used American whiskeys. The next step in the evolution of the American cocktail scene is credited to Jerry Thomas, who, in 1862, completed *The Bartender's Guide,* also known as *How to Mix Drinks, or the Bon-Vivant's Companion,* the first drink book ever published in the United States. Jerry Thomas was so renowned for his creativity, showmanship, and professionalism that he earned the nickname "Professor" Jerry Thomas. He is considered the forefather of today's modern mixologist.

The etymological derivation of the term *cocktail* is disputed, but one of the first known uses of the word as a reference to an alcoholic beverage appeared in 1806, in a New York serial publication known as *The Balance and Columbian Repository*. The publication defined a cocktail as "a stimulating liquor composed of spirits of any kind, sugar, water, and bitters." The article also called a cocktail "an excellent electioneering potion, in that it renders the heart stout and bold, at the same time that it fuddles the head." *The Century Dictionary* formalized the term by 1889, defining the cocktail as "an American drink, strong, stimulating, and cold."

COCKTAILS AND MIXED DRINKS

The terms *cocktail* and *mixed drink* are often used interchangeably. There are, however, several important distinctions that can be drawn between them.

A cocktail is a short drink (one that is typically presented in a small glass) made by mixing liquor or wine with other spirits, fruit juices, egg whites, and/or bitters. A cocktail is created by mixing together two or more ingredients to create a new flavor that is greater than the sum of its parts. No single ingredient should overpower the other. Cocktails are stirred or shaken with ice in bar glasses or cocktail shakers, and served in a short glass (rocks glass or tumbler) or stemmed glass.

Although generally served without ice, the cocktail may be served on the rocks (with ice) if the guest calls for it.

Figure 11.2: The Cosmopolitan Martini is a cocktail, rather than a mixed drink, as it is typically shaken or stirred with ice and served in a small (generally stemmed) glass.

Mixed drinks, on the other hand, are tall drinks presented in a glass such as a highball glass, generally served over ice. Mixed drinks combine liquor with a mixer—one as simple as water or as complex as several kinds of fruit juices or various carbonated sodas. They are generally served in a base (unstemmed) glass.

MODERN MIXOLOGY AND CRAFT COCKTAILS

Modern mixologists are reviving the art of handcrafted cocktails and mixed drinks with an emphasis on freshness, creativity, and customer service. While the term "craft cocktail" is bordering on overuse, a good definition begins with original recipes that use fresh ingredients and quality spirits with an emphasis on flavor and presentation. Fresh juices, house-made mixers, house-made infusions, fresh herbs, freshly ground spices, and custom glassware are often part of a craft cocktail program. Unique customer services, such as customizing drinks to match a meal, providing tableside service, and offering a "bartender's choice" menu item where a bartender creates a customized drink based on the patron's preferences or cravings, are also part of modern mixology.

Revamped and revived "vintage" cocktails from the early years of cocktail culture are also part of the trend. A selection of such classic drinks is found in table 11.1.

KEY INGREDIENTS FOR THE BAR

Key ingredients with which bartenders work include spirits and liqueurs, ice, mixers, juices, simple syrups, bitters, garnishes, and sundries. As in any other dimension of the culinary world, great products can only be created if all the ingredients are of high quality.

SPIRITS AND LIQUEURS

As seen in previous chapters, spirits and liqueurs are produced in a wide array of styles, flavors, and quality levels. Low-cost "generic" spirits generally have more impurities and may have a harsh alcoholic finish. Each spirit and liqueur has characteristics and flavors that allow it to be uniquely integrated with different mixers. Most bars will utilize at least three of the four quality levels of spirits, depending on the clientele they are attracting: generic, premium, super-premium, and ultra-premium. Fine dining establishments may dispense with generic spirits, just as a neighborhood corner bar may choose not to carry ultra-premium brands.

ICE

Ice was a key American ingredient that helped transform the bartender from a mere server to an artist. From the 1830s on, clean ice from New England was widely available, even in summer months, and Americans quickly acquired a taste for it. Accordingly, building drinks shaken with or stirred over ice became a common practice.

Tools and techniques for ice production and use have become much more sophisticated as of late, and it is widely accepted that the size, shape, and quality of the ice used will have a distinct effect on the taste and flavor of a drink.

Small ice cubes melt faster than larger cubes and can lead to watery, diluted drinks. Accordingly, a drink made with small or hollow ice cubes will taste best—and decidedly different—when it is first served, as the melting ice can quickly dilute mixed drinks.

Large, dense cubes of ice are decidedly superior for use in serving spirits on the rocks or in highballs. Larger ice cubes will melt more slowly and release less water into a drink; thus, a drink made with large ice cubes (or ice balls) will taste better—and more consistent—from the first sip to the last.

House-made ice in various shapes and sizes, including the popular ice ball, has become a staple of craft and artisanal cocktail production. Specialty ice machines can now produce ice in a variety of shapes and sizes. Individually produced ice gets even more creative. Ice molds can be found in cubes and balls of all sizes, as well as specialty shapes such as long, narrow tubes for use in highballs and pea-size ice for mists and frappés. Some establishments are even going "old school" (and ultra-high-quality) with their ice programs and hand-carving large ice blocks into balls, diamonds, chips, or cubes to order.

Table 11.1: Selected Vintage Cocktails

	SELECTED VINTAGE COCKTAILS
Bounce	Cherry Bounce was purportedly a specialty of Martha Washington—and a favoritie of the first president of the USA. In colonial times, Cherry Bounce was made from a confit of spiced cherries, strained and served with a spirit. A modern recipe calls for a mixture of fruit cooked with sugar, cinnamon, nutmeg, and lemon juice to be macerated for three months or more with a bottle of rye whiskey. The mixture is strained and served neat.
Calibogus	Calibogus was a popular drink of rum, spruce beer, and molasses. Modern versions are made with rum, molasses, and lime juice scented with a drop of pine tincture or a splash of pine liqueur; served with soda over ice.
Crusta	A fanciful cocktail garnished with a long loop of lemon peel and a sugared rim, Crustas were originally prepared using a mix of cognac, orange liqueur, Angostura bitters, and lemon juice that was shaken, strained, and served over one ice cube in the prepared glass.
Cobbler	The Cobbler is actually a family of drinks; what they have in common is some sort of a base spirit or wine, sugar, and fresh fruit. The original Cobbler was made with sherry. To make a Cobbler, all of the ingredients are shaken with ice and poured unstrained into a glass.
Fizz	A Fizz basically contains a spirit (often gin), lemon juice, and sugar, served tall over ice with carbonated water. There are many variations on the Fizz, including a Silver Fizz (with the addition of shaken egg white), the Golden Fizz (with an egg yolk), and the Royal Fizz (which uses the whole egg). Other variations include the Diamond Fizz, which uses sparkling wine in the place of carbonated water, and the Green Fizz, garnished with a splash of green crème de menthe.
Flip	A cocktail made with a spirit (or spirits), sugar, spices, and a whole raw egg (with cream optional). A Flip is a smooth, creamy drink, made such by first beating the egg with sugar, adding the other ingredients, and repeatedly pouring the concoction back and forth between two glasses or shaking. Egg nog (which includes cream) is a variation on the Flip. Popular Flip recipes included those based on rum, brandy, and Port wine. They were often heated by being stirred with a heated implement.
Sangaree	A wine-based punch, which could be made from table wine, Port, Madeira, sherry, or any other type of wine. Spirits such as brandy or rum were sometimes added, with the entire concoction then blended with water, ice, and nutmeg.
Shrub	In seventeenth- and eighteenth-century England, a Shrub was a sweet, liqueur-like spirit made by mixing rum or brandy with sugar and fruit, fruit juice, or fruit zest. In colonial America, a Shrub was a beverage made using the liquid drawn from a batch of fruit macerated with sugar and vinegar. The syrup-like liquid was then mixed with water, spirits, or carbonated water.
Smash	A Smash is a short drink made with fresh mint leaves, muddled ("smashed") with sugar, shaken with a spirit, and strained over ice. Some versions include fruit in the recipe, to be "smashed" or shaken along with the mint.
Syllabub	A Syllabub is a drink made with a base of sweetened wine, usually a white wine mixed with sugar and lemon juice. The wine mixture is then mixed with milk or cream, and topped with a meringue-like topping of sweetened, whipped egg whites.

Figure 11.3: Garnishes add eye appeal and complement drinks.

GARNISHES

Garnishes are intended to add eye appeal and complement drinks. Still, not all drinks need garnishing. Garnishes should be kept at the appropriate cold temperature to guarantee freshness and eye appeal. Refrigerated or temperature-controlled garnish boxes should be used to store prepared garnishes. Unfortunately, one will frequently see an unrefrigerated garnish tray with citrus fruits such as lemons, limes, and oranges that have become oxidized and wilted. If olives are stored in such a manner and then used to garnish a Martini, for example, they will immediately raise its temperature, resulting in a loss of the Martini's otherwise bracingly icy-cool impact.

JUICES

Fresh juices are always preferable but sometimes impractical, as is the case with tomato juice. When using freshly squeezed citrus juices, one should be aware of the very limited shelf life. Fresh orange juice is best used within four hours of preparation. Grapefruit, lemon, and lime juice are best used within twelve hours. The flavor of fresh orange juice is the first to disintegrate, but all fresh citrus juices are best if used within 12 hours. After 24 hours, fresh citrus juice should be discarded.

Prepared juices, such as tomato, pineapple, and cranberry juices, if used, should be kept under refrigeration or on ice as soon as they have been opened. Such products should be carefully handled using strict product rotation and labeling procedures.

INFUSIONS

In the context of distilled spirits, an infusion is a spirit that has been imparted with a specific flavor or flavors. Examples include blueberry-infused vodka, cinnamon-infused bourbon, or strawberry-infused tequila. Despite the plethora of flavored spirits available, house-made infusions are a creative way to make flavored base spirits, which can then be used in unique signature cocktails or modern variations on the classics.

The infusion of flavor from herbs, fruit, spices, or other foods relies on two principles: osmosis, such as occurs as water flows out of the flavor source (drawing flavor compounds out with it), and dissolution, as flavor compounds dissolve in the alcohol and water of the base spirit. Simply put, infused spirits may be created by macerating a flavor source such as fruit or spices in a base spirit for a short period of time (usually several weeks) before straining. Most infused spirits are best when used within six months.

MIXERS

Mixers vary from homemade infusions, bottled sodas, house-charged waters, crafted sodas, and homemade sours to prepared mixes and packaged products. This allows for countless variations on drink recipes.

SIMPLE SYRUP

Many of today's cocktail recipes have replaced refined sugars with agave nectar, gum syrup, or simple syrup. While many establishments purchase pre-made simple syrup, a homemade version can easily be prepared in advance by dissolving superfine sugar in an equal quantity of water. This basic simple syrup recipe is referred to as "one-to-one." The preferred recipe is to simply heat one cup of water, add one cup of granulated sugar, and stir until the sugar dissolves.

Some recipes require greater sweetness, which can be created by increasing the proportion of sugar to water to two parts sugar to one part water. Many European recipes use this sweeter version of simple syrup, which is referred to as "two-to-one." Simple syrup has an excellent shelf life, especially when stored under refrigeration; however, sugar may support the growth of mold or other pathogens. Therefore, simple syrup should be handled with care, labeled, and rotated like every other perishable product. The maximum shelf life of simple syrup is approximately one month.

COMPOUND SYRUPS

A range of compound (flavored) syrups are used in mixology in order to provide sweetness, flavor, color, or texture to a drink. Such products are commercially produced and widely available—and many experienced bartenders will have a strong preference for a specific brand. However, recipes abound and some establishments prefer to craft their own. Making compound syrups in-house is an excellent way to preserve the flavor of highly perishable products such as fresh mint, basil, pineapple, raspberries, and raw ginger. Most compound syrups are non-alcoholic, but some versions do contain alcohol.

Examples of compound syrups used in mixology include the following:

- **Grenadine:** Grenadine is a non-alcoholic pomegranate-flavored syrup known as much for its bright-red color as its fruity flavor. The name is derived from the French word *grenade*, meaning "pomegranate." Some modern versions are flavored with black currants or other red or black fruits in addition to or in place of pomegranate. Grenadine is a standard component in many cocktails—including the Tequila Sunrise and the Jack Rose—and non-alcoholic drinks such as the Shirley Temple and the Roy Rogers as well.
- **Orgeat:** Orgeat is a non-alcoholic, almond-flavored syrup originally produced with a blend of almonds and barley. Modern versions often have a floral component as well, and may be flavored with rose water or orange flower water. Orgeat is featured in several tropical drink recipes, including the Mai Tai and the Scorpion.
- **Falernum:** The origins of falernum are debated, but most experts agree that this sweet, many-flavored syrup originated in Barbados. The recipes and subsequent character of falernum may vary, but typical versions are flavored with lime, almond, ginger, and cloves. Often used in Caribbean cocktails and other tropically-inspired drinks, falernum may be house-made or commercially-produced; and may or may not contain alcohol. One widely-distributed commercial product, Taylor's Velvet Falernum, is an alcoholic version based a recipe created in 1890 by John D. Taylor of Bridgeport, Barbados.
- **Lime Cordial:** Lime cordial is a very tart and concentrated non-alcoholic syrup flavored with lime. Lime cordial is often used as a substitute for fresh lime juice in mixology and cooking. A widely-distributed commercial product, Rose's Lime Juice, is featured in the recipe for the Gimlet and several other classic cocktails.
- **Ginger Syrup:** While commercial preparations exist, ginger syrup is easy to make and house-made versions provide an excellent vehicle to preserve the potent flavor of fresh ginger.

BITTERS

Commercial cocktail bitters, such as Angostura, Peychaud's, and Fee Brothers, are widely available. When added by the drop, these should enhance the flavor, complexity, and balance of a cocktail or mixed drink. It is not uncommon to find prepared or house-made bitters in upscale bars. Aromatized wines, vini amari, spirit amari, and bittered liqueurs may also be used to add the bitter component in drinks. Cocktail bitters are discussed in greater detail in chapter 10.

Figure 11.4: Bartender Using an Eyedropper to Add Bitters to a Cocktail

TINCTURES

Tinctures are unsweetened single-flavor extracts that are infused or combined with high-proof neutral spirits. Tinctures are somewhat similar to infusions, but are much more highly concentrated. The purpose of a tincture is to add a specific flavor (or flavors) without increasing the volume of a drink. They may be used as an ingredient in the mixing process or added by using an eyedropper as a finishing touch to a cocktail. Useful tinctures include those flavored with clove, cinnamon, nutmeg, orange zest, lemon zest, vanilla, cocoa, basil, or raspberry.

BEHIND THE BAR

BAR GLASSWARE

Today's bar glassware is available in a variety of shapes, sizes, and even colors. One should always use an appropriate glass for each drink, matching the glass size with the correct proportion of ingredients. A typical bar should be stocked with a style of beer glass or mug, white wineglass, red wineglass, flute, Martini glass, coupe, brandy snifter, shot glass, highball, Collins glass, Margarita glass, rocks or Old-Fashioned glass, and Irish Coffee mug. More specialized bars may include other items, such as a frappé glass, chimney or Zombie glass, Hurricane glass, pony glass, or specialized glasses for individual styles of beer or wine.

KEY BAR TOOLS

A bartender is only as good as his or her tools. For consistency, a bartender should always use a measuring device such as a jigger, which is a legal measurement of 1.5 ounces in the US, for measured pours. Many jiggers have a reverse side container measuring a half-jigger to simplify making cocktails that require a ratio of mixing.

Although free-pouring is often used by bartenders, this practice results in inconsistency and unbalanced recipes, which can result in both customer dissatisfaction and unacceptable beverage costs.

In addition to the jigger, there is a wide assortment of bar tools available. The following list of items should be considered essential: mixing glass, Boston metal shaker, cobbler or French shaker, Hawthorne (or spring) strainer, bar spoon (a long stirring spoon), channel knife, ice tongs, zester, muddler, bottle/can opener (church key), corkscrew, hand juicer or citrus reamer, piano whip or whisk, paring knife, French knife, and blender.

THE ONE-STEP RULE

The layout of a bar should be carefully designed so that the bartender will have all necessary ingredients and tools within easy reach. More specifically, almost all tools and ingredients should be available within one or two steps in any direction. The mixing glass and shakers should be inverted and placed on a bar mat on the rail alongside the jigger, Hawthorne strainer, and bar spoon. The bartender should build drinks on the bar rail or bar counter facing the customer so that all ingredients are clearly within view and the bartender's dexterity and skill can be on display.

THE SPEED RACK (THE WELL)

Bar setups vary enormously based on the target audience, the size of the facility, and the type of establishment. Most bars are set up with speed racks that are located in the well, which is mounted to the sinks and the ice bin. They are designed so that bartenders can easily access the most commonly used spirits and mixers. Historically, the least expensive spirits and mixers were placed in the well (or "rail"), and higher-quality products were placed on the back bar and top shelf, where customers could see them.

The setup of the speed rack varies from house to house. At a high-end bar, the speed rack may be stocked with "call," or proprietary, brands such as Smirnoff vodka rather than a generic brand of vodka. No matter the product used, the placement of the products should always remain the same so that every bartender can reach for the correct bottle without even having to think about its location.

THE BACK BAR

The back bar should be set up to display bottles in such a way to promote sales and to market premium, super-premium, and ultra-premium brands. Similarly, liqueurs and cordials are also displayed on the back bar. The manner in which the bottles are arranged will depend on the type of bar, its focus, and the amount of space available, while still maintaining functionality for the bartender. Given that there are, for example, over 750 brands of vodka, many of them produced in a plethora of flavors, it is not surprising that the back bar is premium space for the supplier, distributor, and bar owner(s).

Table 11.2: Bar Terminology

BAR TERMINOLOGY	
Back	A nonalcoholic drink served alongside a shot or a strong drink.
Chaser	A mixer or water served on the side, generally meant to be sipped after a drink of a straight shot of liquor.
Float	The final liquid ingredient added to a drink after the basic procedure is performed. Because spirits and liqueurs have varying levels of density, if the lightest liquid is carefully poured, it will "float" on top.
Free-Pour	To make and mix drinks without using a measuring device like a jigger or measured pour spout. While many bartenders prefer the free pour, it tends to be less accurate than a measured pour.
Light	A drink containing a reduced amount of liquor but the normal amount of mixer.
Muddle	To crush ingredients such as mint leaves or orange slices in order to squeeze out juices, oils, and flavors. A special tool called a muddler (a 6" [15 cm] or longer stick) is used in the process.
Neat	A drink, usually a single unmixed liquor, served without being chilled and without water, ice, or other mixer. This term generally refers to a shot of liquor poured directly from the bottle into a glass.
On the Rocks	A straight spirit served over ice in a rocks or Old-Fashioned glass. When used to refer to a cocktail, it is shaken or stirred with ice and strained over fresh ice into a glass. The type of glass depends on the cocktail.
Rim	To moisten the outside of a glass, typically with fresh citrus, and roll the rim gently into a saucer of uniodized salt or sugar, turning the glass until the rim is coated and tapping the glass to remove the excess.
Short	A drink generally served in a rocks glass with less than 5 ounces (148 ml) fluid in total.
Tall/Long	A drink served in an 8- to 16-ounce (237- to 473-ml) highball glass. The amount of mixer is increased in a "tall" drink, but not the amount of liquor.
Twist	The peel of a citrus fruit, such as lemon, cut lengthwise with little or no pith; used to rim the glass and/or as a garnish.
Up	A drink that is shaken or stirred with ice to chill, then strained and served without ice, generally in a stemmed glass.

MIXING METHODS

The use of the appropriate mixing method is another aspect of mixology. The skilled use of the correct mixing method is important to the quality and consistency of the beverages produced and also impacts speed, service, and costs. The most common mixing methods are the build, stir, shake, and blend. Other, less common mixing methods include the rolling method and the dry shake. As with all things in the beverage industry, these methods have many variations and may be known by different names in different locations.

The Build: Sometimes known as the pouring method, this simple technique is used for mixed drinks requested on the rocks. Using the method, a drink is "built" step-by-step directly into the glass in which it will be served. Highballs such as Rum and Coke and the Tequila Sunrise, and drinks served "tall," are generally made using the build method. The steps for the build are as follows:
- Place ice into the glass to the desired level, always using an ice scoop.
- Pour the measured spirit(s) into the glass.
- Finish by topping off with the mixer (cola, tonic, juice, etc.).
- Garnish as necessary.
- Add the stirrer, sip stick, or straw, and then serve.

Note: In these instructions and several that follow, SWE has chosen to recommend putting the ice into the serving glass or mixing utensil before the spirits and other ingredients are added. While many leading bartenders and professional organizations recommend the same, SWE acknowledges that points of view on the "ice first" or "spirits first" techniques vary, and that many expert bartenders prefer to measure the spirits (and sometimes other ingredients) into the glass or blending utensil before adding the ice.

The Stir: This method is used for cocktails made with two or more easily blended ingredients that need to be served chilled but without ice. The ingredients are placed in a mixing glass with ice, stirred together with a bar spoon, and strained into a chilled serving glass. Removing the ice by straining prevents it from further diluting the drink. Manhattans, Rob Roys, and Martinis are often prepared using the stirring method, but, as is commonly known, some people prefer to have their Martini "shaken, not stirred." The basic steps for the stir method are as follows:

- Chill a stemmed glass by filling it with ice, and then place it on the counter or rail.
- Place ice into the mixing glass until it is one-third to one-half full.
- Pour the base liquid into the mixing glass and add the spirit(s).
- Hold the mixing glass at the base and stir, holding the bar spoon and rotating it around the mixing glass for 20 to 60 seconds, until the liquid is well chilled. Gently remove the bar spoon.
- Remove the ice from the chilled serving glass.
- Using a Hawthorne strainer over the mouth of the mixing glass, strain the ingredients into the serving glass.
- Garnish as appropriate, and then serve.

Figure 11.5: Bartender Making a Drink Using the Stir Method

The Shake: The shake is used for cocktails or mixed drinks containing ingredients such as sugar or cream that do not readily mix with spirits and therefore require a bit of agitation to be thoroughly incorporated into the drink. The shake method can also be used to create a cocktail, such as a Martini, that is lighter in taste than it would be if it were made using the stir method. A fifteen-second shake adds 25% more water and creates millions of bubbles, giving the drink an "airy" texture that many people enjoy. The following steps should be used for the shake method:

- Put ice into the mixing glass until it is one-third to one-half full.
- Measure the spirit(s), mixers, and/or base ingredients into the mixing glass.
- Place the large metal tin over the top of the Boston mixing glass or shaker, making sure that it is sitting evenly.
- Lightly tap the top of the tin, creating a vacuum within the mixing glass.
- Pick up the whole unit from the bar and flip it over so that the large tin is facing downward and the mixing glass is at shoulder height.

- Shake vigorously over the left or right shoulder.
- Continue to shake for fifteen to twenty seconds.
- With the metal shaker still on the bottom, hold the unit in the left hand for balance.
- Press the index finger against the glass mixer.
- Make a ball or fist with the right hand. Locate the frost line on the metal tin and strike the tin on the side to break the vacuum.
- Twist off the mixing glass and strain the liquid through the Hawthorne strainer into a glass.
- Fill to within a quarter inch of the rim, garnish appropriately, and serve.

The Roll: The roll procedure is used with mixed drinks or cocktails that call for thick juices or puréed fruit. The roll, a variation on the shake method, is designed to prevent unattractive foam from forming on a drink, as might occur when using tomato juice in a Bloody Mary, or to prevent a drink from becoming overdiluted. To make a drink using the rolling method, follow the guidelines for the shake, but instead of vigorously shaking, gently roll the ingredients back and forth six or seven times. Another alternative is to transfer the ingredients from one large glass or mixing glass to another half a dozen times.

Figure 11.6: Bartender Using a Hawthorne Strainer

The Dry Shake: Simply put, dry shaking refers to shaking without ice. The dry shake is used to create foam, typically using an egg white. All recipes that involve egg whites should start with a fifteen-second (minimum) dry shake in order to incorporate the egg white with the other ingredients in the cocktail and to give it a frothy, foamy texture. After a dry shake, add ice, shake again, and strain into the glass.

The Blend: This procedure, which uses an electric blender, is for blending ice, ice cream, or other solid ingredients, such as fruit, with spirits and other mixers. Using cracked ice makes the results of this process more consistent. The following steps should be used for the blending procedure:
- Place cracked or crushed ice in the blender jar according to the recipe.
- Add the remaining ingredients, which should cover the ice.
- Blend for a few seconds on the lower setting and then for an additional ten seconds or more on the higher setting.
- Using a cocktail spoon to maintain an even flow, pour the blended ingredients into an appropriate glass.

DRINK FAMILIES

There are likely tens of thousands of different cocktail recipes in use in the world today—and new drinks are being invented all the time. Thus, trying to classify drink and cocktail recipes is a difficult task. There are many systems in use that attempt to categorize drinks, and they all work to a certain extent. The following guide divides mixed drinks and cocktails into twelve basic families. Keep in mind that classifying drinks is a complicated task and that some drinks may fall into more than one family.

A simplified chart listing the twelve basic drink families can be found in table 11.3.

Liquor on Ice: For many customers, particularly aficionados of single malt Scotch, small-batch bourbon, and other super-premium beverages, a single shot over ice is their drink of choice. Drinks in the "liquor on ice" family, such as Scotch on the rocks, are built in the glass—a single liquor poured over ice with nothing else added. Such drinks are usually served in a rocks glass or tumbler. A traditional variation of a drink "on the rocks" is the frappé, sometimes called a mist. A frappé is made using crushed or shaved ice and is served in a coupe or cocktail glass with a straw.

Table 11.3: Drink Families

DRINK FAMILY	WELL-KNOWN EXAMPLES
Liquor on Ice	Scotch on the Rocks, Scotch Mist
Two-Liquor Drinks on Ice	Black Russian, Stinger, Rusty Nail
The Martini Family	Martini, Manhattan, Rob Roy, Old-Fashioned
Sours	Margarita, Daiquiri, Whiskey Sour
Shooters	B-52, Lemon Drop, Mudslide
Highballs	Rum and Coke, Tequila Sunrise, Bloody Mary
Tropical Drinks	Mai Tai, Piña Colada, Zombie
Wines and Punches	Champagne Cocktail, Kir, Fish House Punch
Cream-Based Drinks	White Russian, Grasshopper
Frozen Drinks	Frozen Margarita, Frozen Strawberry Daiquiri
International Coffees	Irish Coffee, Mexican Coffee
Pousse-Cafés	Pousse-Café, Angel's Kiss

Two-Liquor Drinks on Ice: Two-liquor drinks typically combine a jigger of a spirit with a smaller amount of a liqueur. The Black Russian, combining vodka and Kahlúa, and the Rusty Nail, combining Scotch and Drambuie, are classic members of the two-liquor drink family. Generally prepared using the stir method and served in a rocks glass, two-liquor drinks can be strong, as the combined volume of the spirits can total two to three ounces (60–89 ml) of liquor; anything less would look scant in the glass.

The Martini Family: Quintessentially American and the defining international symbol for cocktails, the Martini remains universally popular. There is no universal agreement about what constitutes the recipe for a Martini. The classic recipe of the post-Prohibition era called for three parts gin and one part vermouth. Over the decades, it evolved to include less vermouth. The extra-dry Martini may call for the bartender to merely wave the vermouth bottle over the glass or whisper the word *vermouth* to the completed drink. In addition, the Martini is now made with vodka as often as gin.

The Manhattan, another classic vermouth-based cocktail, is thought to date back to 1874 and is named for the Manhattan Club, where it is said to have been first served. Generally made with blended or rye whiskey, the original Manhattan contained bitters and more vermouth than is generally used in today's recipe. A Rob Roy is a variation in which the blended whiskey is replaced with Scotch whisky. As with a regular Manhattan, a dry Rob Roy and a perfect Rob Roy reflect the kind or blend of vermouth used in the recipe.

The Old-Fashioned, a cocktail based on bourbon, sugar, and bitters—and the drink's many variations, including the Sazerac—is generally considered to be part of the extended Martini/Manhattan family. Drinks in the Martini family are served up in cocktail glasses and are stirred, unless a customer calls for the cocktail shaken or served on the rocks.

Sours: Sours are drinks that combine a liquor (or liquors) with sour mix, lime juice, or lemon juice. Sours can be classified as either short sours or long sours. The classic Margarita, the Daiquiri, the Gimlet, the Pisco Sour, and the Whiskey Sour are classic examples of short sours. Use the shake/strain procedure and a cocktail or sour glass for short sours, unless a customer requests the cocktail on the rocks, in which case the mixing procedure should be used.

Figure 11.7: The Tom Collins, a Member of the "Long Sour" Family

Long sours contain the same ingredients, with the addition of carbonated soda to cut the acidity. Examples of long sours include Rickeys, drinks from the Tom Collins family, and Long Island Iced Tea. Long sours are generally served in a tall glass and are often garnished with a cherry and an orange slice.

Shooters: Shooters are made using one or more spirits; many are made with a combination of liqueurs, or liqueurs and spirits. Shooters can also have nonalcoholic ingredients. They are created using a variety of methods and may be built, shaken, stirred, or blended. Meant to be consumed very quickly, shooters are usually served in a shot glass. Shooters may vary from bartender to bartender and region to region, and they often go in and out of style very quickly. The Mudslide, the B-52, and the Lemon Drop are a few of the more popular shooters that have stood the test of time. Many shooters are actually variations of other styles of drinks. If served in a rocks glass over ice, they could be classified as two-liquor drinks on ice.

Highballs: Highballs are drinks made with carbonated mixers, water, or juices and served tall on ice in a highball glass. Jack and Ginger, Rum and Coke, 7&7, the Tequila Sunrise, and the Bloody Mary are all examples of highballs. Highballs are a popular mixed drink, as the large proportion of mixers and ice to alcohol allows for a slower, more controlled consumption of alcohol.

Highballs with carbonated mixers or water require only the build procedure for their ingredients to be fully incorporated. Those made with liqueurs generally need to be mixed or shaken to incorporate the ingredients. Highballs can be made with many different combinations of spirits and juice or flavored sodas, but the basic highball recipe proportions remain the same: 1½ ounces (44 ml) of liquor is poured over ice in a highball glass, with 4 ounces (118 ml) of soda, juice, or other mixer added.

There are several variations of the story behind the term *highball*. The name may refer to the practice of serving drinks in the dining cars of trains powered by steam locomotives once the engine got up to speed. When the engine was up to speed, the "ball" that showed boiler pressure would be at its highest level, which is known as highballing. Another version claims that highballs were named in the 1800s by railroaders who typically placed a ball on a high pole to indicate to oncoming trains that the track was clear and they could maintain speed. With the track clear, the workers had time to stop for a fast drink of whiskey and ginger ale, which came to be known as a highball.

Figure 11.8: The Bloody Mary, a Popular Highball

Tropical Drinks: Victor Bergeron, the proprietor of Trader Vic's, is credited with starting the tropical drink craze in the 1930s with the invention of the Mai Tai. It is said that Bergeron wanted to create a recipe using aged rum to serve to friends from Tahiti, where the term *mai tai* means *the best.* Bergeron is also credited with the creation of the Piña Colada, although according to Dale DeGroff, author of *The Craft of the Cocktail,* Bergeron "borrowed" the recipe for the Piña Colada from a bartender in Puerto Rico. Nevertheless, the popularity of Trader Vic's, as well as the Don the Beachcomber chain of bars that opened at about the same time, ingrained the "tiki bar" and tropical drinks as part of American culture.

Despite a rather outdated reputation for sweet, slushy drinks with elaborate garnishes (including edible flowers, pineapple chunks and paper umbrellas), tropical drinks are enjoying a modern revival. Contemporary tiki bars featuring authentic Polynesian artifacts and elevated drink recipes are all a part of the growing tiki culture—and, it seems, the collectable tiki mug is here to stay.

Figure 11.9: The Piña Colada, a Classic Tropical Drink, Duly Garnished

Wines and Punches: The term *punch* is derived from the Hindi word *panch,* meaning *five,* reflecting the original recipes which included five ingredients: alcohol, water, sugar, lemon, and tea or spices. Among the first punches introduced to the West by sailors from the East India Company in the early seventeenth century were *wassails* created using a brandy or wine base. It was not long before rum supplanted the other base ingredients.

One of the oldest recipes is for a Barbadian Rum Punch. It reads, "One of sour, two of sweet, three of strong, four of weak," referring to one part lime juice, two parts sugar, three parts rum, and four parts water. Punches became very popular in the eighteenth and nineteenth centuries, as they promoted conviviality by serving a number of guests at one time. Some of these same punches, such as Fish House Punch, Planter's Punch, and Hot Rum Punch, remain popular to this day. Wine-based cocktails such as the Mimosa, the Champagne Cocktail, and the Kir are also included in this category.

Cream-Based Drinks: Cream drinks are rich, smooth, and sweet. They are useful as an after-dinner suggestion in lieu of dessert or in the heat of summer. Cream-based drinks are frequently made using ice cream instead of cream. Examples of drinks based on cream (or ice cream) include the Grasshopper, the Brandy Alexander, and the White Russian.

Cream-based drinks prepared with cream can be made using either the shake or blend procedure. When using ice cream, a blender is required, as it is in any other instance in which solids (such as ice or fruit) are incorporated into a drink.

Serve short cream drinks in a coupe glass. Any short cream drink can be turned into a long cream drink by adding more cream or milk; long cream drinks are generally served in a highball glass.

Frozen Drinks: Frozen drinks, such as the popular frozen Margarita and Strawberry Daiquiri, can be created by incorporating a sour-based drink recipe with crushed ice in the blender. Other popular frozen drinks include ice cream drinks, as discussed above.

International Coffees: The Irish Coffee, which was first prepared by Chef Joseph Sheridan for a group of American passengers stranded at the Foynes Port Airport in Ireland, sets the standard for all international coffee drinks. In the original recipe, black coffee is poured into a mug with sugar and 1½ ounces (44 ml) of Irish whiskey. Heavy cream is poured over the back of a bar spoon. The recipe for Irish coffee has since evolved into many more elaborate preparations. One of today's versions is served using an international coffee glass rimmed with brown sugar, flaming whiskey to caramelize the sugar, and a topping of whipped cream. International coffees of all sorts, made with a wide variety of spirits and liqueurs, are especially popular as after-dinner drinks.

Figure 11.10: Layered Shots

Pousse-Cafés: Pousse-cafés are layered drinks made by floating ingredients on top of one another to create a multilayered effect. Quite difficult to make, they can be a test of showmanship and skill for a bartender. *Pousse-café* literally translates as "push the coffee" or "coffee pusher." In the 1800s, pousse-cafés were popularly served with coffee after a meal.

The secret to layering a drink is to "float" the ingredients into the glass, usually by pouring them slowly over the back of a spoon, in the proper order from heaviest to lightest. A final float of brandy—lit on fire—lends a dramatic flair, as does a float of cream.

The layered effect of a well-made pousse-café demonstrates the variations in density, or weight, of specific liqueurs. In general, liqueurs with the highest amount of sugar are the heaviest. However, there is no easy way to determine the sugar level of a liqueur, so the best guide for creating a layered drink is a chart of specific gravities, which indicates the weight of a liquid in reference to water. Liquids with higher specific gravities are heavier and will sink to the bottom of the glass. The greater the difference in specific gravities between two layers, the easier it will be to keep the layers from mixing into each other. A chart of specific gravities for many types of beverages is provided in table 11.4.

Table 11.4: Chart of Specific Gravities

CHART OF SPECIFIC GRAVITIES	
Spirit, Syrup, or Liqueur	**Specific Gravity**
Grenadine	1.18
Crème de Cassis	1.18
Blue Curaçao	1.13
DeKuyper Crème de Cacao (White)	1.12
DeKuyper Crème de Cacao (Dark)	1.11
DeKuyper Crème de Menthe (White)	1.11
DeKuyper Crème de Menthe (Green)	1.09
Disaronno Originale (Amaretto)	1.08
Drambuie	1.08
Orange Curaçao	1.08
Kahlúa	1.08
Triple Sec	1.07
Campari	1.06
Frangelico	1.06
Bailey's Irish Cream	1.05
Cointreau	1.04
Malibu Coconut Rum	1.04
Goldschläger	1.03
Green Chartreuse	1.01
Water	**1.0**
Vodka	0.95
Tequila	0.95
White Rum	0.95
Gin	0.94

RESPONSIBLE BEVERAGE ALCOHOL SERVICE

In the United States, third-party liability and negligence laws affect anyone who serves beverage alcohol, whether in a food and beverage establishment, at a wine tasting event, or in one's own home. There are a number of states that now require all commercial servers of beverage alcohol to show proof of having successfully completed an acceptable responsible service training program.

While some states require any public server of alcohol to have completed a program offered or approved by the state, most states recognize the validity of two programs that are offered throughout the United States and internationally: the National Restaurant Association's Educational Foundations' ServSafe Alcohol® and TIPS® (Training for Intervention Procedures).

Regardless of state requirements, having such certification can reduce liability insurance premiums for any server or employer. In EU countries, OWI laws are much more stringent than in the United States—and there is a concerted effort to counter alcohol abuse. The Society of Wine Educators regards this as a significant issue and encourages all who take the Certified Specialist of Spirits (CSS) Exam to be properly trained and certified.

Although the food and beverage industry cannot be responsible for all of the problems associated with excess alcohol consumption, servers of beverage alcohol, including members of the spirits trade and educators who conduct any type of tastings, can ensure that their behavior promotes responsible consumption of alcoholic beverages by doing the following things:

- Checking identification as a matter of routine in every case in which there is doubt about a taster's age
- Recognizing the signs of intoxication and refraining from serving anyone who has consumed too many drinks or who exhibits signs of intoxication
- Declining to serve any customer who appears to have consumed excess alcohol elsewhere
- Encouraging impaired customers to call for a cab or contact a friend to get a ride home, or offering to make the call oneself
- Persuading the customer to surrender the car key, when warranted
- Observing responsible and reasonable standards in serving and consuming alcohol so as to set a good example for customers, fellow employees, and friends

CHAPTER TWELVE IMPACT OF ALCOHOL ON HEALTH

IMPACT OF ALCOHOL ON HEALTH

CHAPTER TWELVE

LEARNING OBJECTIVES

After studying this chapter, the candidate should be able to do the following:
- Recognize the potential negative consequences of excessive alcohol consumption
- Discuss the potential health benefits of the moderate intake of alcohol
- Understand how to achieve a healthy balance between the risks and benefits associated with alcohol consumption

Spirits are appreciated in much of the world. In many regions, consumption is on the rise. This presents numerous opportunities for beverage professionals; however, it also presents a unique set of challenges.

Almost every aspect of the beverage professional's job involves the ingestion of alcohol to some degree, including during training, sales, and trade tastings. Even if one expectorates, some absorption of alcohol occurs.

The effects of alcohol consumption can have dangerous consequences for both the professional and the consumer. However, there appear to be some health benefits associated with a moderate daily intake of alcohol as well. This chapter will examine the current research on the risks and potential benefits of alcohol consumption.

Please note that nothing contained in this chapter or in this Study Guide as a whole constitutes medical advice. Such advice should only be obtained from a licensed medical professional.

HARMFUL EFFECTS OF ALCOHOL

Humans have been enjoying alcohol for thousands of years, and it is more widely available now than ever before. It is becoming prevalent in cultures with no prior history of alcohol consumption, and its use is increasing in many cultures that have a long tradition of imbibing.

Alcohol has properties that can act as a depressant, aid in relaxation, encourage social interaction, relieve feelings of anxiety, and enhance a meal. Studies demonstrate that restaurant visits accompanied by an alcoholic beverage are perceived to be more enjoyable and worthwhile experiences than those without.

When ethanol, the main chemical in alcoholic beverages, is absorbed into the bloodstream, it enters the brain, where it induces feelings of pleasure. A moderate intake of ethanol at the appropriate time may be pleasurable; however, some of the effects of ethanol, particularly at higher doses, may be unwanted and have serious consequences. The dangers of the abusive consumption of alcohol are well-known and publicized:

- **Intoxication:** When alcohol is absorbed, it affects the brain's ability to further regulate the intake of alcohol. This can lead to intoxication as the buildup of acetaldehyde in the bloodstream occurs. Acetaldehyde is a by-product of the metabolic process of ethanol in the liver and is more toxic than ethanol itself. When one becomes intoxicated, motor skills, speech, judgment, and the ability to drive become greatly impaired. In some cases, intoxication can lead a person to commit violent acts and exhibit socially inappropriate behavior.

- **Alcohol-Related Diseases:** Consumption of alcohol can increase the risk of serious diseases such as cirrhosis, a potentially fatal liver condition. Additionally, studies have shown that 100 ml of ethanol a day (equivalent to just over a bottle of wine) causes a condition known as fatty liver, in which fat accumulates within the cells of the liver. If alcohol consumption ceases, the condition can be reversed. Cirrhosis, however, cannot be reversed and may result from continued alcohol abuse. Alcohol consumption may also increase the risk of developing many types of cancer, especially cancers of the mouth, esophagus, stomach, and breast. Other risks include stroke, high blood pressure, and heart attack.
- **Alcohol Abuse:** Individuals who abuse alcohol for extended periods of time often develop a tolerance. When this occurs, more and more alcohol is required to achieve past effects and the likelihood of addiction greatly increases. Addiction can lead to severe problems with health, finances, relationships, and career. Prolonged excessive drinking also contributes to several psychiatric conditions such as depression.
- **Binge Drinking:** In developed countries, alcohol ranks third among risks to health and is the largest cause of premature death in people between the ages of 15 and 29. This is largely because young adults may "save up" their drinking for one big night out a week, a practice known as binge drinking. Binge drinking may result in a rapid rise of alcohol in the bloodstream and may also contribute to a host of alcohol-related incidents, such as motor vehicle accidents and fatal alcohol poisoning.

BENEFITS OF MODERATE CONSUMPTION

There is strong evidence to support the claim that some degree of alcohol consumption may be beneficial to human health; however, there is no universally accepted "safe" level of consumption. The USDA recommends up to one drink per day for women and up to two drinks per day for men as a definition of moderate consumption. The definition of one drink is as follows:
- Wine (12%-14% abv) – 5 ounces (148 ml)
- Beer (5% abv) – 12 ounces (355 ml)
- Spirits (40% abv) – 1.5 ounces (44 ml)

Studies have shown that the overall lowest mortality rates occur at this level of alcohol consumption, while the highest rates occur in heavy drinkers. Moderate alcohol intake has been shown to reduce the risk of dementia and Alzheimer's disease, osteoporosis, certain types of cancer, and stroke. Extensive studies indicate that moderate drinkers tend to have lower mortality rates than those who abstain or drink very rarely.

Figure 12.1: Moderation in All Things

Perhaps one of the biggest potential benefits is the decreased risk of developing coronary heart disease. Studies have shown that in people who drink moderately, the risk is reduced by at least 20%. This is due to ethanol's clot- and plaque-reducing properties. However, this effect is only significant in people who are actually at risk of developing coronary heart disease.

Another important point to consider is that alcohol increases blood pressure, so a generalization cannot be made that a moderate amount of alcohol is beneficial for every individual. Furthermore, some individuals may be more prone to addictive behavior than others and should abstain from alcohol, as potential health risks far outweigh any possible benefits.

THE DECISION TO IMBIBE

The decision to imbibe, and how much, should depend on one's specific situation. It would, of course, be ill-advised to consume alcohol to protect from one disease while putting oneself at greater risk for another. For example, alcohol has been shown to increase the risk of breast cancer in women. The risk may be lessened if the alcohol consumed is resveratrol-rich red wine at a moderate level (1 to 1½ glasses per day); however, at higher levels of consumption, this effect is nullified.

The greatest benefits of alcohol consumption to health have been shown to occur when alcohol is consumed with meals, preferably at the same time each day, and not in excess of the recommended servings. Consuming alcohol with food slows down its absorption, which is healthier for the liver, kidneys, heart, and nervous system.

CERTIFIED SPECIALIST OF SPIRITS

ADDITIONAL RESOURCES

ADDITIONAL RESOURCES

GLOSSARY OF SPIRITS-RELATED TERMS

APPENDIX A

GENERAL TERMS

Agave – A genus of succulent plants in the amaryllis family, with approximately 130 known species, mainly found in southern North America, especially Mexico. The blue agave variety is used in the production of tequila.

Aging – A post-distillation maturation process used to impart additional flavor and character to many types of spirits. The length of time that a given spirit is aged depends on its distillation proof, cask size, cask treatment, and storage conditions (temperature and humidity)—and the desired characteristics of the finished spirit.

Agricole – *Fr.*, agricultural. In the production of rum, *rhum agricole* refers to rum produced from sugarcane juice as opposed to molasses.

Aguamiel – *Sp.*, honey water. The unfermented sap of the agave plant that is used to make an assortment of fermented and distilled beverages. Aguamiel extracted from the blue agave plant is used in the production of tequila.

Aldehyde – Any of several chemical compounds—typically quite aromatic and flavorful—caused by the oxidation of alcohol.

Alquitara – A type of pot still used in the production of brandy de Jerez.

Amaro – *Italian*, bitter. An Italian bitter liqueur.

Amatitán Region – A region in Jalisco, Mexico, where blue agave is grown for the production of tequila. Of the two main tequila-producing regions, it is the warmer, lower-lying region.

Americano – A type of aromatized, bitter wine product flavored with wormwood and gentian.

Añejo – *Sp.*, aged. An age classification for both rum and tequila. For rum, there is no minimum aging requirement, but añejo tequila must be aged in oak barrels for at least one year.

Angel's Share – The portion of an aging spirit that is lost to evaporation during barrel maturation.

Applejack – An American brandy produced from the fermented mash of apples.

Armagnac – A French grape-based brandy produced within the delimited area in the department of Gers, in the heart of the Gascony region. It is distilled in a pot or column still and is generally aged in black oak.

Aroma – Any property detected by the olfactory system. Usually reserved for fresh and pleasant odors.

Artemisia absinthium – A green herb often used as a bittering and flavoring agent in aromatized wines and flavored spirits, commonly known as wormwood.

Bacanora – An agave distillate produced in the Mexican state of Sonora.

Backset – The residue left at the bottom of a still after distillation is complete, often used in the production of North American whiskeys. See also: stillage.

Bagazo *(Sp.)*; **Bagasse** *(Fr.)* – The fibrous material left over from either the crushed and cooked agave (in tequila production) or the cut and crushed sugarcane stalk (in rum production).

Baijiu – A distillate produced in China, typically based on sorghum or other base materials such as barley, millet, or glutinous rice.

Barrel – A wooden vessel, usually made from oak, used to age wine or spirits. The barrel's interior may be toasted or charred over an open flame, which imparts oak, vanilla, smoke, and other similar aromas and flavors to the maturing liquid.

Base Spirit – The type of spirit selected in the creation of a liqueur. Base spirits may be a member of a specific spirit category or a neutral spirit.

Beer – In the production of spirits, the term *beer* refers to the result of a mash that has been fermented into an alcoholic liquid of 8–10% abv, which will then be distilled into a spirit.

Beer Still – A pot still in which the beer or wash is boiled, vaporized, and condensed, thereby increasing the alcohol concentration to around 30% abv.

Blanco – A label designation for rum and tequila indicating a spirit that is colorless and unaged; synonymous with *plata* or *silver*.

Blending – A process often used as part of the finishing process in the production of spirits, blending is used to impart flavor and character and/or create a consistent product. The blend may consist of different barrels, different vintages or ages, and/or different types of spirits. In addition, some unsweetened caramel may be added to the blend for color conformity.

Bourbon – An American whiskey and distinctive product of the United States produced using a minimum of 51% corn.

Brandy – A potable spirit produced from the distillation of wine or the fermented mash of fruit. In the European Union, only fruit-based spirits suitably aged in wood may be defined as brandy.

Brouillis – *Fr.,* brew or boil. The result of the first distillation in the production of brandy, usually 25% alcohol by volume.

Cabeza – *Sp.,* head. The swollen central stem of the agave plant used for making both fermented beverages and distilled spirits such as pulque and tequila. Also referred to as a piña ("pineapple").

Calvados – An apple brandy made in a delimited area within France's Normandy Region.

Character – The combination of aromas, tastes, textures, and other traits that define the nature of a spirit.

Charanda – A sugarcane distillate produced in Mexico.

Charcoal – An activated carbon material made by charring a wood product. Often used to filter vodka or other spirits in order to refine their neutrality.

Charcoal-Mellowing – A filtration process used with Tennessee whiskey before the whiskey is aged. The process involves passing the whiskey through a vat filled with a minimum of 10' of sugar-maple charcoal for a week to ten days. The process removes the lighter, pungent aldehydic congener notes, leaving a smoother, mellower whiskey. Also known as the Lincoln County Process.

Cinchona – A genus of flowering plants and trees. The bark of the cinchona tree is used in herbal medicine and as a bittering and flavoring agent.

Clairin – A type of sugarcane-based spirit traditionally produced by independent distilleries throughout Haiti.

Coa – A special cutting tool used for removing leaves during the harvesting of agave plants.

Cognac – A grape-based brandy produced within the delimited regions of the Charente and Charente-Maritime departments of France. Production requirements include double distillation in pot stills and minimum aging in oak barrels.

Cold Compounding – A method for adding flavor to a spirit, most frequently associated with gin, by which essences and/or concentrates of a particular flavor are blended into the spirit.

Cold Method – A method of extracting flavor from fruits, flowers, and herbs during the process of making liqueurs. Generally used for flavors that would otherwise be damaged by the hot method. This is a very time-consuming procedure, sometimes taking up to a year to complete.

Column Still – A large apparatus used in distillation. The main component of a column still is a tall metal column containing porous plates that continually concentrate the alcohol as it moves upward through the plates. This type of still works in a continuous process, eliminating the need for a batch process and permitting the alcohol concentration to reach a very high level.

Compound Gin – One of two types of legally recognized gin (the other being distilled gin). Compounding refers to the method of mixing high-proof neutral spirits with essences of juniper berry and other botanical flavorings.

Congeners – Compounds produced during mashing, fermentation, distillation, and wood aging that contribute to the unique flavor profile of fermented and distilled products.

Corazón – *Sp.*, heart. In the context of spirit production, this is the "heart" of a distillation run, which contains the best aromas and flavors. Usually associated with tequila production.

Cut Points – The points in a distillation run at which the distiller determines where the heads stop and the heart begins, and then again where the heart ends and the tails begin.

Distillation – The separation and concentration of the alcoholic content of a fermented liquid by a series of evaporation and condensation processes.

Distilled Gin – One of two types of legally recognized gin (the other being compound gin), produced solely by the redistillation of a neutral base spirit in the presence of juniper berries and other aromatic botanicals.

Doubler – A type of still that is used to accomplish the second distillation of American whiskey.

Dry Gin – A common style of gin so named because it lacks any sweetness on the palate. Dry gin is often referred to as London dry gin, English dry gin, or American dry gin, although it has no Geographical Indications.

Dunder – The yeast-rich, highly acidic foam leftovers that remain in the still after a batch of rum is finished distilling. Often re-used at some point during the fermentation process and associated with the rums of Jamaica. See also: muck.

Ester – A range of various chemical compounds—typically quite aromatic and flavorful—that result from the joining of an acid and an alcohol.

Ethanol – The principal alcohol produced via fermentation and found in distilled spirits; also known as ethyl alcohol.

Ethyl Alcohol – The principal alcohol produced via fermentation and found in distilled spirits; also known as ethanol.

Falernum – A flavoring syrup typically made with lime, almonds, ginger, and cloves (as well as other ingredients); sometimes used in traditional Caribbean cocktails and other tropically-inspired drinks.

Feints – The portion of the distillation run after the heart that is considered to be nonpotable. Also known as tails.

Fermentation – The process of converting sugar to alcohol through the action of yeast.

Fine Champagne Cognac – Labeling term for cognac produced from grapes grown in a combination of the Grande Champagne and Petite Champagne districts, with at least 50% of the grapes coming from Grande Champagne.

Foreshots – The portion of the distillation run before the heart that is considered to be nonpotable; also known as heads.

Fractional Distillation – The separation and concentration of the mixture of two or more liquids with different boiling points through repeated evaporation and concentration procedures.

Geist – A spirit created by macerating fruit, herbs, or other flavorings in neutral spirits. The resulting solution is then diluted and distilled to create a clear spirit.

Genever – A gin-like spirit produced in Holland, Belgium, and Germany, distilled from a malted grain mash and bottled at 70 to 80 proof. It may have some sweetness on the palate and is often bottled in a distinctively shaped and textured container.

Gentian – A genus of flowering plants. The root of the gentian plant is often used in bitters as a flavoring agent.

Grande Champagne Cognac – Label designation for cognac produced from the highly prized grapes grown solely in the Grande Champagne district.

Grappa – Italian term for a pomace brandy, usually labeled with the designated region of production.

Grenadine – A bright-red, pomegranate- or red fruit-flavored compound syrup used in mixology.

Grist – Ground grains.

Heads – The portion of the distillation run before the heart that is considered to be nonpotable. Also called foreshots.

Heart – The central portion of the distillation run that is considered to be the potable spirit.

High Wines – A distilled spirit after it has passed through a thumper, doubler, or any other spirit still for its second distillation.

Horno – A traditional oven used to cook agave piñas as part of the tequila-production process.

Hors d'Âge – *Fr.*, without age, or more specifically, age unknown. Aging designation for brandy typically specifying a minimum of six to ten years of wood aging, although it may be kept in barrel much longer.

Hot Method – A method of flavor extraction that utilizes distillation to extract the essential oils from a flavoring agent during the process of making liqueurs. Used mostly for seeds and flowers that can withstand some heat and that benefit from a quicker extraction of flavor rather than the slower cold methods.

Hydrolysis – The chemical breakdown of a compound due to a reaction with water.

Hydroselector – A type of column on a continuous still that removes heavy alcohols from the distillate.

Industrial Rum – Rum produced from molasses, as opposed to fresh sugarcane juice.

Industriel – *Fr.*, industrial. In the context of spirits production, rhum industriel (industrial rum) is made from molasses, as opposed to fresh sugarcane juice.

Infusion – A cold method of flavor extraction that involves steeping a flavoring agent in water or alcohol. This process is used for very delicate fruits.

Inulin – The sweet polymers retained in the agave plant's structure as a nutritive reserve. When heated in an oven, inulin is hydrolyzed into fructose and glucose, which can then be fermented to produce alcohol.

Jimador – A skilled field laborer who harvests agave.

Joven Abocado – An age classification used solely for tequila (but not 100% agave tequila) that indicates the tequila is unaged and has been colored and sweetened with the addition of caramel. In export products, these tequilas are labeled as "Gold" or "Oro."

Juniper/Juniper Berry – A female seed cone grown on various species of juniper trees, the most common being the *Juniperus communis*. The berry is used as a spice in cooking and also gives gin its distinctive aroma and flavor.

Lauter tun - A tub-style vessel used in the mashing stage of whisky production. See also: mash tun.

Lees – The sediment composed primarily of dead yeast cells that remains in a tank or cask after fermentation is complete.

Los Altos (Highlands) Region – Region in eastern Jalisco, Mexico, where blue agave is grown for the production of tequila. Of the two main tequila-producing regions, it is the cooler, higher-altitude region.

Louche – The resulting oil-in-water emulsion that occurs when water is added to certain spirits, particularly those flavored with anise, resulting in a milky appearance. Generally referred to as "louching" or "the ouzo effect."

Low Wines – A distillate after it has passed through the first distillation; generally 25% abv.

Maceration – In the context of spirits production, a cold method for extracting flavor whereby the flavor source is cut, crushed, and pressed to expose as much surface area as possible, and then steeped in an alcoholic solution to extract the desired flavors.

Malted Barley – Barley that has been steeped in water and allowed to germinate in an effort to activate the enzymes in the barley to convert the starches to fermentable sugars.

Malting – The process of steeping a grain in water and allowing it to germinate. The germination process activates enzymes that are used to convert the grain's starches into fermentable sugar.

Maltose – A fermentable sugar produced by the enzyme diastase during the malting process.

Marc – The French term for a type of pomace brandy.

Mash – The mixture of base materials (typically ground malted and unmalted grains mixed with water and cooked in a mash tun) that is fermented into an alcoholic wash in preparation for producing a spirit.

Mash Bill – The grain recipe used to produce a specific whiskey. For example, a typical bourbon might be made from a mash bill of 70% corn, 20% rye, and 10% malted barley.

Mash tun – the vessel used in the mashing stage of whisky production, also known as a mash cooker or tub. See also: lauter tun.

Maturation – The process of aging a spirit before it is bottled.

Mezcal – An agave-based distillate produced in Oaxaca and several other Mexican states. The NOM for Mezcal was updated in 2016.

Mixto – A type of tequila made from a mixture of both agave (minimum of 51%) and non-agave sugars. It is no longer an official term, having been replaced by the lone word *tequila,* which distinguishes it from those spirits that are produced from agave alone and labeled as 100% agave tequila.

Molasses – A by-product of sugar production; a thick, black-colored sugary liquid that remains after all of the commercially salable sugar crystals have been removed.

Mosto – *Sp.,* the fermented must of aguamiel that is distilled into tequila.

Muck – A highly aromatic, bacteria-rich, and concentrated substance created by aging the yeast-rich foam "leftovers" that remain in the still after distillation; sometimes used in the production of Jamaican rum. See also: dunder.

Neutral Spirit – A clear liquid distilled at a high ethanol concentration. *Neutral* refers to the singular odor and flavor of ethyl alcohol as well as to the lack of distinct aromas and flavors in the base material.

New-Make – The spirit resulting from the distillation process, prior to any aging or maturation.

NOM (Norma Oficial Mexicana) – An official set of laws or standards regulated by the government of Mexico. Several distilled spirits produced in Mexico, including tequila and mezcal, are regulated per such standards.

Obstler – Term used in the European Union to refer to fruit spirits produced from a mixture of fruits; also known as obstbrand.

Obstbrand – Term used in the European Union to refer to fruit spirits produced from a mixture of fruits; also known as obstler.

Ordinario – The product of the first distillation of mosto in tequila production.

Organoleptic – Relating to the chemical and physical properties of a substance that are perceived by the senses.

Orgeat – A non-alcoholic, almond-flavored syrup sometimes used in tropical drink recipes.

Orujo – A traditional pomace brandy produced throughout Spain.

Oxidation – Chemical changes that take place in the presence of oxygen.

Peat – A compacted form of carbon derived from decomposed plant matter; often used as a fuel in the kilning of grain.

Penca – *Sp.*, the leaf of the agave plant.

Percolation – A cold method of extraction used primarily for herbs and spices and other delicate plant materials. The flavoring material is placed in a percolating chamber, and the base spirit is continuously pumped over and through the material, extracting the aromas and flavors.

Phenolics – A large and diverse category of plant-based chemicals that includes tannins, pigments, aromatic compounds, and flavor compounds (among others).

Piña – *Sp.*, the pineapple-shaped central rosette of the agave plant after it has been harvested and de-leafed. Also referred to as a cabeza.

Pisco – A traditional grape-based brandy produced in Chile and Peru.

Poitín – A traditional Irish distillate—once considered illegal, but now protected by a geographical indication—produced using grains and other allowed base materials.

Pomace – The residue (skins, seeds, stems) remaining after wine has been pressed; the pulpy residue left over after fruit (or vegetables) are crushed and pressed (as in juice, olive oil, or cider production).

Pomace Brandy – A spirit made from the grape solids (pulp, skins, seeds, and stems) left after fermentation and after pressing, which are then diluted with water, fermented into a low-alcohol wine, and distilled. Referred to as marc in France and grappa in Italy.

Potable Spirit – A beverage fit or suitable for drinking.

Pot Still – A type of still used in the distillation of spirits that require a batch process, whereby the liquid must be distilled twice in order to achieve the desired strength. Heat is applied directly to the pot in which the wine or beer is contained.

Proof – A historic scale used to measure the alcohol content of a spirit. In the United States, the proof is two times the percent of alcohol by volume. For example, a mixture that is 50% abv is 100 proof, or $50 \times 2 = 100$. Also designated as 100°.

Proof Gallon – In the United States, one liquid gallon of spirits that measures 50% alcohol by volume at 60°F (15.5°C).

Pulque – An agave-based fermented beverage produced throughout Mexico; generally consumed in neighborhood bars known as *pulquerías*.

Quinine – A bitter compound found in the bark of the cinchona tree.

Quinquina – A type of aromatized, bittered wine flavored with cinchona bark.

Raicilla – A distillate produced in the Mexican state of Jalisco produced using the *lechuguilla* or *angustifolia* subspecies of agave.

Rancio – Term used for describing aging characteristics found in certain cognacs and other wines and spirits whose alcohol has undergone advanced oxidation. Typical characteristics include earthy, cheesy, soy sauce, and/or mushroom aromas.

Rectify – To purify a spirit by repeated distillation. Rectification can also mean any process whereby distilled spirits are cut, blended, mixed, or infused with any ingredient that reacts with the constituents of the distilled spirit and changes the character or Standards of Identity of the distilled spirit, such as the rectification of a neutral spirit with juniper berries to produce gin.

Reflux – A technique used in distillation to control which elements of the liquid are passed onto the condenser and which are returned to the still.

Reposado – *Sp.*, rested. An age classification of tequila designating those products that have been aged at least two months in wood.

Retort – A closed vessel—placed between the still and the condenser—used as an accessory to a pot still.

Rhum – *Fr.*, rum. Used to denote the difference between rum products of the French West Indies and those produced in all of the other islands and countries around the Caribbean Sea.

Rhum Agricole – *Fr.*, agricultural rum. Rum made from fresh sugarcane juice, as opposed to molasses, from which rhum industriel is made. Martinique has an AOC for its rhum agricole.

Ron – *Sp.*, rum. The designation of rum produced in Spanish-speaking areas; almost always molasses-based.

Rum – A spirit distilled from the fermented products of the sugarcane plant in the form of sugar, sugarcane juice, or molasses.

Saccharification – The application of heat to a starch to trigger the enzymatic processes to convert the starch to fermentable sugar.

Schnaps – Term sometimes used in parts of Germany, Austria, and Switzerland to refer to a range of distilled spirits; often used specifically in reference to clear, fruit-based spirits.

Shōchū – A Japanese distillate typically made from barley, buckwheat, rice, or sweet potatoes.

Singani – A Bolivian brandy made using Muscat of Alexandria grapes.

Single-Barrel Aging – A static aging process whereby the spirit is contained in a single small oak barrel. The contents of a single barrel may be bottled on their own, or barrels may be blended together to create a consistent product.

Single Malt Whiskey – A whiskey made exclusively from malted barley (and no other grains) and as the product of a single distillery.

Sloe Gin – A liqueur flavored with blackthorn plums (sloe plums). A similar product, Pacharán, which is also flavored with anise, is produced in Spain.

Small Grains – Grains other than corn that may be used in American whiskey; refers to any grain "smaller than corn."

Soju – A Korean distillate typically made from rice, barley, wheat, or sweet potatoes.

Solera Process Aging – A fractional aging and blending process typically used in the aging of brandy de Jerez, although it may be used with other spirits.

Sotol – A distillate based on the *Dasylirion wheeleri* plant, produced in the Mexican states of Chihuahua, Durango, and Coahuila.

Sour Mash – A type of mash fermented using the highly acidic leftovers—known as backset or stillage—from the distillation of a previous batch of whiskey; typically used in the production of bourbon and Tennessee whiskey. See also: backset, stillage.

Sparge – The liquid extracted from the final rounds of the soaking and spraying of a cooked mash, often added back to the next round of mash. See also: sparging, mash.

Sparging – The final rounds of soaking and spraying a cooked mash in order to extract the sugar and separate the liquid from the solids; an optional stage in the production of whisky. See also: sparge.

Spirit – A liquid containing ethanol (ethyl alcohol) and water that is the product of distillation.

Still – An apparatus for distilling liquids such as alcohols. A still consists of (1) a vessel in which the substance is vaporized by heating and (2) a cooling unit in which the vapor is condensed.

Stillage – The residue left at the bottom of a still after distillation is complete, often used in the production of North American whiskeys. See also: backset.

Tahona – A traditional massive stone wheel used to crush and extract aguamiel from cooked agave.

Tails – Term for the portion of the distillation run after the heart that is considered to be nonpotable. Also called feints.

Thujone – A fragrant, oily substance, naturally found in a variety of common plants and flowers including *Artemisia absinthium*; best-known in connection with absinthe.

Thumper – A type of still used to make American whiskey in which the second distillation takes place, creating increased-alcohol high wines. The thumper gets its name from the thumping sound created by the vapors as they bubble through the alcohol–water liquid in the metal container.

Tuzemák – A traditional Czech spirit produced from potatoes or sugar beets.

Unaged Brandy – Brandy bottled without undergoing any aging in wood. Sometimes referred to as immature brandy.

Vermouth – An aromatized, fortified wine flavored with *artemisia* (wormwood) and other botanicals.

VS – "Very Special." An aging designation for brandy that has been aged a minimum of two years in wood for cognac and one year for armagnac.

VSOP – "Very Superior Old Pale." An aging designation for brandy that has been aged a minimum of four years in wood. Equivalent to the five-star and réserve designations.

Wash – A beer or wine that is the resulting liquid of an initial alcoholic fermentation. The wash is placed into a still to be distilled into a spirit.

Washback – A term used in Scotland for the large covered vessel, often made of wood or stainless steel, that is used to ferment the wort as part of the Scotch whisky production process.

Whiskey – A spirit distilled from a grain product to less than 190 proof, matured in an oak container, and then bottled at no less than 80 proof. Sometimes spelled *whisky*.

Wormwood – A green herb often used as a bittering and flavoring agent in aromatized wine and flavored spirits, also known as *Artemisia absinthium*.

XO – "Extra Old." An aging designation for French brandy that has been aged a minimum of ten years in wood, often used for cognac and armagnac. The minimum requirement for cognac was raised from six years to ten years in 2018.

Yeast – A living, single-celled organism. The yeast cells used in the production of fermented beverages and spirits are generally members of the *Saccharomyces cerevisiae* family. Yeast cells cause fermentation by secreting enzymes that convert simple sugars into ethanol and carbon dioxide.

BIBLIOGRAPHY AND SUPPLEMENTARY READING

APPENDIX B

The following works include sources used in the preparation of this guide and additional references that may be useful to candidates.

Abou-Ganim, Tony, and Mary Elizabeth Faulkner. *Vodka Distilled: The Modern Mixologist on Vodka and Vodka Cocktails.* Chicago: Agate Publishing, 2013.

Barnett, Richard. *The Book of Gin.* New York: Grove Press, 2011.

Begg, Desmond. *The Vodka Companion.* London: Running Press, 1998.

Blue, Anthony. *The Complete Book of Spirits: A Guide to Their History, Production, and Enjoyment.* New York: Harper Collins, 2004.

Boons, Isabel and Du Bois, Frédéric. *Vodka: the Complete Guide.* Tielt, Belgium: Lannoo Publishers, 2018.

Broom, Dave. *Rum.* New York: Abbeville, 2003.

———. *Rum: The Manual.* London: Mitchell Beazley, 2016.

———. *Spirits and Cocktails.* London: Carlton Books Ltd., 2008.

———. *Whisky: The Manual.* London: Mitchell Beazley, 2014.

Brown, Jared, and Anistatia Miller. *The Mixellany Guide to Vermouth and Other Apéritifs.* Cheltenham, England: Jared Brown, 2011.

———. *Spirit of the Cane: The Story of Cuban Rum.* Mixellany Limited, 2017.

Bryson, Lew, and Wondrich, David. *Tasting Whiskey: An Insider's Guide to the Unique Pleasures of the World's Finest Spirits.* North Adams: Storey Publishing, 2014.

Buxton, Ian. *101 Gins to Try before You Die.* Edinburgh: Polygon, 2015.

Calabrese, Salvatore. *Cognac: A Liquid History.* London: Cassell, 2005.

Cowdery, Charles. *Bourbon, Straight: The Uncut and Unfiltered Story of American Whiskey.* Chicago: Made and Bottled in Kentucky, 2004.

Curtis, Wayne. *And a Bottle of Rum: A History of the New World in Ten Cocktails.* New York: Random House, 2007.

DeGroff, Dale. *The Craft of the Cocktail: Everything You Need to Know to Be a Master Bartender, with 500 Recipes.* New York: Clarkson Potter, 2002.

———. *The Essential Cocktail: The Art of Mixing Perfect Drinks.* New York: Clarkson Potter, 2008.

De Kergommeaux, Davin. *Canadian Whisky: The Portable Expert, Second edition.* Canada: Penguin Random House, 2017.

Devito, Carlo. *Big Whiskey: Kentucky Bourbon, Tennessee Whiskey, the Rebirth of Rye and the Distilleries of America's Premier Spirits Region.* Kennebunkport, Maine: Cider Mill Press, 2018.

Dominé, André. *The World of Spirits and Cocktails: The Ultimate Bar Book.* Cambridge, England: H. F. Ullman, 2008.

Emmons, Bob. *The Book of Tequila: A Complete Guide.* Chicago: Open Court Publishing Company, 1997.

Faith, Nicholas. *Cognac: The Story of the World's Greatest Brandy.* Oxford, England: Infinite Ideas Ltd., 2013.

Foss, Richard. *Rum: A Global History.* London: Reaktion Books, 2012.

Gasnier, Vincent. *Drinks: Enjoying, Choosing, Storing, Serving, and Appreciating Wines, Beers, Cocktails, Spirits, Aperitifs, Liqueurs, and Ciders.* New York: DK Publishing, 2005.

Gaytán, Marie Sarita. *Tequila! Distilling the Spirit of Mexico.* Stanford: Stanford University Press, 2014

Haigh, Ted. *Vintage Spirits and Forgotten Cocktails: From the Alamagoozlum to the Zombie—100 Rediscovered Recipes and the Stories Behind Them.* Minneapolis: Quarry Books, 2009.

Herlihy, Patricia. *Vodka: A Global History.* London: Reaktion Books, 2012.

Hoefling, Brian. *Distilled Knowledge: The Science behind Drinking's Greatest Myths, Legends, and Unanswered Questions.* New York: Abbeville Press, 2016.

Jackson, Michael. *Whiskey: The Definitive World Guide.* London: DK Adult, 2005.

Janzen, Emma. *Mezcal: The History, Craft, & Cocktails of the World's Ultimate Artisanal Spirit.* Minneapolis: Quarto Publishing Group, 2017.

Kokoris, Jim. *The Big Man of Jim Beam: Booker Noe and the Number-One Bourbon in the World.* Hoboken: John Wiley & Sons, 2016.

Knorr, Paul. *The Vodka Bible.* New York: Sterling Innovation, 2010.

Kosar, Kevin. *Whiskey: A Global History.* London: Reaktion Books, 2012.

Lubbers, Bernie: *Bourbon Whiskey: Our Native Spirit,* 2nd ed. Indianapolis: Blue River Press, 2012.

Luntz, Perry. *Whiskey and Spirits for Dummies.* Hoboken: Wiley Publishing, 2008.

MacLean, Charles. *Spirit of Place: Scotland's Great Whisky Distilleries.* Chicago: Chicago Review Press, 2015.

Mattsson, Henrik. *Calvados: The World's Premier Apple Brandy—Tasting, Facts, and Travel.* Sofielundsvägen, Sweden: Flavourrider AB, 2010.

Meehan, Jim. *Meehan's Bartender Manual.* Berkeley: Ten Speed Press, 2017.

Morgenthaler, Jeffrey. *The Bar Book: Elements of Cocktail Technique.* San Francisco: Chronicle Books, 2014.

Mulryan, Peter. *The Whiskeys of Ireland, Second edition.* Dublin: O'Brien Press, 2016.

Neal, Charles. *Armagnac: The Definitive Guide to France's Premier Brandy.* San Francisco: Chronicle Books, 2014.

———. *Calvados: The Spirit of Normandy.* South San Francisco: Wine Appreciation Guild, 2011.

O'Connor, Fionnán. *A Glass Apart: Irish Single Pot Still Whiskey.* Mulgrave: Images Publishing Group, 2015.

Pacult, Paul. *Kindred Spirits 2.* New York: Spirit Journal, Inc., 2008.

Parsons, Brad. *Bitters: A Spirited History of a Classic Cure-All.* Berkeley: Ten Speed Press, 2011.

———. *Amaro: The Spirited World of Bittersweet, Herbal Liqueurs, with Cocktails, Recipes, and Formulas.* Berkeley: Ten Speed Press, 2016.

Petzke, Karl. *Tequila: Myth, Magic, & Spirited Recipes.* San Francisco: Chronicle Books, 2009.

Regan, Gaz. *The Bartender's Gin Compendium.* Cheltenham, England: Mixellany Limited, 2012.

———. *The Joy of Mixology.* New York: Clarkson Potter, 2004.

Ruy-Sanchez, Alberto, ed. *Tequila: A Traditional Art of Mexico.* Washington, DC: Smithsonian Books, 2004.

Solmonson, Lesly Jacobs. *Gin: A Global History.* London: Reaktion Books, 2012.

Stewart, Amy. *The Drunken Botanist: The Plants that Create the World's Great Drinks.* Chapel Hill: Algonquin Books, 2013.

Uyeda, Kazuo. *Cocktail Techniques.* New York: Mud Puddle Books, 2010.

Valenzuala-Zapata, Ana, and Gary Nabhan. *Tequila: A Natural and Cultural History.* Tucson: University of Arizona Press, 2004.

Veach, Michael. *Kentucky Bourbon Whiskey: An American Heritage.* Lexington: University Press of Kentucky, 2013.

Walton, Stuart. *Vodka Classified: A Vodka Lover's Companion.* Oxford: Pavilion Publishing, 2009.

Walton, Stuart, and Brian Glover. *The Ultimate Encyclopedia of Wine, Beer, Spirits & Liqueurs: The Definitive Reference Guide to Alcohol-Based Drinks.* London: Southwater Publishing, 2014.

Weir, Joanne. *Tequila: A Guide to Types, Flights, Cocktails, and Bites.* Berkeley: Ten Speed Press, 2009.

Wondrich, David. *Imbibe! From Absinthe Cocktail to Whiskey Smash, a Salute in Stories and Drinks to "Professor" Jerry Thomas, Pioneer of the American Bar.* New York: Penguin Group, 2007.

PERIODICALS

Imbibe Liquid Culture Magazine – http://imbibemagazine.com/

iSanté – http://isantemagazine.com/

The Tasting Panel Magazine – www.tastingpanelmag.com

Wine & Spirits – www.wineandspiritsmagazine.com

For a comprehensive listing of websites covering the study of spirits, please see the "Spirits Links" page of the SWE blog, *Wine, Wit, and Wisdom*: http://winewitandwisdomswe.com/spirits-links/

ADDITIONAL RESOURCES

COCKTAIL AND MIXED DRINK RECIPES

APPENDIX C

THE MARTINI/MANHATTAN FAMILY

Martini (classic): 1½ ounces London dry gin; ¾ ounces dry vermouth; olive or lemon zest.

Extra-Dry Martini: 1½ ounces London dry gin; 1 dash dry vermouth; olive or lemon zest.

Gibson: Follow the Martini recipe but serve with cocktail onions.

Smoky Martini: 2 ounces London dry gin; ¼ ounce dry vermouth with ½ ounce Islay Scotch (float); olive or lemon zest.

Manhattan: 1½ ounces rye whiskey; ¾ ounce sweet vermouth; cherry. The classic recipe includes a dash of Angostura bitters.

Dry Manhattan: 1½ ounces rye whiskey; ¾ ounce dry vermouth; 1 dash Angostura bitters; lemon zest.

Perfect Manhattan: 1½ ounces rye whiskey; ¾ ounce combined dry and sweet vermouth; cherry or lemon zest.

Rob Roy: 1½ ounces Scotch whisky; ¾ ounce sweet vermouth; 1 dash Angostura bitters; lemon zest.

Dry Rob Roy: 1½ ounces Scotch whisky; ¾ ounce dry vermouth; 1 dash Angostura bitters; lemon zest.

Perfect Rob Roy: 1½ ounces Scotch whisky; ¾ ounce combined dry and sweet vermouth; 1 dash Angostura bitters; cherry or lemon zest.

Negroni: 1 ounce gin; 1 ounce sweet vermouth; 1 ounce Campari; ½ slice orange or flamed orange peel. Build over ice in an Old-Fashioned glass.

Sazerac: 2 ounces rye whiskey; 1 cube sugar; splash absinthe; two dashes Peychaud's bitters; lemon zest. Prepare the rocks glass by adding, splashing, swirling, and rinsing out the absinthe, and then add ice. Prepare the drink in a mixing glass and strain into the rocks glass. Note: The original recipe called for cognac as the base; however, as cognac became difficult to source during and after the American Civil War, the recipe changed to feature rye whiskey. Similarly, as absinthe was often difficult to obtain, many recipes feature Herbsaint or Ricard in its place.

Southern Comfort, or Deluxe Manhattan: 1½ ounces Southern Comfort; ¾ ounce dry vermouth; cherry or lemon zest.

Old-Fashioned: 2 ounces bourbon whiskey; 1 cube sugar; 2 dashes Angostura bitters; orange slice; maraschino cherry; splash water or soda. In an Old-Fashioned glass, muddle the sugar, Angostura bitters, orange slice, and maraschino cherry; remove the orange rind and add the bourbon, ice, and a splash of water/soda; garnish with orange slice and maraschino cherry.

SOURS

SHORT SOURS

Aviation Cocktail: 2 ounces gin; 1 ounce maraschino liqueur; ¾ ounce lemon juice; lemon zest.

Bacardi Cocktail: 1½ ounces Bacardi light rum; ¾ ounce lime juice; ½ ounce grenadine; lemon zest.

Bee's Knees: 2 ounces gin; ½ ounce honey; ½ ounce lemon juice.

Between the Sheets: 1½ ounces brandy; 1½ ounces light rum; 1 ounce triple sec; 1 ounce lemon juice.

Caipirinha: 2 ounces cachaça; ½ lime, quartered; 2 teaspoons granulated sugar; lime quarter as a garnish. In a glass mixer, muddle lime quarters with sugar for 15 seconds. Add cachaça and ice, and shake well. Pour contents into a rocks glass and garnish with lime.

Cosmopolitan: 1½ ounces vodka; ½ ounce Cointreau; ½ ounce lime juice; 1 ounce cranberry juice; orange slice.

Daiquiri: 1½ ounces light rum; ¾ ounce lime juice; ½ ounce simple syrup; cherry. Serve in a sour glass.

French 75: 1 ounce gin or cognac; ½ ounce lemon juice; 1 tsp superfine sugar; 2 ounces Champagne.

Gimlet: 1½ ounces gin or vodka; ¾ ounce Rose's lime juice; lime wedge (optional).

Jack Rose Cocktail: 1½ ounces applejack; 1 ounce lemon juice; 1 ounce simple syrup; two dashes grenadine; apple slice or cherry.

Kamikaze: 1 ounce vodka; 1 ounce Cointreau or triple sec; 1 ounce lime juice; lime wedge (optional).

Margarita: 1½ ounces tequila; 1 ounce Cointreau; ¾ ounce lime juice. Salt the rim of the glass.

Pisco Sour: 1½ ounces pisco; 1 ounce lime juice; ¾ ounce simple syrup; ½ egg white (optional); 1 dash Angostura bitters.

Sidecar: 1½ ounce cognac; ¾ ounce Cointreau or triple sec; ¾ ounce lemon juice; orange zest.

Stone Sour: 1½ ounces rye whiskey; 1 ounce lemon juice; 1 ounce fresh orange juice; 1 ounce simple syrup; cherry.

Ward 8: 1½ ounces whiskey; 1 ounce lemon juice; 1 ounce simple syrup; ¼ ounce grenadine; cherry or orange slice.

Whiskey Sour: 1½ ounces bourbon; ¾ ounce lemon juice; ¾ ounce simple syrup; cherry. Serve in a sour glass.

White Lady: 1½ ounces gin; 1 ounce Cointreau or triple sec; ¾ ounce lemon juice.

LONG SOURS

Long Island Iced Tea: ½ ounce vodka; ½ ounce gin; ½ ounce tequila; ½ ounce rum; ½ ounce triple sec; 1 ounce lemon juice; 1 ounce simple syrup; 3 to 4 ounces Coke as a float; lemon wedge or wheel.

Mojito: 1½ ounces light rum; 6 sprigs mint; 1 ounce simple syrup; 1 ounce lime juice; 1 dash Angostura bitters (optional); 4 ounces club soda. Muddle the sprigs of fresh mint with simple syrup and lime juice before adding the other ingredients. Shake and then add the soda.

Ramos Gin Fizz: 1½ ounces gin; ½ ounce lemon juice; ½ ounce lime juice; 2 ounces cream; 1 ounce simple syrup; 1 egg white; three drops orange flower water; 2 drops vanilla extract; 2 ounces club soda. Shake without the club soda; strain into a highball glass and add the soda. Typically served without ice; no garnish.

Gin Rickey: 1½ ounces gin; ½ ounce lime juice; 4 ounces soda; lime wedge. Note: Rickeys are usually served dry but can have simple syrup added if the customer prefers.

Stone Rickey: 1½ ounces gin; ½ ounce fresh lime juice; 2 ounces orange juice; 1 ounce simple syrup; 4 ounces club soda; orange slice.

Tom Collins: 1½ ounces gin; 1 ounce lemon juice; 1 ounce simple syrup; 4 ounces club soda; cherry and orange slice.

Variations on the Tom Collins: Mike Collins—made with whiskey; Joe or Ivan Collins—made with vodka; Pedro Collins—made with rum; Sandy Collins—made with Scotch whisky.

Singapore Sling: 1½ ounces gin; ½ ounce Heering Cherry Liqueur; ¼ ounce Cointreau; ¼ ounce Bénédictine; 4 ounces pineapple juice; ½ ounce lime juice; ¼ ounce grenadine; 1 dash Angostura bitters; club soda (optional); cherry and orange slice. Shake without the soda but add once poured into the highball glass.

Sloe Gin Fizz: 1½ ounces sloe gin; ½ ounce lemon juice; ½ ounce simple syrup; 3 ounces soda; cherry and orange slice.

CREAM DRINKS

SHORT CREAMS

Brandy Alexander: 1 ounce cognac or brandy; 1 ounce dark crème de cacao; 1 ounce cream; nutmeg sprinkle.

Golden Cadillac: 1 ounce Galliano; 1 ounce crème de cacao; 1 ounce heavy cream.

Golden Dream: 1 ounce Galliano; 1 ounce triple sec; 1 ounce orange juice; ½ ounce heavy cream.

Grasshopper: 1 ounce white or clear crème de cacao; 1 ounce green crème de menthe; 1 ounce heavy cream.

Pink Lady: 1½ ounces gin; ¾ ounce simple syrup; ¼ ounce grenadine; 1 ounce heavy cream.

Pink Squirrel: 1 ounce white or clear crème de cacao; 1 ounce crème de noyaux; 1 ounce heavy cream.

Toasted Almond: 1 ounce vodka; ¾ ounce amaretto; ¾ ounce Kahlúa; 1½ ounces cream.

White Russian: 1¾ ounce vodka; ¾ ounce Kahlúa; 1 ounce cream (float).

LONG CREAMS

Girl Scout Cookie: ¾ ounce Bailey's Irish Cream; ½ ounce Kahlúa; ½ ounce peppermint schnapps; 4 ounces cream.

Roasted Almond: 1 ounce vodka; ¾ ounce amaretto; ¾ ounce Kahlúa; 4 ounces cream.

SHOOTERS

Alabama Slammer: 1 ounce Tennessee whiskey; 1 ounce amaretto; ½ ounce sloe gin; 1 dash lemon juice. (This can be shaken and strained.)

B-52: ½ ounce Kahlúa; ½ ounce Bailey's Irish Cream; ½ ounce Grand Marnier or Mandarine Napoléon. Layer ingredients starting with the Kahlúa, then the Bailey's, followed by the Grand Marnier or Mandarine Napoléon.

Black Russian: 1¾ ounces vodka; ¾ ounce Kahlúa.

Godfather: 1½ ounces Scotch; 1½ ounce amaretto.

Godmother: 1½ ounces vodka; 1½ ounce amaretto.

Lemon Drop: 1 ounce vodka; ¾ ounce triple sec; ½ ounce lemon juice. Shake and strain.

Mudslide: ¾ ounce vodka; ¾ ounce Kahlúa; ¾ ounce Bailey's Irish Cream.

Peppermint Patty: 1½ ounces white crème de cacao; ¾ ounce white crème de menthe.

Pousse-Café: ½ ounce grenadine; ½ ounce Yellow Chartreuse; ½ ounce crème de cassis; ½ ounce white crème de cacao; ½ ounce Green Chartreuse; ½ ounce brandy; layer in glass carefully.

Rusty Nail: 1½ ounce Scotch whisky; ¾ ounce Drambuie.

Sicilian Kiss: 1½ ounces Southern Comfort; ¾ ounce amaretto.

Stinger: 1½ ounces brandy; ¾ ounce white crème de menthe.

HIGHBALLS

The Highball: 1½ ounces whiskey; 4 ounces ginger ale.

Bocce Ball: 1½ ounces Disaronno Originale; 1½ ounces orange juice; 3 ounces club soda.

Bloody Mary: 1½ ounces vodka; 4 ounces tomato juice; salt and pepper; 2 dashes Worcestershire sauce; 3 dashes Tabasco sauce; ¼ ounce lemon juice; horseradish (optional); 1 tsp celery salt (optional); celery stalk or lime wedge. Roll, then serve in a goblet or highball glass.

Cape Codder: 1½ ounces vodka; 4 ounces cranberry juice; lime wedge garnish.

Comfortable Screw: 1½ ounces Southern Comfort; 4 ounces orange juice; orange slice.

Cuba Libre: 1½ ounces rum; 4 ounces Coke; ½ ounce lime juice; lime garnish.

Fuzzy Navel: 1½ ounces peach schnapps; 4 ounces orange juice.

Harvey Wallbanger: 1½ ounces vodka; 4 ounces orange juice; Galliano (float); orange slice and cherry.

Jack and Coke: 1½ ounces Jack Daniel's; 4 ounces Coke.

Jack and Ginger: 1½ ounces Jack Daniel's; 4 ounces ginger ale.

Madras: 1½ ounces vodka; 4 ounces cranberry juice and orange juice combined.

Moscow Mule: 1½ ounces vodka; 4 ounces ginger beer; dash lime juice; lime garnish.

Pearl Harbor: 1 ounce Midori; ½ ounce vodka; 4 ounces pineapple juice.

Pimm's Cup: 1½ ounces Pimm's No. 1; 3 ounces lemonade; 1 ounce lime juice; topped with club soda. Apple slice garnish.

Presbyterian: 1½ ounces whiskey; 2 ounces ginger ale; 2 ounces club soda.

Salty Dog: 1½ ounces vodka; 4 ounces grapefruit juice. Rim glass with salt.

Scarlet O'Hara: 1½ ounces Southern Comfort; 4 ounces cranberry juice.

Sea Breeze: 1½ ounces vodka; 1 ounce grapefruit juice; 4 ounces cranberry juice.

Tequila Sunrise: 1½ ounces tequila; 4 ounces orange juice; ½ ounce grenadine (float); orange slice and cherry.

Woo-Woo: 1 ounce peach schnapps; ½ ounce vodka; 4 ounces cranberry juice.

7&7: 1½ ounces Seagram's 7; 4 ounces 7-Up.

TROPICAL DRINKS

Mai Tai: 2 ounces light rum; 1 ounce dark rum; ¾ ounce orange curaçao; ¾ ounce orgeat syrup; ½ ounce lime juice; garnish with lime or chunk of pineapple, cherry, and sprig of mint.

Piña Colada: 1 ounce light rum; 1 ounce coconut milk; 3 ounces pineapple juice; crushed ice; garnish with pineapple chunk and cherry.

Zombie: 1 ounce light rum; 1 ounce Myers's dark rum or similar; 1 ounce orange curaçao; 1½ ounces lemon juice; 1 ounce simple syrup; ½ ounce grenadine; 1½ ounces orange juice; 1 ounce lime juice; 1 tsp brown sugar; 1 ounce overproof rum as a float (optional); sprig of mint and tropical fruit.

WINES AND PUNCHES

COLD PUNCHES

Americano: 1½ ounces sweet vermouth; 1½ ounces Campari; 3 ounces club soda; lemon zest; serve in a highball glass.

Bombay Punch: ½ liter sweet sherry; ½ liter brandy; 3 ounces triple sec; 3 ounces maraschino liqueur; 2 liters Champagne; 1 liter club soda; 6 ounces lemon juice; 5 ounces simple syrup.

Brandy Punch: 1¾ liters brandy; 8 ounces triple sec; 8 ounces dark rum; 24 ounces lemon juice; 16 ounces orange juice; 8 ounces grenadine; 32 ounces club soda; 16 ounces black tea (optional); sliced oranges.

Champagne Cobbler: 1 slice orange; 1 lemon wedge; 1 pineapple wedge; ¾ ounce maraschino liqueur; 4 ounces Champagne. Muddle the fruit in the mixing glass; add ice and stir gently; strain into a Champagne tulip/flute.

Champagne Cocktail: ½ ounce cognac; 1 cube sugar; 2 dashes Angostura bitters; 4 ounces Champagne.

Death in the Afternoon: 1 ounce pastis (or Pernod); 5 ounces Champagne.

Fish House Punch: 36 ounces dark rum; 24 ounces lemon juice; 25 ounces brandy; 4 ounces peach brandy; ¾ lb superfine sugar; 40 ounces water.

Hawaiian Tropical Punch: ½ ounce rum; ½ ounce vodka; ½ ounce amaretto; ½ ounce crème de banana; 2 ounces orange juice; 2 ounces pineapple juice; 1½ ounces grenadine as a float.

Kir: 1 splash crème de cassis; 6 ounces dry, tart white wine such as Aligoté.

Kir Royale: 1 splash crème de cassis; 6 ounces brut Champagne.

Planter's Punch: 1½ ounces dark rum; 1 ounce orange juice; ¾ ounce lemon juice; 1 ounce pineapple juice; ½ ounce grenadine; ½ ounce simple syrup; orange slice and cherry.

Port Wine Cocktail: 2½ ounces port; ¼ ounce brandy.

Sherry Cocktail: 2½ ounces fino sherry; ½ ounce absinthe; ½ ounce maraschino liqueur; orange peel.

Ti' Punch: 2 ounces white rum; 1 ounce simple syrup; 1 fresh, washed lime, sliced. Muddle the lime; add simple syrup; add crushed ice and rum.

HOT PUNCHES

Glogg: 2 bottles full-bodied red wine; 1¾ liters vodka; 20 cardamom pods; 10 cloves; 2 cinnamon sticks; 1 piece orange peel; 1½ cups blanched whole almonds; 1½ cups raisins; 10 dried figs; 1 lb sugar; 4 ounces cognac. Let steep for 24 hours without the cognac. Heat in pan over a stove and bring to a simmer. Add the cognac and sugar to taste. Strain and serve with a few raisins and blanched almonds.

Hot Rum Punch: 1½ ounces Barbados rum; 1 ounce cognac; 3 ounces boiling water; ½ ounce lemon juice; 1 tsp brown sugar; 3 or 4 cloves; spiral of lemon peel.

Spiced Hot Rum: 5 ounces apple cider; 2 ounces orange juice; 1 ounce light rum; ½ tsp sugar; 1 cinnamon stick; 1 clove; 2 ounces lemon juice; orange slice.

Tom and Jerry: 12 eggs, separated; ½ jigger rum; 2 lb. powdered sugar; ½ jigger brandy; 2 tsp cinnamon; ½ tsp ground allspice; ½ cup boiling water; ½ tsp nutmeg; ½ ounce vanilla extract. To make the batter, beat egg yolks with sugar until thin; add rum and spices to beaten yolk mixture. In a separate bowl and using an electric beater, beat whites until stiff. Add cinnamon, allspice, nutmeg, and vanilla. Add the egg yolk mixture half at a time, and blend until smooth. Fill a large mug with 2 Tbsp batter; 1½ ounces brandy; ½ ounce aged rum; and 3 to 4 ounces boiling water. Add freshly grated nutmeg to garnish.

INTERNATIONAL COFFEES

Café Grande: ⅓ ounce Tia Maria coffee liqueur; ⅓ ounce dark crème de cacao; ⅓ ounce Grand Marnier orange liqueur; 1 Tbsp brown sugar; 6 ounces hot black coffee; 1½ ounces whipped cream; lemon wedge to rim the glass.

French Coffee: 1 ounce Cointreau; ½ ounce Kahlúa; 1 Tbsp brown sugar; 6 ounces hot black coffee; 1½ ounces whipped cream; lemon wedge to rim the glass.

Irish Coffee: 1½ ounces Irish whiskey; 1 tsp brown sugar; 6 ounces hot black coffee; whipped heavy cream; lemon wedge to rim the glass.

Irish Kiss: ¾ ounce Bailey's Irish Cream; ¾ ounce Kahlúa coffee liqueur; 1 Tbsp brown sugar; 6 ounces hot black coffee; 1½ ounces whipped cream; lemon wedge to rim the glass.

Mexican Coffee: 1 ounce Kahlúa coffee liqueur; 1 Tbsp brown sugar; 6 ounces hot black coffee; 1½ ounces whipped cream; lemon wedge to rim the glass.

Spanish Coffee: 1 ounce rum; ½ ounce Tia Maria coffee liqueur; 6 ounces hot black coffee; 1½ ounces whipped cream; lemon wedge to rim the glass.

ADDITIONAL RESOURCES

THE SOCIETY OF WINE EDUCATORS' SPIRITS TASTING RATIONALE

APPENDIX D

APPEARANCE

Clarity:	Brilliant	Clear	Dull	Hazy	Cloudy		
Hue:	Water-White Mahogany	Pale Molasses	Light Yellow Brown	Yellow-Gold	Deep Gold	Copper	Tawny	Amber
Colored Spirits:	Light Green Yellow	Dark Green Black	Clear Blue Other:	Dark Blue	Purple	Pink	Red	Orange
Depth:	Water-White	Pale	Medium	Deep	Opaque			
Legs:	Fast	Slight	Medium	Pronounced	Slow			
Other Observations:								

CONDITIONS AND AROMAS

Condition:	Clean	Fresh	Stale	Unclean/Faulty
Aroma Intensity:	Neutral	Light	Medium	Intense

Aromas

Grain:	Malt	Bran	Cereal	Corn	Wheat	Biscuit	Other:	
Fruity:	Citrus	Tropical Fruit	Tree Fruit	Dried Fruit	Candied Fruit	Orange Peel	Other:	
Floral:	Rose	Violet	Perfume	Orange Blossom	Dried Flowers	Other:		
Botanical:	Herbal	Vegetal	Juniper	Tobacco	Peat	Seaweed	Other:	
Sweet Aromatics:	Caramel	Honey	Maple	Molasses	Burnt Sugar	Toffee	Vanilla	Other:
Spice:	Clove	Nutmeg	Anise	Cinnamon	White Pepper	Black Pepper	Other:	
Oak/Wood:	Oak	Cedar	Sawdust	Coffee	Pine	Char	Other:	
Nutty:	Walnut	Hazelnut	Praline	Almond	Marzipan	Coconut	Other:	
Rancio:	Leather	Smoke	Earthy	Acetaldehyde	Ash	Tar	Other:	
Other:								

PALATE

Sweetness:	None	Light	Moderate	Sweet	Very Sweet	
Acidity:	None	Light	Moderate	Sharp	Sour	
Bitterness:	None	Light	Moderate	Sharp	Astringent	
Alcohol:	Soft	Smooth	Warm	Pronounced	Hot	Harsh
Body:	Light	Medium	Full			
Flavors:						
Flavor Intensity:	Light	Medium	Full			

FINISH

Length:	Short	Medium	Long	Lingering	
Aftertaste:	Warm	Smooth	Pleasant	Harsh	Unpleasant

OVERALL IMPRESSIONS

Complexity:	Simple/None	Some Complexity	Moderate Complexity	Very Complex		
Quality:	Faulty	Acceptable	Good	Very Good	Excellent	Exceptional
Maturity:	Unaged	1-2 Years	3-5 Years	6-10 Years	Mature	Very Old

CONCLUSION

Made in the USA
Columbia, SC
04 April 2019